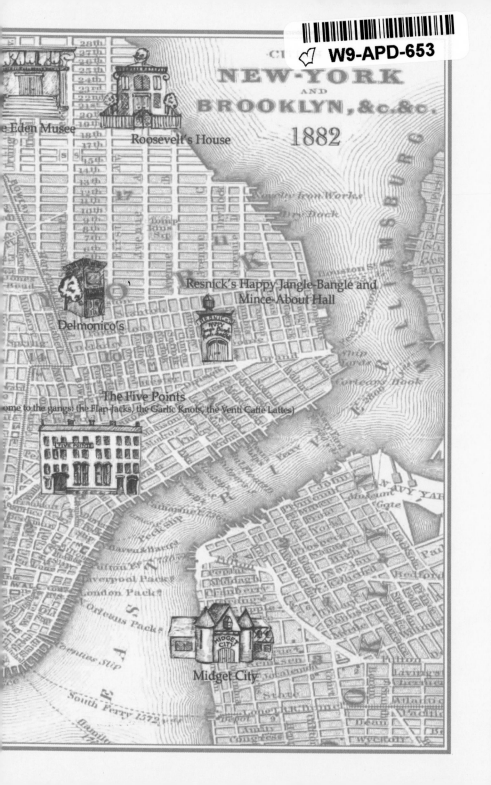

CITY OF

NEW-YORK

AND

BROOKLYN, &c.&c.

1882

The Eden Musee

Roosevelt's House

Resnick's Happy Jangle-Bangle and
Mince-About Hall

Delmonico's

The Five Points
(home to the gangs: the Flap-Jacks, the Garlic Knots, the Venti Caffé Lattes)

Midget City

WILLIAMSBURG

THE
SHROUD
OF THE
THWACKER

THE
SHROUD
OF THE
THWACKER

a novel

CHRIS ELLIOTT

Illustrations by Amy Elliott Andersen

miramax books

HYPERION

NEW YORK

Endpaper map courtesy of John Landers and H & M Production Books,
illustrated by Amy Elliott Andersen.

All rights reserved. No part of this book may be used or reproduced in
any manner whatsoever without the written permission of the Publisher.
Printed in the United States of America. For information address
Hyperion, 77 West 66th Street, New York, NY 10023–6298

ISBN 1-4013-5245-6

First Edition
10 9 8 7 6 5 4 3 2 1

To Jack the Jolly Thwacker, without whom
this book would make even less sense
than it does now. Also to his victims, and,
most of all, to any of their living relatives.
(Please don't sue me.)

How dark the con of the bestseller.

—William Shakespeare

Prologue.

IT STARTED INNOCENTLY ENOUGH. WHAT COULD HAVE BEEN THE HARM, I thought, in investigating an obscure crime that took place over a century ago? It was the year 1882, and New York City was caught in the grip of a serial murderer. His nightly forays into the shadowy streets had claimed the lives of four prostitutes, two women who looked like prostitutes, and, oddly enough, one cow (Bessie LeBlanc, who gave good milk in dark doorways for five bucks a cup). The city's top investigative team was mystified, baffled, and stymied all at the same time. The murder spree lasted one month, driving the innocent citizens of the day into an unprecedented state of mass hysteria—and then it ended, as mysteriously as it began. The killer vanished, presumably, and his crimes were eventually attributed to a mysterious fiend whose moniker has become synonymous with the most heinous and unholy of crimes: "Jack the Jolly Thwacker."

Trying to solve the mystery ought to have been fun. The story did not want for colorful characters, adventure, and derring-do. The investigative team was headed up by Caleb Spencer, then the city's top cop. (At thirty-three, Caleb was the youngest police

chief ever to be appointed by Tammany Hall. He was smart, fit, handsome, and only slightly incontinent.) His partner, and also the recipient of his unbridled infatuation, was the beguiling Liz Smith, columnist for the *Evening Post,* and the person to whom the Thwacker sent his infamous love poems. The third member of the team was their friend the bombastic and thick-headed mayor of New York City, Teddy Roosevelt, who, by all accounts, was fond of bellowing out "Bully!" at the top of his lungs, perhaps even to excess. (But history has forgotten that the well-educated and world-traveled man also coined a number of other popular phrases, such as, "Don't go there," "I'm a happy camper," and "Why don't you just apply it directly to your thighs?" In addition, he was famous for exclaiming "Weehoo!" in falsetto whenever an embarrassing wind escaped his trousers.)

And, in the beginning, it was fun, indeed: Spencer, Smith, and Roosevelt's investigation, as told in these pages, is a harrowing tale worthy of any Hardy Boys mystery, perhaps even an episode of *Murder, She Wrote.* Together they did an admirable job of sorting through the gallimaufry of cryptograms, pentagrams, pagan symbols, and bad haiku left behind by Jolly Jack. Their search for the truth dragged them down into the rarefied annals of ancient secret societies like the Knights Templar, the Knights of Columbus, the Friars Club, and, of course, the Mummers. Still, in the end they came up short.

Utilizing the tools of the modern forensic scientist (who wasn't really using them anyway), I was able to reexamine the mountain of evidence, revisit the crime scenes, reconstruct the murders, and see exactly where Spencer, Smith, and Roosevelt went wrong. In the process, I came up with my own startling revelations about the case, as well as a new, shocking prime suspect. If only it had ended there . . .

Why did I embark on such a project, you ask? Well, I guess you

could say that I've always been fascinated, perhaps even obsessed, with the Thwacker case. You could say that, but it wouldn't be true. The truth is I'd never heard of it until my friend Wendell brought it up.

We were sitting around my apartment in the Dakota, staring at each other and trying to telepathically send thoughts back and forth—an exercise we often indulged in, but never with any real success. (The image I always received was that of a Cavalier King Charles spaniel drinking a bottle of root beer. Wendell claimed he never once sent me that particular thought, but by then, of course, it was all he could think of, because I was always bring-ing it up.) At any rate, one day we were both sitting around my apartment, staring at each other, thinking about the dog drinking the bottle of root beer, when out of the blue Wendell said, "Hey, did they ever find out who that Thwacker guy really was?"

That got me thinking. First it got me thinking that Wendell was really dull, and after I showed him to the elevator and told him that his company was no longer required, it hit me: there might be some cashola to be made in this old Thwacker case! If I could solve it and write a book, I could be rich beyond my wildest dreams.

Sure, I had no investigative skills, but that didn't matter. I have no performing skills and I managed to carve out a career in show business. So I immediately set about the task of gathering research materials, tracking down experts, compiling data, and interviewing witnesses. (Actually there was only one person still alive from 1882, radio shock jock Don Imus, and he was eating peanut butter when we spoke; all I could make out was some inflammatory remark about Teddy Roosevelt, who had appar-ently stolen a girl from him in high school.) The result, my dear

readers, is a conclusive, one-hundred-percent surefire solution to the Thwacker mystery—for all the good it does me now.

You see, in uncovering the truth, I have also exposed something so earth shattering, so mind boggling, so "yeah right, you been huffing again, Chico," that I must take great precautions in relaying it to you. It is a secret with widespread ramifications. This is not just the story of the Jolly Jack Thwacker murders anymore.

Please understand that I, myself, have become personally embroiled in these events. I, myself, am in beaucoup danger. I, myself—that is, me, the author, Chris Elliott, not one of those imaginary narrators that books usually mean when they say "I"— might not get out of this with all my finely buffed body parts intact. I write these pages not from my luxurious appointments in the Dakota on Central Park West, but from an opium den at an undisclosed location in a much less desirable part of town, where I mop up the floors after knife fights in exchange for a heap of straw in the basement.

It is my hope that this manuscript will reach someone in a position to assist me, but lately I have begun to realize that I might have to resign myself to living out my days rifling for change in the pockets of the stoned corpses we haul out to the corner each morning for trash pickup. When you reach the last page of this work, dear reader, it will all become clear. The climactic ending will reveal itself to you with the most unexpected of twists—a denouement so controversial that it will rock the very foundations of religion, politics, and New York City real estate.

One thing is for sure. I am no longer writing this book just for the money. I'm writing it to save my life. (And I guess also for the money, sort of.)

Chapter the First.

In which a damsel is discovered in a most compromising position.

AUGUST 25TH, 1882, 9:00 PM

IT HAD BEEN A PARTICULARLY SWELTERING SUMMER IN NEW YORK CITY, the hottest summer on record (and, not coincidentally, the first summer on record). By all accounts this evening promised to be yet another in the long progression of dog days that oozed like a piece of soft, runny brie served with a hunk of moldy French bread and washed down with a mug of room-temperature Clamato. Each day melting into the next with an excruciatingly, sluggishly slow excruciating monotony. The Santa Ana wind hissed as it blew through the narrow, rough-hewn, cobblestone, gaslit, historically accurate streets, and then it giggled down Fifth Avenue, baking the leaves on the mango and banana trees lining the fashionable boulevard into crisp, brittle parchment. Indeed, the summer of 1882 was nearly as tedious as my first paragraph has been, and I thank you for your patience.

On Twenty-third Street, the sun was setting over the newly built concrete-and-steel Flatiron Building, named for its innovative shape (and coincidentally after its insane architect, José Emmanuel Flitarron). It was the tallest building in Manhattan in

1882, though within a year it would be dwarfed by the Pan Am Building, which was already well under way. The street was strewn with paper streamers, confetti, shredded balloons, and discarded wooden legs. Sanitation workers ran around like madmen, heads upturned, arms flailing, chasing the last of the floating feathers that hovered like small ghosts, refusing to drift within arm's reach. The feathers were castoffs from the annual Mummer's Day parade, which had ended only an hour before. Occasionally two sanitation workers would run into each other and a vicious slap fight would ensue.

A block east, in a nondescript brownstone, the killer put the final touches on a letter addressed to the *Evening Post.* He licked a stamp commemorating Thomas Edison's triumphant electrocution of Jumbo the Giant Elephant, sealed the envelope with a wax crest depicting a skull and crossbones in a bowler hat, and placed the correspondence on top of his stack of outgoing taunting mail. He donned his black overcoat and top hat, grabbed the carpetbag in which he carried his instruments of death—as well as his workout clothes for later—and snuffed out the candle. (Whale oil prices had skyrocketed ever since the sinking of the *Pequod,* and he hadn't paid his bill in months.) Then, with a spring in his step and a song in his heart, he headed out into the dark and steamy night.

Across town, in the "unfortunates' district," there was a ramshackle hovel with nothing more than a bed, a woodstove, and a framed tintype depicting a cat hanging by its paws from an iron rod. The caption read, "I Most Humbly Request That You Hang in There, Baby," a bit of inspiration for the occupant, who sorely needed it. She was a broken-down prostitute by the name of Sally "Old Toothless Sally" Jenkins, and she readied herself for another long night's work by lacing up her worn-out boots, shifting her heavy skirt so that it faced the right direction, and

dousing her underarms with turpentine. She caught her reflection in the mirror and cackled, "Well now, ain't you a pretty one!"

Her cackle was quickly overtaken by a wet coughing fit. The gross hacking seemed to last forever. Neighbors pounded on the walls. Finally, Sally expelled a huge wad of phlegm that shot from her lungs and blew across the room like a cannonball, landing with a *plop* in a pan of simmering porridge atop her stove.

"Oh bother," she said, lighting the end of a half-smoked cigar, "I got phlegm in me porridge." And with that she collapsed back onto her bed.

AT AROUND NINE O'CLOCK, BROADWAY FILLED WITH THEATER PATRONS stepping out at intermission for a breath of stale air. In the poverty-stricken neighborhoods, indigent children opened fire hydrants and splashed about in the filthy gutters, contracting cholera, while uptown the more posh types like the Vanderbilts, the Bloomingdales, and the Trumps sipped their mint juleps, made fun of poor people, and frolicked on their private beaches along the East River, also contracting cholera.

On this night Mark Twain twirled his rope at Lincoln Center, Houdini performed his straitjacket trick at Avery Fisher Hall, and John Merrick, the Elephant Man, did his song and dance routine for a handful of potheads at the band shell in Central Park. All the rummeries and brothels were overflowing, and the restaurants were filled to the brim.

At Delmonico's, Mayor Teddy Roosevelt sat finishing his boiled cabbage and hind-quarters pie. His guest for the evening was Caleb Spencer, chief of police for the NCNYPD.[1] The two

---

1. The Nineteenth-Century New York Police Department.

were celebrating the arrest, earlier in the day, of Dandy Dan, the Water Man. For months now, he had terrified young couples in Central Park. Whilst a romantic tryst was under way, the culprit would hide in the bushes, growling and gnashing his teeth. When the moment was right, he would spring out on all fours, lift his leg, and urinate with great force on the young lady's fine evening frock.

Spencer had apprehended the felon *his* way. Not trusting the officious Detective Thomas Byrnes and his roundsmen with such a high-profile case, he had gone undercover, alone. He disguised himself as both a man and a woman. It was an elaborate costume, but it worked: a man in a tuxedo on one side, a woman in a ball gown on the other. When he twirled rapidly about, you'd swear he was a pair of young lovers doing a steamy, down-and-dirty tango. (Well, maybe *you* wouldn't swear, but it was enough to fool a man who spent the better part of the day hiding in the bushes.) It also displayed a bit of creative thinking on Caleb's part—something of which Detective Byrnes was incapable. Byrnes and Spencer had endured the police academy's rigorous training together, but their strained and often competitive relationship had only further deteriorated after Caleb's quick rise within the department. He was now Byrnes's superior and Byrnes didn't like it.

Roosevelt tapped a glass with a spoon. "I say, my good man, tell me exactly how you managed to corner the dastardly malefactor! I always love a good story."

"Well," Caleb began, "I had just drawn my 'lovely partner' toward me, when I saw this gentleman on his hands and knees, barking. I thought to myself, 'Now, that is highly unusu—'"

"Bully!" interrupted Roosevelt.

Caleb sighed. The mayor loved a good story, but only if it was his own.

"My dear Mr. Spencer, have I ever told you about the time I slept in a hollowed-out four-day-old water buffalo carcass?"

"Yes, I believe that you have, Mayor, several times in fact, but as I have never paid any attention, you may proceed as if you have not."

"Jolly good then!" And with that, the jovial mayor launched into another boring story of his exploits. Caleb was amazed at how his sarcasm flew straight over Roosevelt's perfectly round head. Insulting Roosevelt without the mayor's realizing it had become a game for Spencer's own private amusement. (Spencer had always been a bit of a loner, and he enjoyed nothing more than playing with himself.)

At thirty-three, he was already a seasoned veteran of the force. Having joined when he was a mere five years of age—to work the badge-polishing machine—he rose quickly within the ranks, making lieutenant by the time he was six. His hard-nosed, no-nonsense, look-at-me-indecently-and-I'll-kick-your-posterior-from-here-to-China approach had impressed the older, fatter, and even more incontinent coppers. Upon his appointment as chief, the young crime-fighter garnered a reputation not only for being a good cop, but also, according to an editorial in the *Evening Post:*

... for having looks and appeal so devastatingly dashing as to make any proper woman of childbearing age swoon with delight at visions of the strapping young police chief, buck naked except for a cowboy hat, dancing in her head.

However, much had changed since those words were penned. For starters, he had stopped dating the *Evening Post*'s star reporter, but the times had also been hard on him. Three short years presiding over the most corrupt, crime-ridden city in the world had

aged him. His hairline had begun to recede, and what remained was going quickly gray. To make matters worse, Roosevelt had ambushed him at the scene of Dandy Dan's arrest and insisted that he come to dinner, and Spencer had had no time to change out of his disguise. So there he sat, wearied by the night's ordeals and the mayor's long-winded diatribes, with half a blond wig hanging precariously askew, still bedecked in the now filthy tuxedo and torn ball gown, and scented, faintly, with the pungent effluvium of wine. He looked less like a dashing police chief and more like Bette Davis in *Hush . . . Hush, Sweet Charlotte* after being flattened by a steamroller.

"Oh my, look at the time," he announced, returning his pocket watch to the shiny sequined purse that he clutched to his feminine side. "Mayor, I thank you for a lovely evening. Your self-indulgent anecdotes were both egocentric on the one hand, and long-winded and pointless on the other, but now I must be on my way."

"Let's us two have a toast!" the mayor roared, lifting his goblet of Umbria Vittiono '54, a robust merlot aged with a fine mix of red grapes from the Napa Valley and the essence of pure heroin (which was perfectly legal in the Age of Innocence, and was referred to as "God's Own Medicine").

Caleb was uncomfortable with congratulations of any kind, and he knew that the toast would be in his honor. So, to get the embarrassment over with, he quickly raised his flaming dry martini, laced with uncut cocaine and liquid arsenic (both also perfectly legal, and known as "God's Own Snuff" and "God's Own Rat Poison," respectively).

"In all my years as mayor, I've been privileged to witness several heroic acts of bravery perpetrated by our fine constabulary."

Okay, here it comes, thought Caleb.

"But nothing that could compare with what I faced when

leading a handful of ragtag, battle-weary soldiers on that fateful charge up the great San Juan Hill."

"The Spanish-American War doesn't even happen until 1898," Caleb snapped. "If you are going to force me to endure your stories, at least get your facts straight."

Roosevelt looked hurt. "Are you calling me a liar, Mr. Spencer?"

Caleb sighed. The worst part of his job was dealing with the sensitive emotions of the city's rich and powerful. Still, he preferred Roosevelt, who was merely pompous, to some of the more nefarious types he had to deal with, like J. P. Morgan, the Rockefellers, or the worst of them all, William "Boss" Tweed. He had dined with Boss Tweed on more than one occasion, and he had always left the meal feeling quite dirty all over. Roosevelt, for all his long-windedness—and chronic flatulence—was his only ally against Tweed and his dreaded Tammany Machine.

"Not at all, Mayor. Please, continue."

"There I was atop my trusty steed Bully Boy, bugle in one hand and saber outstretched in the other. All around us—in every direction—bloodthirsty Indians as far as the eye could see . . ."

If this was going to end in a toast to Caleb, it was going to take a while. He sneaked another look at his timepiece. It was now 9:23. The hands blurred and dissolved as Caleb's eyes glazed over. The hypnotic, rhythmic pounding of Roosevelt's garbled voice droned on and on and on.

On Tenth Avenue, Old Toothless Sally had finally gotten it together and was out hawking her goods.

"Hello, gov'nor. Care for a quick bibble in the old bobble?"

A quick bibble in the old bobble cost an even sixpence, while a "wet waggle" cost a ha'penny or two. "A fish in a dish, with

tartar sauce on the side" was a full tuppence. If someone wanted
an all-night "dilly-wonker" or a "triple wraparound digger," that
was extra, and Sally always made it clear up front that she wasn't
into anything weird.

At approximately 9:20, a morbidly obese albino
man coming out of the original Original Ray's
Pizzeria on Eleventh Avenue witnessed Sally wad-
dling up Eighth Street. He later said that she
belched, picked something out of her ear, hawked
up a loogie "of unbelievable size," and then turned
onto Ninth, heading east.

It was the last time she would be seen alive, for
at that exact moment, the killer walked through
the Five Points district of lower Manhattan. He walked
warily; even for him, this neighborhood was dangerous. It was
populated by large street gangs with unusual names like the Flap-
jacks, the Garlic Knots, the Venti Caffe Lattes, and the Toasted
Bialys with a Schmeer. Often these packs would engage in ultra-
violent, riotous brawls that could last the whole night long and
would inevitably end with at least one gang member running
home in tears. Tonight, however, the killer was lucky. It was all
quiet in the Five Points. He made his way up Broadway, where he
paused to buy a cup of mayonnaise from a street vendor. In 1882
a man named Hellmann had just invented this oil-and-egg delight, but he wasn't yet sure how to market it. He started with
street carts, selling it like ice cream. New Yorkers were so crazy
about the new treat that they were more than content, at present, to eat it from a cup with a spoon, or perhaps on a sugar cone
with chocolate sprinkles.

After finishing his mayo, the killer picked up his pace. The
need to murder, maim, and mutilate began to boil up in his veins.

He quickly strode the three blocks to Herald Square, where he hoisted up his woolen trousers and waded through the waist-high manure. Back then there were no cars, and the buggy horses left behind copious amounts of waste. Herald Square's bowl-shaped topography (it was actually below sea level) had made it the repository for most of the city's excrement, as well as most of the city's missing persons.

He was now just one block away from the history books, and ahead, at about ten yards and closing, Old Toothless Sally Jenkins was just one high-pitched cackle away from becoming the first unfortunate victim of Jack the Jolly Thwacker.

". . . AND THAT'S WHEN I DECIDED THAT THE ELEPHANT'S FOOT WOULD make a bully coffee table!" Roosevelt exploded with a boisterous laugh that shook Caleb back to reality.

"So here's to me," bellowed Teddy. "Long may I live. Chin chin, my good friend!" Caleb and the mayor clinked glasses.

"I'll second that, gentlemen," said a woman's voice.

"Well, by golly almighty! Look what the cat dragged in!" Roosevelt bellowed. He stood up, and the tablecloth, tucked into his trousers, pulled up with him, emptying the contents of their glasses into Caleb's lap. This time, the long-suffering police chief didn't even bother to sigh, but merely dabbed at his wet crotch with a handkerchief.

"Why, if it isn't the charming Elisabeth Smith, columnist *par excellence* for the *Evening Post*," Roosevelt schmoozed while taking her hand.

She was the last person Caleb wanted to see, especially in his current condition.

"Oh, Mr. Mayor, you're much too kind."

"On the contrary, miss, I am not kind at all. But I am as strong as a bull moose and you may use me to the limit!" With that the mayor clicked his heels and kissed Elisabeth's hand.

"I have no idea what that means," she said, still smiling.

"But I thought you were on assignment somewhere in Japan," said Roosevelt.

"Close; Egypt, to be precise. I was following the exploits of Mr. Howard Carter and Lord Carnarvon. They were excavating old houses belonging to the slaves who built Ramses the Sixth's tomb. It was all quite boring really, until they reached a door that they couldn't seem to budge. They claimed that something wonderful was on the other side, but by then I was simply fed up with all the sand and all the dirt and grit. It was finding its way into—" She paused, as if looking for the right words. "Every orifice that I have." She paused again, frowning, as if those weren't the right words at all. "I mean, I just had to get back home, and so here I am."

"And we're all the better for it," cooed the mayor. "Tell me, did Mr. Carter and Lord Carnarvon ever get the door open?"

"Beats me. Who's the trannie?" Elisabeth asked, referring to Caleb.

"My apologies. Police Chief Spencer, may I introduce Miss Elisabeth Smith." Caleb reluctantly stood, staring forlornly at his crotch.

"Hello, Liz," he muttered.

"Caleb!" said a surprised Elisabeth. "Why, I'm sorry. I didn't recognize you in drag. Yes, I was reading all about your adventures with Dandy Dan, the Water Man, on the plane back from Cairo." She offered her hand to be smooched.

"That's all right, Liz," said Caleb, making a show of only

shaking her hand. "I'm actually, you know, only half in drag."
He slunk back into his seat.

"Pardon me, but do the two of you know each other?" asked
Roosevelt.

"Well, you might say we do, from a former relationship that
ended very badly." Liz frowned again, as if she had meant to be
more subtle, then shrugged and gave Caleb one of those re-
member-the-great-sex-we-used-to-have smiles.

Caleb couldn't help but notice how great Liz looked. Her thick
brown hair was pulled away from her face, revealing a perfect
neckline, which brought the eye straight down to her shapely
hourglass figure.

"Bully! Then you'll join us for an after-dinner drink! You are
just in time. The evening's entertainment is about to begin. If
you sit here beside your mayor, you'll have a perfect view."

Caleb suddenly spoke up: "You know, I really should be
going—"

"Nonsense," said Roosevelt. "Don't be rude. Miss Smith,
please sit."

"Well, I suppose for just a few minutes."

"Marvelous!" hailed Teddy, as he helped her to her chair.
"How 'bout dessert?"

"No thank you. I'm on a diet. Trying to keep myself shapely
for all those young gentleman callers who seem to be constantly
knocking down my front door." She shot Caleb a look.

"Yes, yes, you're quite right. I should abstain, myself." Teddy
patted his big stomach. "Why don't you just apply it directly to
your thighs, Theodore?" He erupted in a buoyant laugh. Smith
giggled, but Spencer sat glumly. He hated the mayor's catch-
phrases almost as much as he hated his stories.

"What can we get you to drink?" inquired Teddy.

"Maybe something light. Caleb, dear, what was that delightful drink we used to order at Hurley's?" She was looking directly at the police chief, but he wasn't looking back. "Oh yes, I remember. I will have a powdered opium and liquid ether frappe, with a shot of pure laudanum."

"Waiter!" cried the mayor, "One God's Own Enema!"

Caleb rolled his eyes. It was going to be a long night.

A voice cried out, "Ladies and gentlemen. Back for a return engagement here at Delmonico's, please welcome that slaphappy duo of disgruntled lowlifes, forever embroiled in the dismal world of lugubrious matrimony . . . the two and (hopefully) the only . . . Punch and Judy!"

"Oh goody!" declared Teddy. "They're my favorite!"

The patrons applauded as a stubby woman with a big putty nose limped to the center of the room. She was dressed in a red costume, with bells on her shoes and hat.

"Oh woe. What donkey work is this blessed conjugal life," Judy began, and already the audience was booing her. "I hope my helpmate has found suitable employment today, for we need food and have not the means to buy such." The crowd hissed.

Then a huge barrel of a man entered. He was dressed in the same silly red outfit, only his was way too tight for his body. The audience went crazy, pounding the tables and hooting and hollering. Punch was obviously their favorite. "Matron, I am home!" he announced. "Is there a fine meaty banquet for me to partake of? For I am famished and need most assuredly to sup!"

"No, my lord, and master, we have only rotting grub. You have not a craft that pays earnings to buy such fancy edibles!" A hush fell over the audience. They seemed to know what was coming next. Punch pranced about, rolling his eyes and working himself up into a red-faced frenzy. Then he pulled out a long "slapstick" (a doweling rod with a paddle bolted to one end).

"Well then, gentlewoman," he said, "I will have to teach you a lesson!"

"Oh, no! No! Please good sir, no!"

Punch chased Judy all around the dining room, crawling underneath the tables and sometimes jumping on top of them. The crowd was in hysterics. Roosevelt was laughing so hard his face was turning red. Caleb looked like he was about to fall asleep.

Elisabeth leaned toward Caleb. "You suppose that's what our married life would have ended up like?" she whispered.

"Except you'd be holding the paddle," he retorted.

"Well, obviously."

"Why are you really here?" he asked her.

"My dear Mr. Spencer, what *are* you implying?"

"I know you. You would not have left Egypt if there weren't a story brewing."

"You insult me, sir. How do you know I am not back to rekindle the lingering embers of our love?"

"I assure you there are none."

Elisabeth leaned away. "And I assure you there are none on my end, either, Chief Spencer, so you may divorce yourself of any illusions you have in that regard. I am of course here for a story."

The sound of church bells erupted from Caleb's pants. He and Elisabeth looked curiously at his lap.

"Excuse me," he said, and pulled out a large wooden box and placed it on the table. The teak and mahogany frame was decorated with intricate inlaid designs and was marked "Edison" in gold script on the front. Caleb opened a little door in the rear of the box, lit a match, and poured kerosene into the mobile phone's loading funnel.

"I see you use Edison," observed Liz. "I use Bell. The reception is much better and I don't have to wait 'til midnight to call long distance."

"Excuse me again," said Caleb, getting up to move away from the noise of the show.

"Now I have you, you ungrateful ugly wench!" Punch announced, and he swung hard the big slapstick. There was a sickening thud, and a spray of blood hit Roosevelt in the face. The mayor laughed so hard that he nearly exploded.

"Take that!" yelped Punch as he continued to bash Judy with the paddle. The genteel nineteenth-century audience could not get enough of the carnage. Punch bowed to a standing ovation, and two waiters dragged his unconscious wife away. Punch would only have an hour or so to revive her before their next show.

"I gotta tell ya," said Teddy, turning back to the table, "I don't know how many times I've seen that, and it just gets funnier and funnier every time!"

Spencer returned to the table. "That was the precinct. It seems there's been a ghastly murder. You must excuse me."

"Hold on there, Chiefy," roared Teddy, "I believe I'll tag along with you."

Spencer sighed. That was the last thing he wanted.

"My apologies, Miss Smith," said Roosevelt, again kissing Liz's hand, "but I'm afraid what promised to be a most . . . stimulating evening will have to be postponed. Duty calls!"

"You know, Mayor, it's really my duty that calls, not yours. You should stay here and enjoy the rest of this . . . 'show.'"

"Nonsense my boy, I shall assist you in all ways possible. Let us away!"

Caleb bowed to Liz. "Good night Miss Smith, and . . . goodbye." His farewell was cold, and there was a definite permanence to his words. With that, he and the mayor hurried out of Delmonico's to a waiting carriage below.

"Good night to you, Chief Spencer," Liz said softly. "Though I am sure I'll be seeing you again shortly."

AT APPROXIMATELY MIDNIGHT, THEIR CARRIAGE BOUNCED DOWN THE cobblestones on Ninth Street and pulled to a stop in front of the crime scene, between Seventh and Broadway. The police had barricaded the entrance to a dark alley and were now enjoying some well-deserved coffee and "yeast rings."

"What do we have?"

"Jelly, powdered, and cream-filled," said the sergeant in charge.

"I'm talking about the crime," said Caleb, doing a classic slow burn.

"Of course you are, sir. My apologies. Victim is one Sally Jenkins, alias Old Toothless Sally, sixty-three years old, prostitute out of the Mulberry Bend, no family to speak of. She was found by that gentleman over there." The officer pointed to the morbidly obese albino man. "Just about forty-five minutes ago."

"No yeast twists?" asked Teddy.

"Sorry, Mr. Mayor. Them were the first to go."

Caleb was writing in his small notepad. "Who was the last to see her alive?" he asked.

"That would be him, sir." The sergeant pointed to the same morbidly obese albino man.

"You're telling me that the last person who saw her alive and the first person to discover her dead are one and the same person?"

"No sir," said the sergeant.

"But it would seem to me—"

"No sir. *That* morbidly obese albino found the victim. While *this* morbidly obese albino man was the last to see her alive."

Caleb adjusted his glasses. He had not realized there were two of them.

"Are you twins?" he asked.

The morbidly obese albino on the left huffed. "I've never seen him before in my life."

Caleb snapped shut his notepad.

"Sounds like an open and shut case to me!" said Teddy. "Let's get back to Delmonico's."

"You're welcome to return alone if you so desire—"

"Sir, if I may be so bold," said the sergeant. "If you take a look at the body, you'll see that neither of these boys could have done the deed."

"I'll be the judge of that, Sergeant," said Caleb.

"Yes, yes, of course you will, sir," muttered the sergeant. "After all, you're the chief of police, which makes you my superior, and who am I? I'm just a lousy flatfoot, twice your age, who's been passed over for promotion year after year because of a so-called drinking problem, which once, just once, mind you, and it was after a long, thankless day of hard work, may have, and I repeat *may have,* resulted in a minor incident of so-called obscene conduct with my nightstick. Why should anyone listen to me? The crime scene is right down that alley, gentlemen."

"Thank you, Sergeant."

There was still a bit of resentment from the police force about having to report to a young upstart like Spencer, and when he and Roosevelt turned their backs the sergeant stuck his tongue out at Caleb.

Roosevelt and Spencer lifted the rope, bent over, and entered the alley. Caleb picked up an oil lamp and struck a match on the wall. Suddenly the match exploded in a huge fireball that singed his eyebrows.

"Weehoo!" exclaimed the barrel-chested Roosevelt.

"Delightful," hissed Spencer, who knew all too well what the

mayor's weehooing meant. "I don't know which I love more, Mayor, your stories or these little . . . outbursts."

"Well, fear not, young Caleb. I've a million of them both." Roosevelt slapped his belly.

"I'm overjoyed. Now, if you would kindly step back, I need to examine the crime scene."

"I've seen my fair share of violence, young man, like the time I was hunting giant iguanas in the dusty outbacks of Australia. The females can get quite feisty, and—"

"Now is not the time for stories, Mr. Mayor!"

"You're just jealous because you've never seen a female iguana swallow a fully grown wild Aborigine. Now that, my boy, will put hair on your chest."

"Gentlemen," called a familiar female voice, "why don't we put our testosterone back in the old billiard pockets for the time being and observe the crime scene, shall we?"

"Oh, hell," muttered Caleb.

Elisabeth Smith stepped out of the shadows. "I'm quite sure there will be ample opportunity later for the two of you to compare your . . . best . . . um . . ." She concentrated. This time she was going to find the perfect phrase. ". . . muscular protuberances." She sighed. *Oh, Liz,* she admonished herself, *why do you even bother to open your mouth?*

"How the hell did you get in here?" Caleb demanded.

"Don't talk to the little lady that way," said Roosevelt, stepping quickly to her side. "But how the hell did you get in here, honey? This is supposed to be a sealed-off crime scene."

"The officers were kind enough to let me in. I simply explained to them how much you required my assistance."

"Very resourceful," said the mayor.

"Yes, well, we are not in need of your help," Caleb said, "and

I'll thank you to leave now, so we—that is, *I*—can get down to work."

He took Elisabeth by the arm and started to escort her out of the alley.

"T. R.," she pleaded, "there isn't any harm in my observing, now, is there? I would absolutely love to watch a top-notch investigative team at work."

"We are not a—" Caleb began.

"The young lady might learn something, Chief Spencer."

"She might learn what your weehooing means."

The mayor whispered into Caleb's ear, "But she's a hot tamale." Then he turned to Liz and wagged his finger. "Just swear you won't print anything you see here, tootsie roll."

"You have my word, Your Honor," she said.

"Please, all of you, I prefer to work alone. My . . . solitude is of great value to me, and—"

"Now, hold on there, buckaroo banzai, I think there's only one mayor standing here. And as far as I know, mayors outrank police chiefs. It goes mayors, bookies, leg-breakers, ice cream, then police chiefs. I say the little lady stays!"

The mayor seldom pulled rank with him, and Spencer stood still, not sure of his next move. He didn't like being told how to run his investigation, didn't like the mayor being there, and definitely didn't want his snoopy ex-girlfriend hanging around. But what could he do?

"Okay, just stand to the side and keep your trap shut, understand?"

"Oh, we're feeling bossy, aren't we?" Liz replied. "As per usual."

Spencer ignored her, lit his lamp, held it up, and illuminated the horrible scene.

The three stood slack-jawed. At first glance, the bizarre display in front of them appeared more like a tableau from a wax museum than a crime scene. The body was standing (not lying face-up with an embroidered pillow under the head, hands folded neatly over the chest, and legs crossed in a ladylike fashion, which was the customary way to leave a murdered prostitute in a dark alley in that era). Rigor mortis had set in early, allowing the killer the ability to manipulate the body like a fully articulated doll. He had even propped it up, using a stick and a wooden box for a stand.

"It's an atrocity," said Caleb.

"Ritual murder," Liz whispered.

"Shark attack!" exclaimed the mayor.

Old Toothless Sally Jenkins, the poor unfortunate victim, had not only been murdered (clubbed from behind, possibly by a bag of apples), but the killer had taken the time to do some rather outlandish things to her body.

Spencer took out his new Edison tape recorder and turned its crank several hundred times. Then he spoke into its horn-shaped microphone in a professional, unemotional manner.

"The victim's dress has been cut, and the hemline raised a good fifteen inches above the knee."

"That isn't the way the ladies wear their skirts today," Liz interjected.

"Quiet!" Caleb admonished. "In addition, numerous brightly colored, round pieces of cloth . . . I would say about two inches in diameter, have been meticulously sewn into the garment, creating a random polka-dot pattern. It looks like her boots were removed by the killer, resoled, painted white, polished, and returned to her feet.

"The victim's, um, intestines have been removed and placed

atop her head. They have been fashioned into a hairdo shaped like a . . . beehive?" This staggered him for a moment, and he switched off his tape recorder and turned to Liz.

"Why would he do such a thing?" he whispered. Liz shrugged.

"I've never seen a hairdo like *that* before."

The killer had also made his mark on Sally's face: a small incision under her jawline allowed the jowls to be pulled up and pinned back behind her ears, giving her essentially what we would today call a face-lift. Liz observed that the heavy mustard and lard makeup that Old Sally was accustomed to wearing had been wiped away, and a fine layer of a makeup of exquisite quality had been applied in its place (Max Factor Light Foundation Number Two, actually, according to a "friend" of mine who, um, knows a lot about makeup). Her lips were painted shocking fuschia, long black eyelashes were glued to her still-open eyes, and a strange insignia had been inscribed on her cheek with an eyebrow pencil. None of the three could identify the sign. It consisted of a circle bisected by a straight vertical line and two opposing radials extending from the center point to create two acute angles.

"Pey-ah-cey," Roosevelt said, sounding out the inscription on the symbol. "What could it mean? Do either of you know Latin?"

But something else had grabbed Caleb's attention: her smile. Anyone who knew Old Toothless Sally knew of the brown, rotting nubbins that had given her the nickname. But now the prostitute's frozen mouth displayed a set of gleaming white Hollywood choppers. The killer had capped her teeth!

Taking into account the last time Sally had been seen alive, outside the original Original Ray's Pizzeria, until the time that the second morbidly obese albino discovered her dead, plus all the fine tailoring and extensive dental work, Spencer determined that the encounter between Sally and her killer had to have lasted at least three minutes.

Teddy Roosevelt threw up his arms. "What the hell are we supposed to do?" he bellowed. "The way I see it, our suspect is a skilled surgeon, dentist, cobbler, tailor, and makeup artist—*and* he enjoys styling ladies' hair! Jesus H. Christ! There's got to be at least a thousand guys like that in this city."

Spencer was trying desperately to contain himself.

"Plus, he can't spell." Elisabeth said, drawing their attention to a corner of the alley. As if the killer hadn't left enough clues already, there on the brick wall he had scrawled a cryptic message in chalk:

da mummers are da wonz dat dont get blamed and
wees da wonz dat get thwacked. Im no dandy dan the
water man, yooz can just call me Jack. Jack The Thwacker
cause Ize like to thwack.

The End (I hope you like my poem)

Roosevelt clenched his fists. His eyes turned red with what looked to his companions like rage. Thick, oily liquid from his

pupils condensed into round droplets that spilled over his eyes, onto his hot cheeks, and—in the suddenly chill night air—became a fog upon his spectacles. The big teddy bear was crying.

"That has got to be the most beautiful poem I have ever read," he whimpered as he pulled out his snot rag and blew a loud foghorn into it. "Weehoo," he added half-heartedly, the blowing effort having shaken something loose.

"Okay, that's it! I can't take this anymore! I want both of you out of my crime scene, now!"

"Caleb, stop!" Elisabeth ordered, then her tone changed from admonishment to one of urgency. "Listen to me. We have a major clue here. The killer mentions Mummers in his poem."

"Yeah, so? The clowns that dress up like birds and run around drinking beer?"

"Not exactly," Liz said. "The Mummers are about more than an annual parade. They are an ancient secret society that has its origins in Sussex, England, hundreds and hundreds of years ago. The word 'mummer' refers to a person who is mumming. It comes from the Greek word 'mommo,' meaning 'mask.' Wearing masks and costumes became quite popular in the fourteenth century. Besides dressing up, performing plays, and holding parades, the Mummers also worship pagan gods of fertility."

"Sound like my kind of gods, if you get my drift," said the mayor, gesticulating wildly with his pelvis.

"But what does all this mean?" Caleb asked.

"So now you admit you need my help?"

"I admit your insight at this particular moment might save me some time, yes—"

"Bully!" cried Roosevelt. "Then the tamale is on the team."

"There's no team!" Caleb exclaimed.

Roosevelt looked as if he might cry again. "No . . . team?"

Liz furrowed her brow. "I don't know exactly what it means,

but the annual Mummers Day parade was held here today, down-town. I say we head down there and start putting the pieces to-gether." Caleb seemed about to protest. "You'll need me on this. My father was a Mummer, so I might spot something."

He could not argue with that logic, but he was not comfort-able with the situation.

"And if this killer does any more styling, you'll need my fem-inine wiles."

Roosevelt whispered into Caleb's ear, "Plus, if things get rough, we might get to see her with her shirt off!"

"All right. Let's go," Caleb finally said.

"Bully!" shouted you-know-who. "Now I am a 'happy camper!'"

Liz suddenly became extremely animated. "Caleb, listen to me: every year, members of the secret society of Mummers hold their convention here in New York. If our killer is a Mummer, he's probably still here. But only for one more day. We have no time to waste."

"Right," said Roosevelt, finally comprehending the direness of the situation. "Let's hurry back to Delmonico's and quickly finish our after-dinner drinks!"

THE NEWLY FORMED INVESTIGATIVE TEAM HAD DONE SOME EXPERT ANALY-sis. In fact they were ahead of their time in terms of decipher-ing forensic evidence, but in their exuberance to follow the Mummer lead, they had ignored one blatant clue left behind by the killer: the position of the prostitute's body! Was it some-thing they just missed? Or was it something they just couldn't understand?

Yes, Old Toothless Sally was left standing, but she was also

posed with one knee up and both arms extended, her hands bent down at the wrists. Considering the way the killer had arranged the entrails into a lovely bouffant hairstyle, as well as the white boots, the makeup, the polka-dot miniskirt, the body position, and the peace sign on her cheek, the picture couldn't have been clearer. But, of course, it could never be clear to someone from the nineteenth century. It was obvious to me in the twenty-first century that the tableau the murderer created with Sally Jenkins was unmistakably that of a late-1960s go-go dancer!

A week or two later, it occurred to me that there was definitely something out of the ordinary going on.

"Shark attack!" exclaimed the Mayor.

Chapter the Second.

In which a dreadful epistle is dreadfully received and quite prudently responded to in a manner most befitting dread.

I needed someone to bounce ideas off of, someone with wit and insight. Unfortunately, I have no friends except Wendell, and even he would only come over to my luxurious Dakota apartment if I promised to make him a cheese sandwich.

"Wendell, my fine African-American buddy," I said. "In one week's time I may have solved a case that's gone unsolved for over a hundred years."

"Guess who I saw in the elevator," he replied.

Wendell had a hard time focusing. I chalked it up to the result of his two chosen professions: by day he was a New York City cab driver and by night he blew himself up at carnivals.

"Wendell, I am talking about the Jack the Jolly Thwacker case, here. The one you said had never been solved. I think I might actually be able to figure it out."

"Yoko Ono," he said. "Stood right beside me. Asked me to press eight, I told her I'd already pressed it. Then she told me to look up at the ceiling, where she'd written 'yes' in very tiny letters."

I wasn't particularly impressed. My apartment was adjacent

to hers in the Dakota, and we had exchanged pleasantries in the elevator many times. Or rather, I had offered pleasantries while she examined me for signs of age or disease—she wanted me out of my place in the worst way, so she could add a gallery or something to hers, and she was eager for either me or my lease to expire.

"Wendell, pay attention here. Look at these crime scene photos and tell me if you see anything out of the ordinary."

"Do you think it was Yoko who came up with Bagism, or was it John?"

"The victim, the way she's standing, doesn't it look odd to you?"

"Personally, I think crawling inside a bag isn't a bad way to—" His eyes settled on the picture. "Are her intestines supposed to be on her head like that?"

"Oh, just eat your sandwich."

"Can do."

"Here's what I think," I began. "The killer seems to have some kind of foreknowledge of modern American cultural trends. Either he's hip enough to have predicted the emergence of go-go dancing one hundred and fifty years in advance, or he's some kind of magician or prognosticator. Of course, both of these theories are completely preposterous, which leaves me with only one conclusion . . ."

I paused for dramatic effect.

Wendell sat chewing his cheese sandwich.

"Go-go dancing has been around much longer than we thought! The Mummers might even have been go-go dancing since their inception. It could be one of those pagan ritual things that only became popular traditions later, like Easter or the Kentucky Derby."

Wendell took a big swallow of grape juice to wash down his

cheese sandwich. He looked thoughtful and for a moment it seemed as if he might actually say something helpful.

"There is no way," he pronounced, "that anyone could keep something like go-go dancing a secret for hundreds of years."

His obstinance was vexing. I tried to telepathically send him a picture of me hitting him over the head with a baseball bat, but I couldn't stop thinking of the dog drinking the root beer. After he finished his sandwich, I showed him to the door, so I could get back to my research in pey-ah-cey.

AUGUST 26TH, 1882, 5:30 AM (THE DAY AFTER THE FIRST MURDER)

In the nineteenth century, before the birth of the modern skyscraper, New York's skyline was simpler. At dawn, its most famous landmarks would have stood out strikingly against the open sky: the Brooklyn Bridge, the Flatiron Building, the Nabisco Pork Fat and Hardtack Company, and the famous copper statue of Nathan Bedford Forrest, founder of the esteemed brotherhood of the Ku Klux Klan.

The ninety-meter[2]-tall hooded statue was presented to the Union by the defeated Confederate states in 1865 as a peace offering at the end of the Civil War, and it stood on Bedloe's Island at the mouth of New York harbor for over thirty years. With its burning cross held high in the Grand Wizard's right hand, it served as a welcoming beacon to millions of immigrants seeking refuge in America's bosom. It was their first sight after a long

---

2. Meters are an antiquated form of measurement employed by nineteenth-century Americans, although they are still used in many of the more backward parts of the modern world, such as Africa, Asia, Europe, most Pacific islands, the Middle East, Antarctica, and Australia.

Chris Elliott

journey across an angry Atlantic. Schoolchildren loved to race up the klansman's 350 steps to the giant hood and peer out from its big eyeholes, while below, their parents shed tears at the moving inscription:

> Give us your tired, your poor, your huddled masses from no further south than Spain and no further east than Russia (unless they're good with railroads).

Unfortunately the landmark was destroyed late one snowy night in the winter of 1896, when a drunken zeppelin captain crashed his dirigible into the figure's groin. The zeppelin's cargo, five hundred gallons of Texas tea, spilled into the Hudson, resulting in the nation's first true environmental disaster. Indigenous life forms—pigeons, wharf rats, and eels—were covered with the sticky crude oil for decades to come. Frederic Bartholdi and Gustave Eiffel's eyesore was erected in the statue's place some years later, and the gaudy Lady Liberty remains a source of heated debate amongst New Yorkers to this day.

Now, the morning after the first murder, the penny papers already had the grisly story:

"Sporting girl mutilated in Herald Square!" yelled the newsies.

"Read all about it! Plus, tonight's Powerball drawing up to nearly forty dollars! Match two numbers, get a free frying pan handle!"

Penny papers, the rag papers of yesteryear, specialized in the darker, more gruesome side of city life. Although Liz had kept her promise and had not yet filed the story with the *Evening Post*, other journalists had scooped her by bribing chatty coppers and weaseling their way into the makeshift morgue now set up at the Manhattan Abattoir. (Back then people had a tendency to die off in large numbers, and the slaughterhouses were employed to

take in the overflow.) There, amidst cattle carcasses suspended by their hind legs in various stages of butchery, reposed the body of Old Toothless Sally Jenkins, cold, lifeless, and also suspended by her hind legs.

RAP, RAP, RAP. RAP, RAP, RAP.

The loud knocking woke the sleeping man in the nondescript brownstone.

"Coffee and strudel, it is!" announced Mrs. O'Leary, the boardinghouse-keeper, and from the other side of the door she heard the occupant fall out of bed with a loud thud. Later she would describe to investigators hearing what she thought were wet footsteps clumping and squishing their way across the room. Then the heavy door creaked open a crack.

"Your breakfast, Doctor." There was no response, and Mrs. O'Leary, her neck stretching like saltwater taffy, bobbed her head to and fro, straining to see inside.

"Did you hear the news?" she offered. "It's in all the papers, it is. A gruesome murder last night, not far from here, it was. They say the lady was beheaded, de-armed, de-legged, cleaned, and deveined, they do. They say he sawed her right in two, he did. Imagine that. In our own neighborhood, no less. It was!"

A hand reached out from the narrow opening. It was covered with dried blood, from wrist to fingertips.

"Oh my," she said, as she nervously placed the cup of coffee in the palm and balanced the pastry on top of it.

"Enjoy your breakfast, Doctor."

The bloody hand gingerly retreated through the narrow opening, careful not to spill the hot liquid.

"So I'll be back then, this afternoon, I will, and . . ."

Blam!

"Ow, ow, ow, my foot! My foot!" Mrs. O'Leary was screaming in agony.

"Doctor, please! My foot is . . . in . . . the . . . door . . . it is!"

The door quickly opened to release her foot, then slammed back shut. Hobbling back down the stairs in pain, Mrs. O'Leary muttered to herself.

"What an incorrigible donkey's crupper, he is!"

By seven AM the city was abuzz with talk of the murder. Gossip and speculation were everywhere. "Who could do such a thing?" "It couldn't be an American!" "It most certainly was the work of a crazed immigrant, or one of Barnum's ungodly freaks, or worse yet, an insane Negroid."

But at the nineteenth precinct on Sixty-eighth Street, Police Chief Caleb Spencer, with cool, level-headed objectivity, was already hard at work trying to determine exactly which crazed immigrant or insane Negroid was responsible. Having received plenty of volunteers to interview prostitutes in the Tenderloin district, and having doubled the patrols in Herald Square, Caleb, at the mayor's insistence, now ordered warning signs to be posted throughout the city:

Dreadful!

Evil-Doer at Large.
Watch your Derrieres!

After their search of the parade grounds had turned up nothing but cast-off feathers, Caleb had agreed to meet with Liz Smith and Teddy Roosevelt later today, but now he sat at his desk with his stereopticon, quickly shuffling through his Gallery of Surly and Suspicious Foreigners. It was a long shot, but that was how all criminal investigations began.

At the top of his list was Hans Von Copple, an Austrian who had emigrated from his hometown of Hal's Ass five years earlier. Von Copple was also known as Rawhide Face, because his nose had been sheared off by a corn-detasseling machine in the old country and then reconstructed using polished leather. He was a good suspect. He was a big man with a bad temper, especially when he had a cold. His arrest record indicated three convictions for sneaking into women's apartments and styling their hair while they slept. Coincidentally, he was also a Mummer. A shudder of excitement ran through Caleb. Could this be his man? But, after reading that Copple had also lost both his eyes in a wild turkey attack (a handful of leather now stuck out of each eye socket), and reasoning that whoever committed the crime had to have been able to see, he crossed Hans off his list.

Why did that woman appear at Delmonico's? he thought to himself, allowing his mind to drift away from mutilation to Liz, then back to mutilation again and then back to Liz. *What could she possibly require from me now? It's over!*

He sighed, pulling out the file on the next possible suspect, Larry "the Li'l Leprechaun" Lupo. Still he found it hard to concentrate.

"Get a grip, my good man, she's just a dame," he told himself.

Born of hardy New England stock, raised on the rocky coast of Maine, and imbued with a plucky Katharine Hepburn–esque disposition, Elisabeth May Smith was anything but "just a dame." She was a true modern woman in every sense of the word. She was young, handsome, and stubborn to a fault. She was intelligent and romantic, and her fierce insistence on dating only men with good childbearing hips and smaller breasts than hers set her apart as a woman of integrity and standards.

My in-depth research revealed that Liz and Caleb first crossed paths many years before, at a rally for women's rights in

Washington Square Park. Back then women couldn't vote, but it was still early in the struggle, and all they demanded at present was the right not to have their intellectual abilities repressed and their hopes and dreams quashed by an uncaring, rigidly patriarchal social system, and to belch out loud in restaurants.

Caleb, a flatfoot, was assigned to crowd control, and Liz caught his eye right away. Sitting on the stage behind the guest speaker, she shifted in her seat and recrossed her legs. Caleb caught a glimpse of a fine, shapely calf bedecked in a bright red stocking (unheard of in the day, and actually unheard of today as well). He thought to himself, *Now that's a lady with* chutzpah.

When Victoria Woodhull, the first woman to run for president, took the stage and began to rant and rail hysterically from the podium about injustice or somesuch, a group of disgruntled restaurateurs, cooks, and waiters filed out of the eateries along Washington Square. The angry men began to stir up a ruckus. When Woodhull lit up a cigar and burped into her megaphone, that was the last straw. The men rushed the crowd, and pandemonium broke out.

"Kill the distasteful ladies!" they shouted. They whooped and hollered, swinging champagne bottles, rolling pins, and ears of corn on chains.

Young Caleb was taken by surprise at the sudden riot. He pulled out both his long nightstick and his short daystick and joined in the melee, swinging to and fro, bashing heads right and left. A frozen duck was hurled at the stage. Liz jumped from her chair and pushed Victoria Woodhull away. In so doing, she received the full impact of the rock-hard poultry. Caleb watched in horror as Elisabeth swayed and then, unconscious, fell forward into the crowd.

When Liz finally regained her senses, she was reclining on

a daybed. Caleb sat over her, gently holding an ice pack to her head.

What follows is not conjecture on my part, but the actual transcript of their first conversation. In the Victorian era, it was a common practice for a stenographer to be present whenever a young, unmarried couple were to be alone.

"Where am I?" she asked.

"You're safe. You're in my flat. You took quite a bonk from a frozen duck out there, but you're gonna be fine."

"Ow, my head hurts," she groaned, trying to focus on the young man hovering over her. Perhaps it was her blurred vision, but she found him attractive, in a queer sort of way.

He removed the ice pack.

"Looks like your duck laid a purple egg," he said. He reached into a small vial and handed her two pills. "Take these."

"What are they?"

"Prussic acid. Best thing for a headache. Also good for killing insects. 'Course, if you had ants on your brain you could kill two birds with one stone." He laughed, then immediately shook his head. "Sorry, wretched joke."

Liz took a gulp of water and swallowed the acid pills. Then she sat up and looked around the room: a classic nineteenth-century bachelor pad with forest-green walls, darkly varnished wainscoting, pornographic tintypes here and there, a number of female mannequins, a pair of ladies' undies flung over the coatrack, and the stenographer typing away in the corner. She turned back to Caleb inquisitively.

"Who are you?" she asked.

"Your humble servant, ma'am. Officer Caleb R. Spencer of the NCNYPD. I was at the rally. I, um, I saw you sitting up there on the stage and, I don't know, something about you . . . I just

couldn't keep my eyes off you. Of course, when you got knocked out, well, that was the perfect opportunity for me to—"

"For you to *what?*" she demanded.

"Take care of you," he said, quite oblivious to any untoward subtext. "I live just across the square."

Elisabeth smiled as if to ask, *Are you for real?* She pulled herself together and tried to stand.

"Well thank you very much for taking care of me, humble servant Spencer. But I must get back to the paper and file a story on the riot. I'm a stringer for the *Evening Post.*"

"You should probably rest."

"Thank you, but I'm really fine."

"No, I insist. You can sleep here. I'll watch you—I mean, watch *over* you. I mean, I won't take any pictures or anything . . . unless you want me to. But they'll be tasteful . . . that is, unless you don't want them to be."

Liz walked to the door, then stopped with her hand on the knob. She turned. He was right behind her, still holding the ice pack. There was a pause filled with anticipation, and then their lips met. In the next few moments their entire future, their destiny, and the gravity of their love would be born out in the warmth of that pure, innocent kiss, which led almost immediately to second base.

That's how it all began. The next night they made love like drunken sailors. Every hour on the hour, every which way but loose, higgledy-piggledy, until they were plum out of nature's gum. This was according to the stenographer, who added:

like two shameless hottentots ignorant of the Lord's commandments and the damnation that awaited them, neither moral nor chaste, nor lonely, nor dried-up, nor hopelessly chained to a notepad for the rest of their few remaining

childbearing years, and certainly not residing at 15 Fowler's Hat Place, Apt 3¾, waiting in bed behind an unlocked door . . . oh for Heaven's sake, I'll even cook you a meal!

Their relationship lasted three years, but when Elisabeth became a full-time columnist and Spencer made chief of police, their responsibilities tore them apart. (Of course, it was also impossible for them to remain friends after the ugly events surrounding their breakup, especially the incident with her mother's crinoline bustle and the pinking shears, which Caleb still swore was a mistake anyone could have made.)

But those were just memories. Now, the morning after the bizarre murder of Sally Jenkins, while Caleb sat at his desk at the nineteenth precinct and mused, Elisabeth sat at her desk at the *Evening Post* and fumed. She was not one to take being scooped by the competitors easily. She rifled through her mail, took an important-looking letter out of the middle, and then immediately dropped it. Somehow she knew it was from the killer. Maybe it was her reporter's gut instinct, or her woman's intuition. Or maybe it was because it was sealed with a skull and crossbones in a bowler hat. She tore it open, squinting to decipher the strange handwriting. The message was cryptic, threatening, and full of bad grammar, which she instinctively corrected with red ink. The last line she read out loud: "Very truly yours, Jack the Jolly Thwacker."

She swallowed hard. The letter slipped from her fingers. She gazed out into space, her eyes fixed on something far away, some frightening memory, a memory from another world, a cold, dark world, a world that she was loath to revisit (because of the aforementioned darkness and coldness). She gave little voice to what she whispered next:

"Daddy," she said.

WHEN I REACHED THIS POINT IN MY RESEARCH, A COLD CHILL RAN through my body, as I pray it ran through yours. (If it didn't, then I haven't done my job, and perhaps I need to rewrite the section, or maybe you could just pretend for my sake.)

As I sat on the floor of my living room in the Dakota, amidst a mountain range of research material strewn hither and thither in ill-organized piles like so many peaks and vales, I felt really creeped out. "What is going on with this Liz chick?" I thought. "Is there a connection between her and the Thwacker? If so, why wasn't that fact included in the official record of the investigation?" My heart began to pound. What had I stumbled on to? My apartment was dark and silent. I don't mind admitting to you that I was scared. I seemed to know information that had been intentionally kept secret for over a hundred years. Somebody didn't want it in the reports. For the first time in this process, I thought, *Could my life actually be in danger?*

Ring!

I nearly jumped out of my skin. I went to the door and peeked through the spyhole. Despite the fact that the murder I was studying happened over a hundred years ago, I felt sure that the killer himself had come for me. But the reality was far, far worse.

It was Yoko.

I opened the door.

"You know, Yoko, sweetheart, this really isn't a good time."

She brushed past me without a word.

"I'm kind of in the middle of something, here."

She took out a measuring tape and began to measure my kitchen.

"Hold this end for me," she commanded. As annoyed as I was, I found her quaint Japanese charm impossible to resist.

"What are you doing, exactly?"

She didn't answer. Instead she motioned for me to hold the tape in the corner of my dining room.

"Look, Yoko, I appreciate the visit, but I'm in the middle of some heavy research, here."

"Research," she said, in an eerie gallery-attendant monotone, "like art, is a form of time travel. One recreates the past with the impressions it has left on the present. This is possible because of what remains. Sometimes, the shadow of the thing is the thing itself." She took an apple out of the bowl on my counter, like she owned the place. "The apple has not changed in one hundred years. To bite into it and to taste its flavor is to be transported back in time." To demonstrate, she took a big bite.

Go ahead and make yourself at home, Yoko, I thought.

"See? Now I am back in time," she said.

I decided to challenge her: "What about pesticides? Fertilizers? Modern agriculture? How do you know for sure what an apple used to taste like?"

She huffed and closed the measuring tape with a *snap*.

"Trust me, I know," she said, and returned the half-eaten apple to the bowl.

She took out a stethoscope and began to listen to my heart.

"How are you lately, Chris? Feeling strong?"

"You're welcome to take that apple with you. I'm sure no one's going to want it now."

"Any heart pains? Blurred vision? No?" She sighed. "Oh well, I'll be seeing you."

When she was gone, I locked and double-bolted the door behind her, and dropped and did fifty push-ups. Well, five push-ups.

I mean, I thought about doing some push-ups, but I figured I should probably lose some weight first. Besides, I had a case to solve!

"Now where was I?" I said. "Oh yes, my life was in danger."

THE RELATIVELY BORING EXTERIOR OF TEDDY ROOSEVELT'S HOME AT 28 East Twentieth Street belied the tasteful opulence within. On the outside, it was a gray row house done in a semi–French Renaissance style. The front was symmetrical and predictable. The only notable accent was the hideous limestone relief separating the second and third floors. It depicted a smiling Roosevelt sitting cross-legged atop a pyramid of naked pygmies. The base was inscribed with his famous aphorism:

"Speak softly but carry a big stick."

Once inside, it was quite different. Upon entering the foyer, one was greeted by a giant stuffed gorilla. The dead animal was actually an early automaton that utilized a wind-up clockwork and music box mechanism perfected in Germany. It had the ability to move its arms up and down and to talk.

"Howdy, folks," it said in a voice that sounded a lot like Baloo the Bear from the *Jungle Book* cartoon (according to my research).

"Teddy will be right with ya. In the meantime, why not take a load off in the parlor?" Beyond the gorilla you passed through two giant Corinthian columns to enter the parlor and sit on your choice of a leopard-, zebra-, or human-skin sofa. Roosevelt's collection of mounted wildlife and stuffed Zulu tribesmen was the best in the land.

To the rear of the home was the conservatory, a glassed-in sunroom filled with giant ficus and palm plants and all sorts of live wildlife specimens. Tortoises lumbered across the tile floor as a

ten-foot anaconda slithered its way towards the piranha pond. Giant colorful parrots and rare butterflies flew back and forth, and in the corner was a cage, home to an extremely rare endangered species indeed: Ishi, the Last Uncivilized Indian in North America. The only known descendant of the Yahi tribe, whose ancestors could be traced back to the Stone Age, Ishi was captured by Roosevelt on one of his many expeditions into San Francisco. When the wild man wasn't on loan to anthropological museums, he lived a relatively peaceful life in Roosevelt's home, munching on cabbage and communing with the wildlife that roamed freely around him in the conservatory.

Bing bong!

At about 9:00 AM the morning after Sally's death, the doorbell rang at Roosevelt's residence. There was no answer.

Bing bong! Bing bong! Bing bong!

The door flung open and Caleb came flying through.

"Howdy folks," said the gorilla, "Teddy will be right . . ."

"Yeah yeah yeah," said Caleb. He blew past and headed for the parlor. "Roosevelt! Roosevelt! Where are you?"

"My good man, I am in the conservatory. Please join me," Roosevelt called back.

Caleb rushed to the rear of the house, tripping over a stuffed dingo. He reached the conservatory excited and out of breath.

"Is Miss Smith here?"

"Not that I'm aware of," said Roosevelt. "Why don't you check the hopper?"

"She sent me an urgent message. She said to meet her here. She said she had something to tell us both about the murder, and she sounded . . . she sounded like . . . like she . . . was . . ." Caleb slowed down to catch his breath and to attempt to comprehend the rather intriguing scene in front of him.

Roosevelt was standing in the middle of the conservatory

stark naked. One hand held a rose to his nose while the other stretched out behind him. His right leg was extended and the plump toes on his right foot were as pointy as he could make them.

Caleb shot a look at the artist, who stood at an easel painting Roosevelt's nude. The artist just shrugged, as if to say *What can I tell you, it's a living.*

"My official portrait," bellowed T. R. "I thought it would be bully to do something different. Not the same old stodgy, 'Look at me, here I am in my three-piece suit, aren't I just a handsome devil?' sort of thing, but something with a little *panache,* a little allure to it."

"The only things you are going to allure are your pet hippopotami."

"My point exactly, my good friend!" boomed Roosevelt, the cutting insult eluding him once again.

Caleb shook his head. Suddenly, from the foyer, came a familiar simian voice.

"Howdy folks . . ."

"More visitors! How gay!" exclaimed Teddy.

"Spencer? Roosevelt?" It was Liz.

"Back here!" Caleb yelled. "For God's sake, Mayor, put something on before the lady arrives."

Roosevelt barely had time to wrap a zebra pelt throw rug around his waist before Liz bounded into the conservatory.

"You really should keep that door locked, Teddy," she said.

"Yes, yes, I'm quite aware of the security gap."

"Are you all right?" Caleb asked. "You sounded dreadfully frightened on the phone." If Liz was touched by his concern, she didn't show it. If anything, Caleb's presence seemed to stiffen her steely demeanor.

"I received a correspondence at the *Post* this morning. It's

signed Jack the Jolly Thwacker. I think you two should take a look at it."

She handed it to Caleb. While he read, Liz regarded the large pink blob to her right. Teddy grinned and waved his rose at her. She returned the smile and nodded, then slowly looked back to Caleb.

"That's it!" said Caleb, finishing the letter. He dropped to one knee, pulled out his mobile phone, uncorked the receiver, opened his canister of kerosene, and began to fill it up.

"What are you doing?" Liz asked.

"I'm calling the station. I'm having an armed guard escort you home. He's going stay with you day and night."

"I'll volunteer," Teddy said. "Though I'm out of uniform," he purred.

"Do I have a say in this, Caleb?"

"You're off the case. It's too dangerous. I won't jeopardize a civilian." Caleb tapped the bottom of the kerosene canister, trying to coax out the last bit of accelerant.

"Whoa horsey, I thought we covered all this last night!" bellowed Roosevelt, hitching up his zebra pelt and stepping over. "That's all for the day, François. Thank you." He handed the artist a wad of cash.

On his way out, François muttered to Caleb, "Beats scrubbing whale bumps at the candle factory."

"Now let us have a look at this silly letter," said Roosevelt. "I'm quite sure there's no reason to get all spooked." He adjusted his glasses, cleared his throat, and began to read.

Elisabeth knelt beside Caleb.

"You and Teddy are mentioned as well. It's not just me! I know you care about me, but you can't do this."

"I can and I will. It has nothing to do with my affections, which I assure you I keep separate from my work."

"I know you too well, Caleb," she said, "and if there's one thing you don't know, it's your own affections."

"Mother of Zimbabwe!" Roosevelt gasped.

The old mayor had turned as white as a ghost. Something in the letter had clearly upset him.

"Is it actually possible to do all that to one man's head?" he asked.

Liz took the letter. "This freak has threatened all three of us, but he wrote to *me*. Not to you, Caleb. And you can bet these letters will stop coming the second I'm taken off the case."

"You're not on the case. You're a reporter, not a cop—"

"You're right."

"I—I am?"

"I am a reporter, so I'll deal with this like one. I'll write the killer back—on the front page of the *Evening Post!*"

She started to leave.

"Wait!" Caleb ordered, rising to his feet and slinging his heavy mobile phone over his shoulder. "I'm out of kerosene. I—um—can't make the call anyway. You'll have to stay with me until I can find someone to look after you."

Liz turned, smiling, and reached out to hug him.

"I knew you cared!" she said.

"All right, all right, let's try to keep our heads," Caleb said, enduring the hug with his arms stiff at his sides.

"Please don't mention heads," said Roosevelt, rubbing his neck. "I'm going to be dreaming about corkscrews and egg slicers for months."

Caleb began to pace.

"Okay, let's get down to business. He thwacks Old Toothless Sally from behind. Then he turns her into some kind of a clown. I can definitely see a connection between that and the mention of Mummers scrawled on the wall."

"Possibly," said Liz. "But that was no ordinary clown."

"In his letter he threatens all three of us and warns us to stay out of it, but at the same time he tells us he's going to kill again tonight in preparation for the Mummers' death ritual, which he says will happen at midnight tomorrow. And then there's this strange poem:

Erce, Erce, Mother Earth,
Hail to thee, mother of men.
Be fruitful in death's embrace,
Filled with food, for the use of man.

PS: Roosevelt is a big fat ape.
PSS: Why is Roosevelt so fat?
PSSS: Roosevelt can kiss my . . .

"Well, it goes on in this vein for a while."

"One man's fat is another man's thin," declared Roosevelt. "A, um, fatter man's."

"He obviously wants us involved, but he doesn't give us any clue as to where the secret death ritual will take place. Why?"

Roosevelt said, "Maybe he's just pulling our legs. Homicidal maniacs have the best senses of humor, or so I've heard." He tore off some orange sections to throw to the wild Indian through the bars of its cage.

"You know, I think our corpulent mayor actually has a point," said Caleb. "I mean, it's too obvious."

"What is?" asked Liz.

"This Mummers' ritual thing. I don't buy it. If he's playing a game with us, maybe that's part of it. Maybe our man isn't a Mummer at all."

"Oh, he's a Mummer all right," said an unfamiliar, cultured voice behind them.

"Who said that?" asked Liz.

"I did."

It was Ishi, the caged Indian. He was sitting in a loincloth on a wooden stool, speaking with a stuffy Oxford accent.

"Ishi!" admonished Roosevelt. "Leave the nice people alone." To Caleb and Liz, he apologized, "He does this sometimes. Kind of like a parrot."

"Your suspect," continued Ishi, "is quoting a heathen incantation to the earth. The goddess—"

"The goddess Erce," completed Elisabeth, with dread in her voice. "But how do you—"

"I read a lot," Ishi sighed. They noticed that, strewn about his cage, buried under fruit peels and fish skeletons, were stacks of leather-bound volumes. "There is not much else to do around here. The conversation is quite intolerable."

Roosevelt said, "He likes to play with the books from my library, sometimes. They're so cute when they think they're people."

"What's going on here, Liz?" Caleb asked. "Is there something you're not telling us?" As Liz spoke, the conservatory became very quiet. She had everyone's full attention. Even the animals seemed to be listening.

"The incantation was used by the Anglo-Saxons in pre-Christian times as a kind of charm," she said. "To bless their harvest, their soil, and their fertility. The Mummers are descendants of these Anglo-Saxons. Their parades may seem fun and harmless, but they are full of hidden spells."

Ishi yawned. "It would be obvious to a five-year-old that your supsect is practicing heathen goddess-worship in the *worst* way."

"Meaning?" questioned Caleb.

"Meaning," said Liz, "sacrifice. A death ritual is part of the worship ceremony."

Roosevelt said, "*Good boy,* Ishi," and threw him a handful of orange pips. "Bath time!" and with that Teddy grabbed a hose and proceeded to bombard Ishi with a powerful cannonade of cold water.

"And Old Toothless Sally Jenkins?" asked Caleb.

"Sally is just the first," said Liz. "Expect more. The Mummers believe that Erce requires sacrifices before, during, and after the ritual itself."

"And you know all this because your father was a Mummer?" Spencer asked.

"My father was a Mummer, my mother was a Mummer, and I was a Mummer!"

Roosevelt pointed at her.

"Good lord, she's the Thwacker. Call the constable!"

"Imbecile," muttered Ishi.

Caleb said, "Calm down, Teddy, she's not the Thwacker, and I am the . . . the constable."

"Oh, of course you are, I knew that. My apologies, Miss Smith, but the events of last night have put me a tad on edge. Plus I find myself terribly bound up this morning. Too many spermaceti crepes."

"Lovely. But we don't have much time, gentlemen," Elisabeth warned. "We have to find out where the death ritual will take place. Lives depend on it. Possibly our own."

Caleb paced some more, then said, "There's only one person I know who could help us, and his name is Phossy Phil. But it's going to be dangerous; he lives downtown in Bandits' Roost."

"So?" queried Elisabeth.

"So, Liz, Bandits' Roost is not a place for a lady," said Caleb.

"Good lord," muttered Ishi. "We're not going to go through

this tiresome ritual again, are we?" He put a pair of spectacles on and opened a book. "Why don't you two just mate already and be done with it!"

"We're all in equal danger here, Chief Spencer," said Liz. "That's not going to change. So I say we meet it, together."

"Bully! Now we're talking!" charged T. R. "I love a perilous adventure. Remember: cowardice in a race is an unpardonable sin! Perhaps on our way down to Bandits' Roost, we could stop at Delmonico's for a quick sour head cheese croissant? A mug of hot bacon butter might just loosen up my spleen."

Roosevelt threw off his zebra pelt and bounded up the conservatory's spiral staircase. "We will meet outside momentarily, where I shall be better dressed for derring-do."

Caleb thanked Ishi for his help. "If there is ever anything we can do for you . . ."

"Just don't let that buffoon put my bones in the British Museum."

After Caleb and Liz left the parlor, Ishi made sure he was alone and then reached under his loincloth and pulled out an Edison mobile phone, lit its burner, wound its crank, spun its whirligig, and began to dial.

Across town on Eleventh Avenue, a phone rang in the elaborately carved kiosk outside the original Original Ray's Pizzeria. A morbidly obese albino man, who bore a striking resemblance to the two morbidly obese albino men from the night before, answered the phone. He didn't say anything at first, he just listened.

"I'll pass it on. Praise be to Erce." Then he hung up.

"I received a correspondence. It's signed Jack the Jolly Thwacker."

Milk, milk, lemonade,
'Round yon corner,
Chocolate is made.

—Walt Whitman, commenting in 1882 on the
relentlessness with which industry was popping
up all over the then-young New York City.

Chapter the Third.

In which a baleful wraith abets the loss of a dear and corpulent colleague.

I WAS ALONE IN MY COVETED RENT-CONTROLLED APARTMENT IN THE Dakota (which, legally, I shouldn't even have had, because technically I'm a resident of Ecuador—long story), surfing the great Internet that seems to be all the rage with the kids these days, when it occured to me how much we take our modern technology for granted. For instance, back in 1882, the World Wide Web was only available in a penny arcade zeo-opticon at the Crystal Palace, and it only offered one page, showing a man being kicked repeatedly in the head by an angry mule. Now, after a mere two hours of fumbling with spark plugs, coaxial cables, and blinking lights, I'm able to find the *On* switch, power up my computer, and, in a mere eight to sixteen hours of repeated phone calls to all my friends' children, I can be pouring over a bounty of alternate Thwacker theories at www.alternatethwackertheories.com.

One scenario had Abraham Lincoln's assassin, John Wilkes Booth, as the killer. The theory was that Booth had not been shot on a tobacco farm in Virginia in 1865, but had escaped, moved to New York City, and opened the first erotic bakery in Greenwich

Village. He then went on a killing rampage in 1882 when the Saudis jacked up the price of flesh-tone penis icing.

Another theory was that the murders never happened, that it was all a misunderstanding, and that Spencer, Smith, and Teddy were not an investigative team at all but rather a folk music trio with one big hit called "Swing, Sweet Thwacker, Swing." According to this theorist, there was a popular recording made of the song in the 1930s by Woody Guthrie. Supposedly, after it was broadcast over the radio, a misinterpretation of the song's lyrics fueled a nationwide Thwacker-mania panic. Horrified citizens scoured the countryside, clubbing apple vendors to death with their own sacks. Thousands of entirely innocent prostitute-murderers were needlessly slaughtered, and Woody Guthrie was forced to make an apology on national radio, before being summarily executed.

This theory had two flaws. One was that it ignored all the photographic evidence, police and medical records, newspaper stories, and actual dead bodies. Two, it was put forward by a ten-year-old kid, whose website also included a theory for integrating Pokémon characters into the Star Wars universe. (Oh, and third, Woody Guthrie was never executed.)

I even submitted a theory of my own, in which famed artist Vincent Van Gogh was the murderer. Of course, as many of the posts to the website pointed out, he was in Paris during the murder spree, and all sources suggested he was painting non-stop while under constant supervision by his brother, Theo. And it is quite true that he had absolutely no motive or opportunity whatsoever, but have you ever actually seen his paintings? The guy was nuts! If not for the defamation of character lawsuit threatened by his surviving family members, I would have pursued the possibility more vigorously. Let this be a lesson to all of you: next time you try to blame a murder spree on

an innocent dead artist, make sure he has no living relatives. (Like say, Walter Sickert. He'd be perfect.)

Then it hit me! Evidence! There was evidence! I ought to examine it! I rifled through my bag, and I retrieved the daguerreotype of Sally Jenkins. "Go-go dancer," I thought. Of course! "Go"! The word "go"! It kept popping out at me. Not "go-go," but just "go." Clearly it was the beginning of a message from the killer.

As I cogitated on this, I glanced out my window at Central Park and thought, *Look at all those sorry bastards down there. I bet I make more money than all of them combined!*

"Go . . . blank . . . blank . . . blank . . ." *Go somewhere?* He must be referring to some sort of *place!* I was interrupted by a phone call.

"Yes, this is he. Oh hi, Myron. How's tricks in La-La Land?" Whenever possible, I refer to L.A. as La-La Land; it puts people at ease and seems fitting for me, a "funny man."

It was my agent calling to tell me I had an audition set for later that day.

"Really? What's it for? . . . oh, that's wonderful. Yes, I'm so excited. I'm—how do you say it out in Hollywood—'jazzed!' Thank you, Myron. Jingle bells!" And I hung up. The audition was for the part of Elderly Change Basket in a children's production of *The Phantom Toll Booth,* and although I was 'jazzed' to start preparing, I first wanted to finish my research into the team's meeting with Phossy Phil down in Bandits' Roost.

IN 1882 THE DIVIDE BETWEEN THE "HAVES" AND THE "HAVE NOTS" AND the "will never haves" and the "wish they had what the others have" and "the ones that have what they have just because their

mommies and daddies have it, too," could not have been more apparent than in New York City. Uptown, Fifth Avenue boasted the mansions of Cornelius Vanderbilt, as well as John J. Astor's estate, Henry G. Villard's castle, and Mademoiselle Stewart's French chateau: *Le Grande Turkey Mound*.

Downtown, where Broadway, Sunset Boulevard, and Route 66 intersected, forming a triangular district known as the Mulberry Bend, things could not have been more different. This area was the poorest of the poor. The filthy slum was a hodgepodge of multifarious gloomy streets and narrow alleyways laid out in an incomprehensible manner. Squalid tenements, boardinghouses, wooden boxes, and L. L. Bean tents were the makeshift chateaus of thousands of wayward waifs, street Arabs, rag-pickers, chimichangas, and bad stand-up comics—the cursèd inhabitants of the bend. Bandits' Roost was just one of the many unwelcoming haunts located in an alley near the heart of the district.

In Jacob A. Riis's 1885 exposé "Mulberry Bend—Hopeless Squalor, or Developer's Dream?" the author describes firsthand what life in the Bend was really like:

Half-eaten mules, cows, and pies lay baking beneath the blistering sun, the sport of flies and maggots. Emaciated pigs, scrubby dogs, and disoriented sea lions foraged freely about in the streets. Raw sewage flowed in the gutters, while the sidewalks were strewn with every vile combination of human waste—disgorged garbage, vomit, barf, and throw-up. The odor on Mulberry Street alone was enough to make the residents' eyes water and forced many of them to breathe through gas masks improvised from pungent old socks, the smell of which, though horrible, was like a heavenly waft from the pits of a snow-white virgin compared to the air that surrounded them. Murder, thiev-

ery, hunger, and starvation were rampant, but where others see Hell Itself, a wise investor sees Opportunity! Never has a rent gap been wider! Real estate prices clearly have nowhere to go but up!

But life in the Bend wasn't all work and no play. In fact, as there was very little work, it was mostly play. On Tuesdays the charity wagons would make their way down from Fifth Avenue and drop off barrels of pre-chewed victuals and wine-flavored sputum on every street corner. And when there was no charity to be had, the locals would frequent the illegal dives, saloons, and stale-beer cellars, where they might prey upon "easy marks"—also known as "free spenders," "untraceables," "the sublime want-wits of whom we can easily take advantage," and "tourists." These hapless souls could easily find themselves thwacked from behind, jackrolled, and dropped through a trap door into the swift "mystery sludge" that flowed below. Underneath the Bend, the rush of befouled brown ooze flowed west, eventually emptying out with great force into the Hudson. Then the thieves and pimps and whoresons and whoredads would fritter away their meager booty either by whoring, whoremongering, whorejiggling, or by partaking in that cruelest of all sports—rat baiting.

Rat baiting was a controversial practice even by the era's pre-ASPCA standards. On the one hand, there were people who felt that the rats should be given three square meals a day and a clean place to sleep, whereas there were others, like the patrons of Kit Burns's Sportsmen's Hall, a popular rat-baiter's haunt, who just liked to watch the rats get squished.

It was late afternoon by the time the investigative team's carriage drew up to the mouth of that maze of alleys known as Bandits' Roost. Teddy's "quick stop" at Delmonico's had turned into a ten-course brunch, and Caleb and Elisabeth were

anxious to find Phossy Phil before the Thwacker could strike again.

"Mmm. Smell that air," a satisfied Roosevelt roared, flaring his nostrils and filling his lungs. "Now that's what I call fresh!"

"You'll stay here until we come out," Caleb instructed their carriage driver through a handkerchief he had pressed to his nose.

"As you say, gov'nor," replied the driver. But as soon as their feet were on the cobbles, the driver whipped his horses and the carriage bolted out of sight.

The three stood alone—no means of egress if the situation turned precarious.

"Now what are we going to do?" asked Caleb.

"What else?" said Elisabeth. "Onward to Bandits' Roost."

Roosevelt sampled a tin cup of grub from a charity barrel at the corner.

"Odd," he said to himself after swallowing the swill. "Tastes rather like something I ate at Maxwell Shermahorn's last week." He eyed another barrel down the block. "Wine-flavored sputum!" he cried.

"Roosevelt, we have had enough of your dilly-dallying," Caleb said. "The Thwacker could have thwacked his fill and retired in the time you've wasted this evening."

But Roosevelt was already raising the dipper to his lips, a look of bestial serenity on his face.

"Don't worry about him, Caleb. You've got me to keep you safe."

Elisabeth locked her arm in his. Normally Caleb would have reacted to the obvious slur against his manhood, but he realized that Elisabeth was shaking with fear.

"No, we had better all stick together. It will be awfully crowded in the *tavern,* and we might lose each other."

"Tavern?" cried Teddy.

"Yes, Kit Burns's Sportsmen's Hall. Some of the finest ales in the Roost, or so the survivors say."

"Bully!" cried Roosevelt, running to catch up as Caleb and Elisabeth entered the dark mouth of the Roost.

It seemed that they were being watched from every shadowy crevasse. Above them, curious faces appeared behind the seeded glass of the tenement windows. Pale with hunger, eyes listless from long lives devoid of hope, they resembled ghosts more than human beings.

The alley curved steadily to the right, quickly swallowing the entrance behind them. A piece of forgotten laundry—a bedsheet, perhaps a shroud—rippled from a clothesline above them. In the silence, they heard a low noise, a kind of hiss.

"Quiet," said Caleb. "Is someone whispering?"

The noise came again, higher-pitched this time.

"It sounds like a child's laugh," said Liz.

The sound erupted suddenly into a kind of roaring bark, the sound one would imagine would come from a rabid camel. Liz jumped close to Caleb, who turned to face whatever was behind them.

But there was nothing but shadows, and Roosevelt staring meekly at his feet.

"Weehoo?" he ventured.

Caleb could not help but shout, "For God's sake, Mayor, do try to control yourself! We are exposed enough out here as it is."

Before the mayor could respond, Elisabeth cried out, and Caleb turned forward again—only to see an approaching mob of goons in tattered overcoats and bowler hats, which quickly surrounded them.

Faces disappeared from the windows; shutters smacked closed one after another and another. Elisabeth squeezed Caleb tightly.

"Don't worry," he said. "I've got you." Looking up at him

with gratitude in her eyes, she thought, *Caleb's got me. He is, after all, such a strong man. But the years have been unkind to him. Is he losing his hair? And why is his skin so greasy? My God, how could I have ever slept with him?*

The group's leader was a tall man, scarred and pockmarked. His beady red eyes barely blinked. But his most distinguishing feature—or lack thereof—was his chin. He quite simply did not have one. He had no bottom jaw whatsoever. It was completely gone. Instead, his neck joined his throat in a sheet of ravaged skin the texture of lettuce. His yellow upper teeth hung over like a strange rock formation, while his bloodred tongue darted in and out of the cave that was the remains of his mouth. From his palate saliva cascaded unchecked.

Liz and Caleb looked around. The goons were all afflicted with the same revolting disfigurement.

"My Lord," gasped Liz.

Teddy exclaimed, "They're all wearing the exact same hat!"

The leader gazed wickedly at Liz. He winked, cocked his head, and attempted to speak, scoring only a chow-chow garble of incomprehensible gibberish.

Liz looked frightened, as if to say *Please don't kill me, I'm as pure and innocent as the morning snow! Well, sort of. Maybe more like an evening snow.*

"No, Phil," said Caleb to the tall man. "I assure you, she won't do 'it' for *any* amount of 'shiny gold doubloons.'"

He turned to Liz. "It's all right, my dear. This is the man we came for."

KIT BURNS'S SPORTSMEN'S HALL WAS A DINGY BASEMENT BARRELHOUSE with low ceilings, a bar, and a few tables. A couple of flickering

oil lamps hung on the walls, and a red curtain in the back marked the portal to the rat pit.

Phil motioned them to follow him through the taproom, which was already jumping. A clamorous rabble of foul-mouthed ruffians, cutthroats, whores, and harlots were all jammed into the cramped and putrid-smelling rummery, squeezing in at the bar like a herd of starved cattle converging upon a salt lick. (There was, in fact, a salt lick at the far end of the bar, popular with the young students at Mulberry U, who took a lap or two off it before downing the newfangled drink tequila, which was a Spanish name for a highly communicable tongue disease.)

Teddy cried, "Barkeep, a swig of your most potent aqua vitae, if you please!" He threw down a shilling.

"Mayor!" cried Caleb. "We do not have time—"

"Just one moment, my dear police chief. The salty food at Delmonico's has left me rather parched."

Phil was already disappearing through the curtain.

"Just leave him," Liz said. "We'll find someone to wheel him home when we're through with Phil."

The two followed their informant out of the taproom as the bartender directed Teddy to the three giant wooden casks sitting on the bar. Each cask was open at the top and painted with a la-bel. From the one labeled VILE SWINE XXX stuck the hind end of a dead pig, gently bobbing. Another one marked CHINAMAN'S FIRE TIPPLE had a decapitated head sticking out of it, his race—Chinese, of course—only barely recognizable. But it was the third keg that caught Teddy's eye—or rather the live, naked, obese whore protruding from the keg itself. Her chubby legs were splayed, sticking up in the air, while her round rump was completely submerged in the intoxicant. She laughed and beck-oned Roosevelt with a coyly curled finger.

Her barrel was marked TOXIC FAT WHORE GROG—WARNING, COULD BE FATAL TO YOUR HEALTH AS SUCH.

"I believe I will sample the lovely, fat *fille de joie*'s potent potables!" said Roosevelt as he stuck the hose connected to the wooden cask into his mouth and began to suck. Back then, in the lower-class dives, few used glasses, preferring the rubber "hose 'n' keg" method.

"Weehoo!" the looped mayor exclaimed, having sucked generously. "Now let's see what that Chinaman has to offer a discriminating palate!" He threw down another shilling and then started to suck hard on the Fire Tipple hose.

A plug-ugly and a hooligan joined Teddy at the bar. They could tell a good want-wit when they saw one. Unseen by Roosevelt, in a dark corner of the pub, obscured by the mottled shadows cast by a flickering oil lamp and various other sinister-mood-inducing phenomena, sat a figure shrouded in a black, hooded robe, watching the good mayor's every move.

"WHAT ARE YOU GOING TO DO FOR US TODAY, MR. ELLIOTT?"

The voice came from the darkened audience. With the bright follow spot blinding me, I squinted to see if I could connect it with a face.

"Hello?" I said.

"Yes, Mr. Elliott, hello. We see you. Now what would you like to do for us?"

"Hello?"

"Yes, hello again, Mr. Elliott. Would you please proceed with what you've prepared? We're a little short on time."

"Hello?"

The first rule of any good audition was to establish a rapport with the director.

"Just do something!"

"Have we ever worked together before?" I asked.

"No, we have not."

"Because you sound very familiar to me. Are you Chita Rivera?"

"I'm a man, Mr. Elliott," said the increasingly impatient voice from the audience.

"I want you to know I'm honored to be auditioning for the Harlequin Children's Theater production of *The Phantom Toll-booth*. It's my favorite Edgar Allan Poe short story," I said. But there was no response from the faceless voice. Maybe he only knew the corrupted Norton Juster version, the one where the boy survives.

"Next, please," called the director.

The spot moved off of me to see who was waiting in the wings. That was when I saw it—in the audience, sitting two rows behind Chita Rivera, a figure shrouded in black, wearing a tall black top hat and holding an oil lamp in its lap for some reason, maybe to give his face that menacing glare.

My body began to shake uncontrollably. Sweat materialized at the soft spot on top of my head and ran into my eyes. My vision blurred.

"Um, could I start again?"

"You haven't done anything yet, Mr. Elliott."

"Then why do you sound so mad?" I said, beginning to feel exposed up there on that stage. My knees knocked together.

The figure drew a finger across its throat. I knew what it was thinking. It wanted me to choke.

"Now I will—I will be performing a little ditty you might have heard of—um, if you're into little ditties . . ."

I wanted to cry. I could feel warm urine on my leg. My flop sweat had loosened the glue that held my hairpiece on, and it was sliding down my forehead. The strange figure extinguished its lamp, and I gasped, choking on my temporary front tooth cap, which I had to spend a few minutes coughing back up. During the fit, my fake hair fell off altogether, but I was so nervous that I thought it was some sort of rodent attacking me, so I began to stomp on it, bursting the plantar wart on my foot. I screamed in pain.

The voice from the audience seemed somewhat exasperated now.

"Mr. Elliott, will you please audition or please leave! We have a lot of people to see today."

"Yep, yep, okay, I get it. No time for chitchat," I said, limping over to the piano player and handing him my sheet music. The light was back on me, and I couldn't see if the figure was still in the audience. I wanted to grab him after the audition and tell him how much he resembled someone I couldn't quite put my finger on . . .

"You can do it in D minor or C major or F sharp, whatever's easier for you," I told the pianist. "I'll just follow." And I limped back to center stage. "Okay, here goes nothing."

"Finally," said the voice from the audience.

"What?" I said.

"Nothing. Nothing. Just go on! Jesus Christ!" the angry voice yelled.

"Okay," and I gestured to the piano player to start the music. He didn't. I began to sing:

"Iy yiy, yiy, yiy, I am a Frito . . ."

Then I glanced off stage right. The figure was there, in his top hat and cape, making an elaborate hand gesture that was meant to indicate the removal of someone's head and its subsequent

use as a bowling ball. Then I realized who he was—a headhunter! He must have been some sort of talent scout! Now this was about more than a children's production! The pressure was really on.

"Eek," was suddenly all I could muster. "Eek eek eek eek."

"Thank you! That will be all."

The steel door of the stage entrance to the Harlequin Children's Theater slammed shut behind me with a disquieting permanence. As I stood outside, alone in the dark alley, I couldn't help but crack a smile.

"Yes!" I said. "I nailed it!" And I ran off, anxious to get back to the Dakota and call my agent, Myron, to tell him how great my audition went.

It might seem to you, dear reader, that the audition for the role of the wise old change basket in *The Phantom Tollbooth* did not further my investigation of the Thwacker murders one iota. But first, you must remember that I'm primarily an actor, then a dancer, then an occasional purveyor of contraband, and then, and only then, am I a forensic detective. Second, I was to discover later, that the so-called talent scout was not "exactly" what "he," as they say, "seemed."

Now back to the story, already in progress . . .

Liz sat uncomfortably at a small wooden table across from Phossy Phil in his tenement flat. There not being enough chairs, Caleb stood, leaning against the wall by the door to the only other room. Muffled yet ungodly sounds emanated from back there, and Liz tried not to imagine their source.

It was difficult for her to look straight at Phil, but there was not much else to see: a bucket, a few pornographic tintypes on the walls, and a shelf with a bunch of wooden jaws resting on it.

Each jaw was a different size and marked with a different name: Uncle Hyman, Aunt Dorothy, Little Heather, Mikey, Bubba the Fish, etc.

What happened to them? she asked Caleb with her eyes.

Phil attached a wooden jaw to his face and gave it a couple of experimental clicks to make sure it was in properly. Now he was able to speak flawless English.

"A result of this city's neverending desire to expand, my dear," said Phil, who had clearly read the curiosity in her look. "More mansions on Fifth Avenue mean more steam-powered equipment to build 'em, and that means more oil. More oil means more oil barges . . . that means more horses . . . and . . . horses eat corn and that means . . . that . . . well . . . the bottom line is matches! Everyone needs matches nowadays."

Suddenly two teenage boys bounded out of the other room. "Hey, get back in the parlor!" Phil yelled. "And put your jaws in when we have company!"

Before the boys could close the door, Liz caught a glimpse of the rest of the family heaped in a pile one on top of one another in the small adjacent room, nearly fifty of them—children, aunts, uncles, grandmothers, and grandfathers—and not a one had a jaw, not even their cat.

"You see, we all work at the match factory," Phil said, but Liz still seemed confused.

"It's the phosphorus, Liz," explained Caleb. "When you make matches, you use phosphorus. Prolonged exposure can lead to deterioration of the joints, especially the cartilage connecting the mandible with the skull."

"Phossy jaw, my dear," said Phil, rolling a cigarette. "Dreadful thing. But I don't suppose you've heard of that up there on Fifth Avenue?"

"I don't live on Fifth Avenue," retorted Liz.

"No?" said Phil. "Well you should. A pretty little jewel like yourself." He took her hand to kiss it—rather gallantly, albeit in a crass sort of way—but before he could, his jaw fell off and hit the table. He muttered something incoherent and then snapped the wooden prosthesis back into his face.

"Phil, we need information," Caleb said.

"I know why you're here," said Phil, lighting a smoke. "It's about the murder last night."

"We think it might be connected to the secret society of the Mummers," said Caleb.

"And what do you think, Miss Smith?" asked Phil. "After all, you have personal experience with the Mummers, don't you?"

Elisabeth turned to Caleb.

"It's all right, Liz," reassured Caleb. "The best informants know everything."

"That's right, Chief Spencer, we do. But then again, the best informants don't inform . . . for free. Do we?"

Caleb glared at Phossy Phil, then reached into his coat pocket and produced a large wad of cash that he tossed onto the table.

IN THE RAUCOUS BACK ROOM OF THE SPORTSMAN'S HALL, LARGE WADS OF cash were also being tossed on a table. The wagering on rat baiting was fast and furious. One half of the fulminating crowd chanted "Roosevelt! Roosevelt! Roosevelt!" while the other gave thunderous voice to "Rodents! Rodents! Rodents!" In the pit Roosevelt puffed out his chest and strutted around, wearing the standard-issue black boots with lead soles. His pockets were full of cash, and a number of rats lay pulverized at his feet.

"Weehoo!" Roosevelt vociferated, and the crowd—not having any idea what it meant, but knowing he had been yelling it all

night—weehooed back in unison. A man in a silk top hat and a red plaid vest made his way through the crowd holding up a big, burlap sack.

"No more bets!" he yelled, and the crowd quieted down. Roosevelt combed back his unkempt hair and parted it perfectly. He took out his white handkerchief, wiped clean his spectacles, and with a dramatic flourish returned them to his nose. Then he squatted in the traditional sumo wrestler's stance and waited.

"This is the final and deciding round!" cried the man in the silk top hat.

As the announcer went on to describe the fearsome characteristics of the rats he was about to release, one of the men from the bar—the plug-ugly, not the hooligan—took a large, vicious black rat from his own sack. Retrieving an ampule from inside his coat, he drew a green liquid from a vial labeled PIZZIN and squeezed a generous dose into the rat's throat.

When the man in the silk hat opened his bag and let drop three dozen nasty rats into the pit, no one noticed when one more entered the fray—nor did they notice the deadly green foam frothing from its mouth.

The army of hairy animals immediately formed up ranks opposite Roosevelt and let out an ear-piercing squeal. Roosevelt stuck his fingers in his ears and squealed back at them. The spectators shook the floor with their pounding feet. The sound was deafening.

A bell rang.

Teddy pulled an imaginary sword from his belt and yelled: "Charge!"

The crowd went wild as Roosevelt rushed the onslaught head-on. He ran around the pit clomping and stomping, squashing the attacking rodents into flat rat pancakes with his giant lead boots.

A rat seized hold of his pants leg, but T. R. shook it off, and as he tromped down on the rodent, it exploded in a splattering blast of gore. The rats tried to outflank him, but the chubby mayor was surprisingly nimble on his feet.

"I know your tactics! You yellow-bellied bastards!" he yelled.

One by one, he eradicated the mongrel hordes. Panicking rats tried to squeeze out under the sides of the pit, but they were easy targets for the adrenaline-crazed, drunken mayor.

It was a massacre. The rats were decimated. A few wounded, half-flattened ones lay motionless, pretending to be dead. Then the black rat, driven into a frenzy by the "pizzin," sprang at Teddy and landed on his newly parted hair, where he began scratching and pulling and chewing at it.

"Why you little son of a . . ." He grabbed the animal and threw it to the floor. The rat looked up at the mayor, shaking with fear. Its front claws were clasped together almost as if it were pleading for mercy.

Roosevelt said, "Well, my little friend, a man who is good enough to shed his blood for his country is good enough to be given a square deal afterwards."

The rat seemed confused, and the last thing it would see in this beautiful world was the giant lead bottom of Roosevelt's shoe, smashing down.

Moments later, Roosevelt grew dizzy. The room began to spin. Colors became more vivid. Everyday objects seemed to bristle with annoyingly excessive significance. He licked the blood on his lips, as if sampling a wine. A look of cheery nostalgia crossed his face.

"Why, if it isn't Venezuelan death dart poison! Made from the extract of a boiled warted pygmy. I haven't taken this stuff since college!"

And with that, much to the dismay of the plug-ugly and the

hooligan, and their hooded master in the back of the room, Roosvelt began his victory dance.

"YOU WANT TO KNOW WHERE YOUR KILLER MIGHT STRIKE NEXT. AM I right?" Phil's short, glowing cigarette was jammed between his fake jaw and his yellow teeth.

"If there's a ritual connection," said Caleb, "there must be a pattern, maybe something symbolic. Our killer is too—well, not smart exactly, but too *meticulous* to be killing at random."

"Ah yes, the Mummers. The most dreaded and labyrinthine of secret societies." Phil puffed on his cigarette, which was now burning down close to his wooden jaw. Liz watched it, a bit concerned that Phil seemed oblivious to the danger.

"Up until yesterday I could have sworn they were just a bunch of clowns," said Caleb.

Phil snorted. "Clowns? Clowns! Do you have any idea how high up this goes? There are very important people in this city, very powerful people who practice Mummery. We're not just talking about the Masons or the Shriners or the Friar's Club for Christ's sake, we're talking about the Mummers! I'm not sure you know what you're getting into!"

The red tip of his cigarette was now scorching his wooden jaw, but of course he couldn't feel it. Liz didn't want to be impolite. Instead of coming right out and saying, "Hey Phil, your chin is burning," she awkwardly shifted around in her chair and hummed out loud, trying to signal him.

"All I know is that a woman was brutally murdered last night, and it is my job to find out who the culprit is," said Caleb.

"A woman of questionable standing in our society, who won't

be missed. Maybe this one is best left alone," said Phil, his jaw now beginning to smolder. Liz exaggerated a loud cough.

"Damn it! She was a human being, Phil!" said Caleb, pounding his fist into his palm. "Now I paid you good money, so I want information. Tell me everything you know. Why would the Mummers want to decorate a woman's head with her own entrails? What does it mean?"

"Perhaps it doesn't *mean* anything, Mr. Detective. Or perhaps it has nothing to do with the Mummers. Perhaps," Phil winked, "the killer is trying to send you a message." Phil winked five more times. It seemed the smoke was getting in his eyes. "Maybe he doesn't even know it."

"What do you mean?" bellowed Caleb. "How could he be sending us a message without knowing it?"

"There are wheels within wheels, and bitty bits of things all over. People do things without meaning to. Perhaps you should pay close attention to his next victim."

"There's not going to be a next victim."

"Oh, there'll be more. You'll stop 'im in the end, I'm sure, but there'll be more."

A small flame leapt to life on the end of his chin.

"Um, Phil," began Liz.

"Relax," said Phil calmly. Evidently he was used to this happening. "Where's my water?"

Liz, panicking, reached for a red bucket marked FIRE.

"I got it. I got it," she said and threw its contents straight into Phil's face. *Blam!* Two pounds of coarse sand hit his burning mug hard, extinguishing the fire. He stood for a moment. Then, unruffled, he removed his charred jaw from his face and placed it on the table. He looked at Liz and made some disgusting guttural sounds.

Caleb translated, "He says he was talking about his glass of water, but he thanks you just the same."

AT THE SPORTSMEN'S HALL, ROOSEVELT WAS NOW ON TOP OF THE BAR, shirtless and dancing with the fat whore's rubber hose in his mouth. The crowd cheered for him as he flung down his winnings for round after round of drinks. Sticking out of the wall above the kegs were the various implements of death that the plug-ugly and the hooligan had been hurling at him during his dance—knives, throwing axes, darts, crossbow bolts, and a prized swordfish which had been removed from its plaque. All to no avail. The poison, rather than killing him, had granted him a supernatural alertness. No matter what his would-be assassins threw at him, he thought it was some kind of game and jumped out of the way, only to launch into a story about throwing-axe contests with Utah plains Indians. The plug-ugly and the hooligan conferred in the corner with the hooded figure, who appeared exasperated—or as exasperated as a figure in a hooded robe could appear.

"Boy, I haven't had so much fun since the time I beat that bastard J. P. Morgan's derriere at strip poker," announced Roosevelt. "Have I ever told you fellas about that one? We were on a singles' cruise steaming west aboard the White Star Line's grand vessel the *Behemothic,* when . . ."

As he told his story, the hooligan advanced, motioning for him to come down.

". . . I'll tell you, I've never seen a man shrivel up so fast in all my life!" bellowed Roosevelt, and he burst out in a loud guffaw.

"Egh, Mr. Rosie-veldt," began the hooligan. "Weh don't ye come have a seats here an' let us buy ye a drink for once?"

The suggestion was met with general applause. Roosevelt clambered down onto a stool.

"I say, my good man, the only thing better than a free lunch is a free drink!"

"Nah, not that'n. Sit here, instead." The hooligan motioned to a place two stools down. "It's, er, the special seat. For people what's we like so much."

"Certainly, my good man. Who am I to turn my nose up at the customs of your stinking lowlife establishment . . ."

Roosevelt trailed off, the effects of the pygmy extract beginning to peak, or, as they called it in 1882, "inspire kinship with the howling abyss, in which life is reflected as in a mirror darkly, or somesuch, oh boy, I need to lie down." Teddy sat still, staring at his pudgy hand.

The hooligan turned back to the shrouded figure. This time the figure nodded at the thugs. They knew what it meant. The plug-ugly bellied up next to Roosevelt and reached for a lever under the bar.

"My hand," gasped Teddy. "It looks just like that of an infant. Why, we are all just chil—"

The rest of that sentence is lost to history, as the mayor plunged through the trapdoor and into the mystery sludge below. The patrons heard a distant "Weehoo!" followed by a splash. Used to such spectacles, they returned almost immediately to their ruckus.

"IS THAT ALL YOU CAN TELL US, THEN?" SAID CALEB, CLEARLY IRRITATED. "This case will go round and round."

"And up and down. Don't forget that," said Phil, who had

now replaced his wooden jaw with another one that was much too small for his face. It was marked LITTLE MISSY.

"I didn't pay good money for riddles."

"Your money is good, I'll give you that. But not even the whole city of New York could pay me enough to run afoul of the Fancy Brigade."

"Not the Fancy Brigade!" said Elisabeth.

"What?" asked Caleb. "Who are they?"

Liz said, "The Fancy Brigade is the most elite of Mummer factions. They are typically called upon only to guard the most important of ceremonies, or to dispatch the Mummers' enemies. If they're involved, then we're all in real danger."

"Is that all you can tell us, Phil?" asked Caleb.

"I've already said too much. I'll just say this: this is going to be a real 'freak' of a case, if you get my drift. A real 'sideshow.' One might even go as far as to call it an 'amusement park containing a large Ferris wheel.'"

"That's it!" barked Caleb. "I've heard enough of this mumbo jumbo. Come on, Liz."

"Wait! There's something else," said Phil, lighting another cigarette. Liz rolled her eyes. *This guy never learns!*

"What?" asked Caleb. "The case is going to be like 'swallowing a sword' while 'diving into a glass of water'? Please, enlighten us."

"Ah, I'm going to regret telling you this, but . . . you're being followed."

"By who?" asked Liz.

"By someone or somethin' that doesn't want you to solve this case."

"You got a name?" asked Caleb.

"No." Phil puffed on his short cigarette. "But have you thought that maybe the Thwacker is warning you to stay out of

Teddy pulled an imaginary sword from his belt and yelled: "Charge!"

his nasty business for some other reason besides his fear of being caught?"

"What other reason could there be?" asked Liz.

"Maybe he knows he's being used. Maybe he's worried you'll get bumped off and there'll be no one to admire his pretty work. All I can tell you is that someone wants the three of you exterminated, and it's not necessarily just the Thwacker."

From somewhere came the sound of a harpsichord playing "Greensleeves." The three looked at each other. Then Phil spoke.

"Oh, sorry. That's me."

He retrieved his Edison mobile phone from under the table. As befitting his class, he had one of the older and bulkier cast-iron models, powered by rats running on a wheel.

"Yeah?" he said. "Uh-huh. Yeah? Hmm. I was worried something like that would happen."

He put the phone away.

"That was my man downstairs. You better put an APB out on your friend with the big mustache. He's gone." Caleb and Liz looked at each other in fear and then rushed out to find Teddy.

"Careful, the two of you are surely next!" Phil shouted after them in the doorway of his hovel, but they were already gone. Then he heard a *creak*.

"Yes? Is someone there?"

Chapter the Fourth.

In which a pair of sorrowful souls meet— with a certain degree of understandable angst—a gruesome cessation at the hands of the deleterious malefactor.

EIGHTEEN EIGHTY-TWO WAS A BANNER YEAR FOR HISTORICAL EVENTS IN NEW York City. Besides the Jack the Jolly Thwacker murders, Robert Odlum became the first man to successfully jump off the Brooklyn Bridge (the jump was successful, the landing was not). New Yorkers witnessed the last public execution (Rainy Bethea, for spitting in Times Square) and the city endured the goiter epidemic, the phlebitis, gout plagues, and the conjunctivitis outbreak of '82–'83.

The year 1882 also saw the first New York City Marathon. Olympic champion Lewis Tanner was the official winner but was disqualified for wearing shorts that concealed a block of ice (apparently for cooling purposes), and because he used steampowered sneakers. The 1884 stock market crash was in 1882 (close enough), but by far most notable was the grand opening of Röntgen's X-Ray Funhouse and Race Transformation Salon on Madison Avenue. Some years earlier, Wilhelm Conrad Röntgen won the Nobel Prize for his discovery of X-rays. Now with the advent of the Funhouse, everyday New Yorkers could experience the thrill and magic of radiology. In the Transformation Salon people of color entered through the back door. Inside,

they were bombarded with massive amounts of scattered radiation until their skin turned a ghastly grayish white. Next they were presented with a crisp Brooks Brothers suit and allowed to exit via the front door into a whole new world of racial privilege, where—as long as they were male, and well-to-do, and owned property, and knew someone who knew someone—they would be treated with the equality and respect accorded all citizens, at least for the six to nine months they had left to live.

As you might be able to tell from my little history lesson, I had at this point hit a dead end in my investigation. This was the dark period when I thought I might even give up, but fortunately, I called my friend Wendell, and he suggested we go down to Caleb's old precinct, the nineteenth, and look around the police archives.

I was a bit surprised when the desk sergeant claimed not to have even heard about the Jack the Jolly Thwacker case.

"Fellas, tell me again what you want? We're kind of busy here, as you can see."

Wendell and I exchanged frustrated looks. We had already told him twice.

"The Thwacker case," I said. "I'm doing research for a book."

"Jack the Thwacker," added Wendell.

"The whacker?" said the sergeant.

"No, that's something different," said Wendell.

The desk sergeant yelled over his shoulder. "Theo, you know anything about a Jack the Whacker?"

"We don't need any information on Jack the Whacker," I said. "We're *very* familiar with him."

"Yes. In fact, I see him at least three times a day," said Wendell.

"At least," I said.

"You boys trying to make trouble, here? We don't put up with any of that funny business in this precinct."

"No, sir, we're serious," I said. "It was a case that was handled out of this precinct in the nineteenth century. T-h-w-a-c-k-e-r."

"The nineteenth century? What is this, *The Jetsons*? Hey Theo, these boys say they're from the future."

"No, the 1800's. 1882 to be exact," I said.

"1882?" said the sergeant. "That was like two hundred years ago. Hey, these kids are asking me about a case that happened before I was even born yet."

"What did they say they want? The Slacker?" shouted Theo from the back room.

"Look, boys, we've got this thing called the statute of limitations. Somebody robbed somebody back in the Middle Ages, it doesn't count anymore, get it?"

"Look, sir," began Wendell, "don't you keep archives—*records*—of past cases? So that you can maybe compare them to present events and thereby learn from previous mistakes?"

"Archives, huh? Like on *CSI*?"

"Yes," said Wendell, sighing gently. "Like on the television."

"Hey Theo, we got any of those, what you call 'em, *archives*?"

"Yeah, it's that room in the basement wid all the boxes."

"Oh, you mean like the Box Room. Well, why didn't you say so, boys? Goin' on about whackers and stackers. Box Room is on the basement level. Take the elevator to your left."

We started for the elevator.

"And kids, no funny business down there, understand? We don't put up with that around here. We ain't that kind of police station."

"Yes sir," I said.

It was kind of nice to be called a kid, I thought as Wendell and I boarded the elevator, *especially considering that we're both forty-four.*

After a similar go-around with the archivist in the basement,

we were ushered to a table and handed two big boxes marked THWACKER CASE EVIDENCE.

Before allowing us to peruse the evidence, the archivist required us to first wash our hands, then don surgical gloves, then green gowns and face masks, which he retrieved from under a sterilizing UV light.

"Some of this old stuff must be pretty sensitive, huh?" I asked.

"Naw," said the archivist. "Just filthy."

Wendell and I began to peruse the boxes of evidence.

"Look at this," said Wendell as he pulled an item from his box.

It was the coroner's daguerreotype of the Thwacker's second and third victims. I was interested in whether or not the "go" clue that I had found in Sally's death photo would continue in these. But when I looked at them, I gagged and almost lost my cookies. What the Thwacker had done with the intestines of these two was simply nutsola! (We'll have to go into more detail about that later, when I recount the second murders for you, after I first return home to eat my stuffed chicken breast din-din.)

Looking into my box, I pulled out a burlap bag marked MCINTOSH APPLES. Was this the Thwacker's weapon of choice?

Wendell pulled something out of his box and was smelling it through his face mask. It was a bra. I quickly snatched it away from him.

Examining the undergarment, I noticed that it was embroidered with the initials "E. S." *Why would Elisabeth's bra be in the evidence box?* I wondered, and then I took a turn smelling it as well. I shrugged and stuffed it in my pocket for later.

We spent the better part of the day sifting through police reports, witness statements, newspaper clippings, etc., etc. But there wasn't much there that I hadn't already found in published accounts of the events.

We were about to leave when I made a significant discovery in the bottom of my evidence box. Something was wrapped in a lace handkerchief and tied with a ribbon. I pulled it out, slowly undid the lace, and pulled away the hanky.

There before me lay two small books. The worn brown leather one was embossed with the NCNYPD detective shield, and the other, a black hardbound book, was decorated with a pink French poodle.

"Wendell, I think I have something here."

The two of us put on our monocles and opened the books to their title pages. Mine read,

The personal recollections of Police Chief Caleb R. Spencer as they pertain to the dreadful case of the notorious Jack the Thwacker.

Wendell's title page read,

The personal diary of Miss Elisabeth Smith as it pertains to nasty Jolly Jack, as well as my love affair with the dashing chief of police, Caleb R. Spencer.

"Bingo!"

"We hit the mother lode!" cried Wendell.

"Caleb and Liz's diaries! Who could ask for more?"

"We're closing," called the archivist.

"Oh, yes sir. Thank you very much. We're all done here, sir," I called.

Wendell and I looked at each other. We knew what we had to do. We each slipped a book underneath our surgical gowns and stuck them into our pants. Then we quickly got up and beat a hasty retreat to the elevator.

As we were leaving, the archivist said, "Strange. Been a lot of interest in the Thwacker case lately."

"Oh, really," I said, waiting for the elevator while trying to conceal the bulge in my pants, a problem I'm used to.

"Well, one other person anyway, which makes three more than usual, heh-heh. Odd little fellow in a black cape and a top hat. Didn't talk much. Sounded like he had a cold or something. Had to shoo him out after I caught him sniffin' that bra."

"The talent scout? What would he want—"

But the elevator had come, and Wendell, fearing discovery, pulled me in.

"'Bye, Sergeant. Thank you! You've been a doll!" I called out as we rushed out of the precinct, still in our masks and gloves.

"Asshole kids," mumbled the desk sergeant.

I couldn't wait to get back to the Dakota and start devouring the diaries, not to mention finish smelling that bra. Surely they would shed some light on the case and give me some insight as to why it had gone unsolved for all these years. But first I had to call Myron and let him in on my latest discovery—that talent scout was no talent scout at all, but a Hollywood producer interested in making a movie of my book! Finally, after thirty years of slaving away in obscurity, my career was going to take off!

But first we should return to the story you bought this book to read, you miserable, selfish readers. No, no time for Chris Elliott's problems. You probably want to hear all about how Caleb and Liz had tried in vain all night to locate Roosevelt. How they had found the trapdoor at the Sportsmen's Hall, the plug-ugly and the hooligan long gone and no one in the tavern talking. Well fine, I'll tell you all about it.

AN ALL POINTS BULLETIN WAS OUT AND CALEB HAD CHARGED EVERY MAN
he could spare with the task of finding the mayor. He dispatched
a handful of coppers to stand ready at the storm pipe where the
black sludge flowing underneath the Bend blasted into the Hudson River, with hopes that Teddy would come shooting out
sooner or later. Five hours after his disappearance there was still
no word of his recovery, so, in a last-ditch effort, they decided to
search his home.

"Howdy folks. Teddy will be right with ya."

Caleb and Elisabeth, exhausted, entered Roosevelt's darkened house.

"Teddy? Teddy?" cried Elisabeth.

"Roosevelt, where in the blazes are you?" yelled Caleb.

They were greeted only by the chirping of nocturnal birds in
Teddy's vivarium. Caleb lit an oil lamp, and its glow settled onto
the naked portrait of the mayor. Liz studied the painting closely.

"Wow," she said. "I never knew he had a pierced, that is to
say a piercing through his, um, or rather in his—"

"He had it done in Fiji," Caleb said nonchalantly. "*Everyone*
was doing it back then. It's actually made from a pearl he choked
on when he was eating raw oysters with King Bowser Koopaloopa. He wanted something to remember the evening by."

"It rather makes it appear as though he has two . . . you
know . . . two . . ." Liz sighed. "Oh, Caleb, I fear the worst has
happened."

"Liz, whatever evil has befallen Roosevelt, it threatens us, as
well." Spencer cast his light around the house. "We must be extra
vigilant now and take great pains to protect ourselves. There's

something I want you to have. It's been in my family for years. I didn't want it to come to this, but you may need it. Just be careful with it, it's dangerous."

He reached into his pocket and handed her a pearl-handled police whistle. Liz rolled her eyes.

"Listen, I'm sure Teddy will turn up somewhere," said Spencer. "And hopefully in one piece! He's come through worse situations, God help him. But in the meantime we've got to try to find out where the Thwacker's going to strike next."

"Finding the Thwacker is one thing, and I have every confidence that you will. You found that 'Peter Pisser' character rather quickly. But we can't leave Teddy out there. He's helpless, Caleb, and quite possibly retarded."

"If he's dead, he's dead, Liz, and there's nothing we can do. If he's alive and free he'll find us, and if he's trapped somewhere the only way we're going to find him is by penetrating this mystery."

"How can you be so coldly rational?"

"Because I have to be. It's a crazy world and real people's lives are at stake. Now, if the Thwacker is responsible for Teddy's disappearance—or if he knows who is—then he knows we would eventually exhaust our options and return here, and since he's so partial to leaving messages, we might find one in the house somewhere."

Spencer shined the light around the perimeter of the conservatory. His face turned stern, his eyes searching for clues.

Liz gasped.

"Spencer, look!"

"What? Oh no!"

He shined the light on Ishi's cage. The door was wide open and the cage was empty, except for some orange rinds and half-eaten heads of cabbage. Someone had let the wild Yahi Indian loose.

"Be careful Liz, and keep your hand on that whistle. We may not be alone."

Caleb began to sniff the floor of the cage.

"What on earth—"

"Shh! This stool's still warm," he said, gesturing to a pile of excrement. "And this copy of *Moby Dick*'s been left open in the middle of a chapter. He must have left in a hurry."

"Now you're just showing off."

"Oh, of course!" Caleb smacked his head. "What did Phil say? 'Freak!' Ishi's a freak. And what else? 'Round and round,' 'up and down'?"

Caleb turned in a circle, panning the light around the conservatory.

"You are grasping at straws, Caleb."

"Wait! Look!"

"What?"

The light shone on the spiral staircase.

"Round and round. Up and down."

"You're out of your mind."

Caleb raced up the stairs with the oil lamp. Liz plodded after him. In Teddy's bedroom, nothing was out of the ordinary except for lots of oversized corrective underwear with all manner of pulleys and cords and block-and-tackles attached to them.

"Hernias," whispered Caleb, racing on to the next room.

The oak floors of the dark house creaked while Caleb searched high and low to no avail. He tore through trunks, ruffled under beds and knocked over the contents of Teddy's numerous commemorative spitoons, his shadow tap-dancing on the tall walls and high ceilings (literally tap-dancing, I looked it up). At the end of a long hallway on the third floor, he came upon a closed closet door. "Now I wonder what's behind this door." He flung it open.

Elisabeth screamed and groped for her whistle.

A man was standing in the closet, the biggest man they'd ever seen.

Then Caleb started to laugh.

"I'm sorry, Liz. I couldn't resist."

"You insufferable infant," said Elisabeth, and she smacked Caleb in the arm. "We're possibly about to die, and you're playing jokes."

"I really had you going, though, didn't I? Round and round, up and down! *X* marks the spot!" Caleb laughed and dodged Liz's attempts to stuff the whistle down his throat. "It's not real. It's just another one of Teddy's little toys, like the gorilla downstairs. It's harmless."

"This is no toy," said Elisabeth, taking the oil lamp from him and shining it on the huge man. "And it's anything but harmless."

It was made of iron and tin. Its face had two big rings for eyes and a bigger ring for a mouth. The appendages were connected to the body with menacing grommets and even more menacing rivets. It wore a metal helmet and held a rifle. Two belts of bullets crisscrossed its barrel chest.

"*Supériorité des Anglo-Saxons,*" Liz said. "'Superior man.' A killing machine. Create an army of these, and no human would ever have to die in battle again. Its official name is Boilerplate, but Teddy used to call it his mechanical mule. It's a robot really. A prototype soldier and a deadly weapon."

"This tin can?"

"I assure you, Boilerplate is not just a tin can. It was quite effective when it fought side-by-side with Teddy and the Rough Riders during the Spanish-American war."

"Oh Christ, not you too! That war doesn't happen until 1898!"

Liz looked at Caleb like he was out of his mind.

"Well, it doesn't," groused Caleb. "So . . . if it was so effective, why didn't we build an army of Boilerplates?"

"Yes, well that's one of history's great ironies, isn't it? Boiler-plate was a technological milestone and yet it was a soulless sol-dier. Wars are not just physical ventures, Caleb. They're also highly charged emotional experiments . . . much like relationships."

(That was what Elisabeth said, but I knew what she was really thinking. She was thinking, *I'm talking about us, but you think I'm talking about Boilerplate, because you're so thick you just don't get it! But I still might have sex with you by the end of this book.* I sniffed her bra ravenously and resumed my account.)

"Anyway," she continued, "the human qualities of honor, valor, and sacrifice are absent in Boilerplate. So any victory on the battlefield would be a hollow one, devoid of emotion. Who cares how many Boilerplates come home in body bags? They're not human! As long as everyone had enough Boilerplates, war would never end. There would be no reason for it to."

"And you're an expert on *this* topic because . . . ?"

"Because I knew the inventor. A Professor Archibald Cam-pion. A rather idealistic man. A very complicated man. But an oh-so-brilliant man." Liz seemed lost in the memory.

"Another old boyfriend, huh Liz? How many of us do you have mounted on your wall?"

Liz chose to ignore him. "Unfortunately, he went insane. Last I heard he was in the Bellevue Lunatic Asylum."

Spencer was already starting back down the stairs.

"Yeah, well I'm not surprised. Anyone who invents some-thing like that has to be a tad cobbled in the head."

"Non compos mentis," Liz said softly and followed him back down.

In the conservatory, Caleb stopped in front of the portrait again.

"The fat old fool."

"Oh, stop acting so tough and admit that you miss him," Liz said.

"Like a hole in the head," Caleb sighed, "a hole . . . that I nonetheless . . . irrationally cherish. I hope he's okay."

"There, that wasn't so hard, was it?" Liz pulled a stray hair back from Caleb's rapidly expanding forehead. "You know, you're rather handsome for a man of your age."

"Oh, Liz. Even in the midst of all this ungodly mischief, I still can't help but notice it."

"Notice what?"

"It is rather amazing."

"What?"

"You look exactly the same as the day we met."

Liz believed herself incapable of blushing, but she blushed anyway, the compliment having touched a surviving romantic nerve. She made a show of clearing her throat. (But I know what she was really thinking. She was thinking, *Let's just get back to work, shall we? Otherwise I may be forced to throw you to the floor and have sex with you right here and now and that just wouldn't be right because it's still way too early in the story.* I should probably add that the dye in bras in the nineteenth century was made of a volatile mixture of turpentine and radium, and was never meant to be inhaled.)

Suddenly there was a loud *pop!*

A skylight pane shattered. The oil lamp went out, and the conservatory plunged into darkness.

Liz screamed. "Caleb, where are you?" she cried.

Something big hit the floor. She felt around on the carpet for what had fallen. Her hands found the prone body of her ex-lover, who was now groaning in pain.

"Caleb. Caleb, can you hear me?"

"Supériorité des Anglo-Saxons," said Liz. "A killing machine."

"Liz," he said weakly, "I'se tinks I'se been hit." And then he lost consciousness.

HISTORY, IN PAINTING THE STERILIZED PORTRAIT OF THE SO-CALLED GILDED Age, has long forgotten Franny Rose Tiddles and Emma May Pinch. Our memories have a wonderful way of erasing the embarrassments of our past. (At least that's what my mom and dad always say when they talk about me.)

Franny Tiddles and Emma Pinch were two dwarf prostitutes from the Mulberry Bend. Friends since childhood, they were rarely seen apart. Throughout their arduous fifty years on earth, they held a variety of occupations: rag pickers, snot gatherers, rodent groomers, and Sabrett hot dog stuffers. But it was the skin-for-hire trade in which they found their true calling.

The eccentric duo were cute, as far as filthy harlots go. In another life, they could have been dear old Aunt Emma and sweet old Aunt Franny, but in this life they were known as "Emma the Finger" and "Franny the Sprinkler."

There was nothing extraordinary about these two (except for the fact that Emma was actually the granddaughter of the Duchess of Wales and stood to inherit a large fortune had she only known about her true geneology). No, these two raffish creatures were simply more flotsam and jetsam afloat in the sea of the Mulberry Bend. Their only claim to fame was sharing the unfortunate privilege of being Jack the Jolly Thwacker's second and third victims (and boy were their intestines in for a big surprise!).

Uptown in the nondescript brownstone, the killer (dressed to kill) latched the door to his flat and headed downstairs.

At the foot of the steps, Mrs. O'Leary, the nosy housekeeper, stepped out of the parlor's pocket doors.

"Oh, good evening, Doctor. Out for a night on the town are we? I hear the Little Foys are performing at the Orpheum, they are. Or perhaps it's a minstrel show that's more your fancy? 'First on de heel, den on da toe. Every time I wheel about, I jump Jim Crow!' That 'Shuffling Throng' can sure tap up a storm, they can. And those painted white lips of theirs, my gracious but they're—"

The killer pressed his index finger over Mrs. O'Leary's lips. He shoved a letter into her hands and then ever-so-slowly removed his finger.

"Oh, pardon me," said Mrs. O'Leary. "I do tend to go on, don't I? I suppose you'll be wanting me to post this for you then?"

The strange doctor nodded, picked up his carpetbag, and exited out the front door. Mrs. O'Leary shouted after him, "Have a jolly evening, then!"

At 10:20 PM, Franny Rose Tiddles and Emma May Pinch exhausted their meager supper of "poor man's cud" and returned to the streets. Their plan was to make enough money to pay for one night on a mud mattress at the newly built Hyatt Flophouse and Suites. But business was sluggish, their bobbles being bibbled only every other half hour or so.

"I'm telling you Emma, it's the way of the future."

"What's is?"

"Unions!"

"Onions?" queried Emma.

"No, unions! Listen, one day them cutthroats and ruffian goons are all gonna have their own whataya call . . . intanational broderhood, so why shouldn't we?" Franny was perpetually optimistic in a sweet and naive way.

"You mean a whore union?"

"Sure. Now you got it!"

"I don't know, Franny, I don't want to have to dress up and go to no meetings or not'in.'"

"Meetings? Oh hell. You won't have to go to no meetings."

"No?"

"No, you'll vote by proxy. Just leave everything up to me. Okay, deary?"

"I don't know what I'd do wit'out ya," said Emma.

"Sweetheart, we're what they call a couple of old dames at sea," mused Franny, throwing her arm over her pal's shoulder. "Now give your old soulmate a li'l nip off that natty flask of yours."

"Of course, Franny. But just a li'l nip now, remember . . . too much of this stuff makes you . . . sick."

"Oh, pish posh."

A breeze ruffled Franny's filthy hair as she took a li'l nip . . . then another li'l nip . . . then gulp after gulp after gulp, draining the flask and sucking it inside out.

"Oh Franny," began Emma, "I don't know nothing about no onions, but wouldn't it just be gay if one day we could take the paddle boat up to Saratoga, just the two of us, and maybe open up a little tea-tasting shop with all manner of fancy lace and fine china right there on Main Street? Wouldn't that just be gay now? . . . Franny? Wouldn't it? Franny?"

Without warning Franny slugged Emma right in the face, sending her straight to the cobblestones.

"What did I say? What did I say?" a stunned Emma asked.

"You dirty, li'l, filthy, stinkin', ugly piece of horse excrement. I'm gonna wallop you to a bloody pulp. And heres I come, lady!"

And with that Franny jumped on top of Emma and proceeded to pound away. Franny was not so sweet after she got a little kickapoo joy juice in her system.

The sight of two intoxicated prostitutes brawling in the street was not an unusual one in nineteenth-century New York. Pedestrians and policemen alike would have taken little notice of the altercation. So Franny and Emma were shocked when a long dark shadow fell across their embroiled mass of rags and flesh, and they were even more shocked when the stranger attached to the shadow spoke.

"Good evening, ladies. Tch, tch, tch, such an unfortunate rowdydow. Can I be of some assistance? I'm a doctor."

The two sat up. Emma spit out a wooden tooth and blood trickled from her beak. They straightened their hair and tried their best to look presentable.

"It weren't nothing for a fine gentleman like yourself to bother over," said Franny.

"Li'l squabble, that's all," added Emma.

"I see," said the mysterious man. "Well then, I suppose I should be on my way and allow you two lovely ladies to continue your . . . discussion."

"Well hold on there, gov'nor. Care for a quick bop-bop in the old yam shop?" offered Franny.

"Only cost ya a quid," added Emma.

"My my," said the stranger, as he mulled over the proposition. "What an enchanting possibility . . . and I assume it's buy one, get one free?"

The two little prostitutes laughed. Franny poked Emma with her elbow.

"Buy one, get one free! That's funny! I like this one! He's a saucy one, isn't he?"

"Oh yes, he's a clever, saucy one, he is," said Emma.

The man stepped closer and hovered over the still-seated unfortunates.

"But, my dear ladies, you have me misjudged."

"What you got there, mister?" asked Franny, noticing the man pulling something heavy from his carpetbag.

"You see, I'm not saucy at all. In fact, my friends say I'm rather jolly."

When Caleb regained consciousness, he found himself under a blanket in the back of a carriage. He was cold, and his head hurt. Elisabeth sat across from him, smiling.

"Oh, good, you're awake."

"Where are we going? Am I being taken to hospital?"

Elisabeth snorted. "Hardly."

Caleb felt over his chest. There was a sore spot on his rib cage, but no bullet hole.

"What—what happened?"

"You were shot. Don't you remember?"

"But I—"

"With this." Liz held out a wax bullet. "A blank. A warning shot, clearly. And then you fainted."

"I—I fainted?"

"Like a little girl, hitting your head on the parlor floor in the process. It was all we could do to haul you into the carriage."

"We—who is we?"

"Tally-ho!" cried a familiar voice from the driver's seat. "Yippie-ki-eye. Tippecanoe and Tyler, too."

Caleb lifted his head enough to make out Roosevelt's portly silhouette at the front of the carriage.

"You're alive?"

"Stout as a powder keg with twice the blast!"

"What happened?"

"He came home, just like we thought he would. And the fall

seems to have done him some good. It certainly, uh, expanded his vocabulary."

"Whatever tickles your fancy, my dear," T. R. cried.

"So, Liz, about before. What I said—"

"Oh, no, I was flattered, really. Coming from a big strong man like you, it really means something. I feel so safe and secure—as long as the Fancy Brigade isn't armed with pop guns."

"Very funny." Caleb patted himself down. "Where's my mobile?"

Liz kicked a trunk at her feet. "I had Teddy drag it along. I figured you would want to contact the precinct and have them send a couple of men over to protect me from having you faint all over me."

Caleb ignored her, winding the crank that retrieved his messages. A ticker tape wound out into his hands, and he read it.

"We're too late," he said. "There's been another murder. Or should I say . . . murders." He paused. "No, seriously, should I?"

Chapter the Fifth.

In which a curious simulacrum is encountered by the author and aids to perpetuate a further deepening—if conceivable—of the conundrum.

Dear Diary,

It is a dreadfully beleaguered hand with which I compose this evening's entry, for I have experienced no less than a whirlwind twenty-four hours, and find myself now drenched with fatigue and plagued by a wretched cranium discomfort. Therefore, I feel that it is most incumbent upon myself to apologize humbly in advance for the following prose, for I fear it will not rise to my usual superlative artistry. I do pray this will not detrimentally affect my ranking within the circles of society that are most frequently visited by yours truly.

"What the hell is she talking about?" asked Wendell.

"I don't know," I said, "I guess that's just the way they wrote diaries back then."

"She's writing all this right before she goes to bed?"

"Yep."

"She's got a motormouth on her, that's for sure."

"Well, it was a different time, Wendell. People paid more attention to language."

"Yeah, well skip the fancy-cracker crap and jump to the shit."

"Right."

The day began like any other. I enjoyed a cup of figs and warm rice yogurt in my rooms at the Cairo Arms, and then readied myself for another day of sifting through rubble with Lord Carnarvon. (What a bore! And I don't think he has much betwixt the legs! Not like that juicy Howard Carter, boy what I wouldn't give for a quick you-know-what with him!)

At 10:00 AM, the porter (cute!!!! but too short. Not my type) brought the mail and it was then that I discovered a correspondence from a long lost "acquaintance" of mine. It was a warning. Lives were in danger, and I was to keep my distance. Hardly. I hopped the first transport back to the States and not so coincidentally happened upon T. R. and my old boyfriend Caleb (I think you remember him, don't you, diary?).

"We know all this already."

"No, there's something new here," I said. "She was warned. She received a letter in Cairo warning her about something. That's why she came back. Plus, she puts the word 'acquaintance' in quotation marks. Curious."

"Why can't she just come out and say what's going on?"

"I'm not sure she knows at this point. But it's obvious that she's keeping something from Caleb."

"I'm late. I got to get out to Englishtown, New Jersey, and blow myself up at Raceway Park."

After Wendell left, I walked aimlessly about my apartment for a good three hours mulling over the strange entry in Liz's diary. Dakota apartments are huge and it's easy to wander around for hours on end without ever visiting the same room twice. I

heard Yoko "strangling a cat" in her recording studio next door, and my blood pressure shot through the roof. So I brewed myself a pot of chamomile tea and retrieved my ex-wife's old plaid skirt from the closet.

I've found over the years that cross-dressing in my ex-wife's clothing is the most efficient way for me to relax. So I put on the skirt and a pair of shiny, patent leather Mary Janes and curled up in a comfortable easy chair with my cup of chamomile tea and both Caleb's and Elisabeth's diaries in my lap.

It occurred to me that I was in possession of something very real—something tangible from the past. Something that Caleb and Liz had both touched and cared about. I remembered Yoko's words about the apple and felt a chill run through my body. *Were they trying to send me a message from the grave?*

Then something struck me: Liz and Caleb were real people! They had lived and loved over a hundred years ago! But they were real! They weren't made-up characters from some cheap, waste of money, trashy novel, written by a hack D-list actor who thinks he's a big writer now. No, they had been living flesh and living bone (and living hair, ew!). They most certainly walked the same streets that I walk now and perhaps even visited the Dakota, for it stood just as it does today back when they were alive.

I wondered if the three of us would have been friends or if they would've thought I was a bonehead. I weighed the question and resolved that the three of us would've been the *best* of friends! (And that Liz would've wanted to do me.)

For a moment the room seemed to get all liquidy, like it was a TV show having a flashback, and I felt as if I were in the nineteenth century. It was so near to me that I could almost smell the unwashed masses. Then the Dakota reasserted itself.

I was suddenly energized by a renewed passion. I wanted to

exact a solution to the case more than ever. But now I wanted to help my new friends from the nineteenth century solve it as well.

I would read just a little more, I thought, then sleep and get a fresh start in the morning.

Cinematically, at that moment an old, faded daguerrotype marked PRIME SUSPECT fell out of Caleb's diary. I picked it up and looked at the face in the picture. That face would keep me up all night.

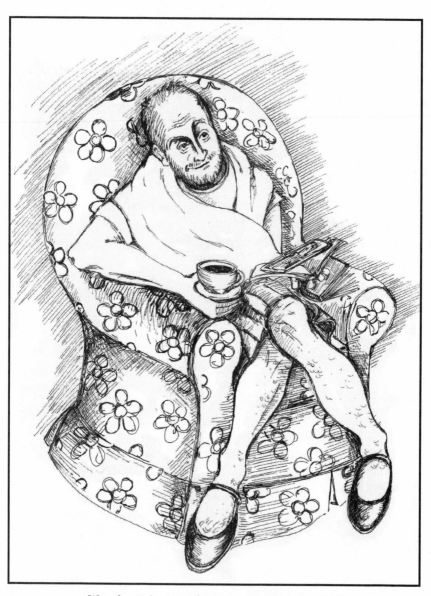

Were they trying to send me a message from the grave?

A crime preserved in a thousand centuries ceases to be a crime, and becomes a virtue.

> —*Mark Twain,* forecasting the inevitable commercialization of Jack the Jolly Thwacker and his murderous deeds—which was realized in the twentieth century with the propagation of Thwacker T-shirts, plastic top hats, and Mattel's screaming burlap bags filled with rubber McIntosh apples.

Chapter the Sixth.

In which Police Chief Spencer becomes mistrustful of an affable confidant, causing Miss Smith to become most egregiously affronted.

NINETEENTH-CENTURY NEW YORK WAS A CITY VERY MUCH IN DENIAL, especially when it came to the welfare of its children, namely the hordes of juvenile delinquents who roamed freely about the neighborhoods. From the Five Points to Harlem, from the East Side to the West Side, tribes of marauding gangs, pickpockets, toddler finks, diaper-runners, and pacie-chompers ruled the night. Although the Society for the Prevention of Cruelty to Livestock had added children to their cause a few years earlier, records at the nineteenth precinct indicate that out of a hundred thousand arrests made in 1880, ninety thousand offenders were under the age of five and the remaining ten thousand were over the age of ninety-six.

We often forget that in the Gilded Age people lived within a strict class structure favoring the wealthy and cruel. Children, especially those of the "unfortunate classes," grew up quickly, often obliged to beg, borrow, and (mostly) steal before they could even waddle upright on both legs. While the affluent children, in their little sailor outfits and delicate lace, were afforded the luxuries of fine educations, arranged marriages, arranged affairs, and arranged divorces—as well as oodles of boodle whenever

they wanted it—the sons and daughters of the city's hardscrabble were compelled to leave home by the time they were five. They were forced to choose between toiling in a sweatshop or joining a street gang, which ironically had their own class systems and often drove the lower-class members out by the time they were seven—at which point they would go back home and work in a sweatshop until they were about thirteen and then have kids of their own, whom, in turn, they would kick out by the time they were five. This vicious cycle produced hundreds of *Lord of the Flies*-style colonies, which sprouted up along the riverfronts, in the holes of the dock rats, and underneath the stinking dumps along the polluted water's edge.

One such community was known as the Mud Tot Tribe, and its fifty or so members made their home beside the Hudson River beneath the dump on Rivington Street. Aged from two to seven, the clan was composed of both males and females of all races and minorities (an equal opportunity gang of infants, rare for those days). Its leader was a fierce six-year-old called Chickabiddy. His second-in-command was a tough Mexican kid named Bambino, and the third of the top dogs was a five-year-old African girl, the daughter of freed slaves, who preferred to go by her Christian name, Molly Coddle.

Foraging in the dumps, setting hobos on fire, and robbing pedestrians whenever they could, the Mud Tot Tribe struggled to lead a serene life, only waging war with neighboring gangs if they felt their territory had been infringed upon, or if they were intoxicated, or if it was raining and the hobos were too slippery to grab onto and too wet to catch.

A smoldering fire pit under the overhang on Rivington Street gave little hint of the wild debauchery of the night before when the Mud Tots had performed their tribal rain dance. Now, the morning after the murders of Franny Rose Tiddles and Emma

May Pinch, they lay sleeping, huddled in tight groups on the harsh concrete gravel that was their beach (all the sand in their district had long ago been taken to make the beaches bigger in the Hamptons). They slept so peacefully that one would almost think they were at a summer camp, rather than engaged in a day-to-day struggle for survival.

Their mascot and lookout, Bud, an odd mix of Irish setter, beagle, and porcupine, sniffed along the water's edge, where he found a crab shell worthy of a bite. After gobbling it down, Bud noticed a large load of laundry that had washed up overnight. There was something unusual about its smell. He let out three loud barks and rustled his quills, the signal for an interesting discovery.

Molly Coddle fumbled beneath her makeshift bed of rags and pulled out a club 'n' spikes, ready to do battle.

"What is it? Surprise attack? I'll destroy the lot of 'em. Bambino, wake up!"

Bambino sat up.

"What, what is it?"

"Bud barked and rustled."

Bambino sighed, "Aw, he's just found somethin'. Where's Chickabiddy?"

"I'm already halfway there. Move your carcass."

Several members of the gang were awake now. The children's bodies, extremely muscular for their age, were painted with mud that had dried and cracked. They wore jury-rigged motley bits of fabric fashioned into skirts and tunics with bits of rope, wire, and chain, and their bare feet were so callused and filthy that it looked like they were wearing black boots. They stretched their aching limbs, stuck their weapons into their belts, and then walked down to the riverfront.

Chickabiddy stood over the big blob of black cloth covered in mud and seaweed. Fabric of any kind was always a welcome

commodity. Not only was it useful, but it fetched a pretty penny on the streets.

"Roll it over," he said, and, using a stick, Bambino did just that. But it wasn't laundry at all. It was a human body. And it was still breathing.

The children looked at each other, unsure of what to do. If they went to the police, they would assume it was the Mud Tots' handiwork. It would be far better for the tribe to push the unconscious man back out into the river and let him wash up on some other gang's front porch, but it was Chickabiddy's decision to make. He paced back and forth, thinking. Despite his ferocious demeanor, there was a soft side to him as well, and he showed it when he turned around, dropped his pants, and took a long piss. When he was finished, it was obvious that he had made his decision.

"Runabout!" he called out. He stuck a corn cob pipe between his teeth and lit it. Bambino and Molly Coddle exchanged looks. They knew they were in for another of their leader's "inspirational" speeches. A chubby, two-year-old baby girl in diapers, also smoking a pipe, crawled up.

"Yes sir?" said Runabout.

"Hurry to the Cherry Street Cantina and fetch the growler."

"Yes sir."

"And get somebody to change ya!"

"Yes sir."

With that the babe crawled away at a pace so furious that any adult would have had to run to keep up with her. Chickabiddy clapped his hands three times, and Bud the dog and the rest of the tribe joined in hoisting the body out of the river.

AT 6:20 AM, A HANDFUL OF GAWKERS ATTRACTED BY THE EARLY-MORNING police activity gathered in front of the alleyway on Twenty-sixth Street between Eleventh and Twelfth. Having roped off the area about ten minutes before, the coppers now stood around waiting for the investigative team to arrive, passing the time by gorging themselves on coffee and jellied yeast rings.

This time the bodies had been discovered by an Italian manure collector, who was in the process of hauling his wagon of excrement over to the West Side Recycling Center. In the nineteenth century, manure was used in the manufacturing of many household items, especially holiday fruitcakes, ladies' winter hats, and gentlemen's codpieces and merkins. The recycling center paid handsomely per pound for the harvested crap.

At approximately 6:22 the buggy carrying Caleb, Liz, and Roosevelt pulled up to the crime scene. Magnesium-powder flashes popped, billowing smoke as the three stepped out and were immediately besieged by reporters from the penny papers.

"Is this the work of the Thwacker?"

"Has the fiend struck again?"

"Are you and Liz Smith an item?"

"Is it true the mayor has a pearl earring in his pe—"

"Get these people back!" ordered Caleb, and a trio of flatfoots pushed the photographers behind the barricades.

"Names?"

"Tiddles and Pinch, sir."

"Damn, I knew those two," Caleb said, shaking his head and looking down.

"I believe we all knew them two at one time or another, sir. If you get my meaning." The sergeant winked. And then he explained: "I mean they were prostitutes and we all—"

Caleb looked up at him sternly.

"Where are they, Sergeant?"

"In the alley, sir."

"Great, another alley."

"Maybe it's a pattern," said Liz.

"I'm beginning to wonder if there's any pattern in this at all."

Teddy surreptitiously pulled from his pocket a pamphlet entitled, *Bartlett's Memorable Sayings of the Nineteenth Century*, glanced at it, then returned it to his jacket. He cleared his throat and blurted out,"The average man's a coward, Huck!" His round face blossomed with a satisfied expression.

Liz, Caleb, and the sergeant stared at him.

"That will be all, Sergeant," said Spencer, and the sergeant moved off.

"Teddy, are you feeling all right?"

"Never better, my boy. Never better. Remember, 'Cauliflower is nothing but cabbage with a college education!' "

"Eh, right."

As the three entered the alley, Liz whispered to Caleb, "Have you understood a word Teddy has said lately?"

"No. We better keep an eye on him. He's acting a little oddball—I mean more than usual."

The alleyway was yet another dark, narrow brick corridor reminiscent of where Old Toothless Sally's body had been found. The place was damp, and rusty water dripped down the walls into brown puddles at their feet. The oil lamp Spencer held added little illumination to the dreadful place.

"Something's up ahead," noticed Liz.

"I see it, too."

"Weehay!" exclaimed Teddy.

His companions looked at him with puzzled expressions.

"Weehee?"

No response.

"Wee . . . wee? Weewee! That's it—wee-wee!"

Smith and Spencer shook their heads and the three walked further in. They could just make out a small flame flickering in the darkness.

"There," said Liz.

The tableau the killer had created this time was truly macabre. Franny and Emma's bodies were seated at a child's table, apparently celebrating a birthday party. They were both wearing paper hats, and Franny seemed to be blowing on a little noisemaker shaped like a horn, while Emma was cradling a doll. Franny's intestines had been fashioned into a cake with a lit candle and placed in the center of the table. Emma's intestines were strung about the scene like decorative streamers.

"What the hell is wrong with this man?" asked Caleb. "Does he think this is some kind of, kind of—"

"Party?" offered Liz. "I agree, it's horrible, to use someone else's life for your own amusement."

"Amusement . . ." Roosevelt said, stroking his chin. "Might I suggest that perhaps this scene might have some connection with whatever Phossy Phil told you two last night? Did he not tell you to examine the murder scenes for clues?"

Spencer and Smith were astonished. *Roosevelt was actually saying something helpful. How could that be possible?*

"You may be on to something there, Teddy," said Caleb, and then he whispered to Liz, "Maybe the fall has transformed him into an idiot savant."

"Just trying to do my civic duty, Caleb. Remember, kings is kings, and you got to make allowances. Take them all around, they're a mighty ornery lot. It's the way they're raised."

"Ah, yeah . . . I guess I would have to agree with you there, Teddy." Caleb retrieved his notepad.

Liz felt Teddy's forehead. "Are you sure you're feeling all right, Teddy?"

"Woman, where I come from that's an invitation to jump your bones!" he roared and laughed lasciviously.

Liz frowned. Teddy had always been lascivious, but he had seemed more or less harmless. Suddenly she felt a little afraid of him.

"Let's see here . . . Phil talks about matches . . . Fifth Avenue . . . phosphorous . . . 'How many gold doubloons for the wench?' Then all that mumbo jumbo about freaks and balloons. He stressed Ferris wheels."

"Ferris wheels?"

"There you go! Now we're cooking with oil!" said the mayor.

"But what could Ferris wheels possibly have to do with Tiddles and Pinch?"

Roosevelt cleared his throat. "Did not your informant say something about 'freaks'?"

Caleb slapped his forehead. "Freaks! Of course. Not Yahi! Midgets! There is an entire midget colony in Coney Island!"

Liz exclaimed, "And it's an 'amusement park containing a Ferris wheel.'"

"Very good, very good my little duckies," said a voice behind them and out of the gloom emerged a bearded man, bigger around than even Teddy, and considerably softer. "Good to thee our preciouth tax dollars aren't going to waitht."

Despite his flabbiness, his presence exuded pure domination. He wore a white sack-suit and spats, held a gold-tipped walking cane, and crowned his head with a furry white top hat. His satin vest shimmered as the light from Caleb's lamp danced upon it, creating the illusion that the garment itself was alive, rather than merely tacky. The man's voice would have been fierce had it not been for a slight hint of the feminine in its tenor. Caleb, Elisabeth, and Roosevelt recognized him right away.

William "Boss" Tweed was a three-hundred-pound corrupt

city politician. He had been an alderman and even a state sena-
tor before most recently being anointed Grand Sachem of the
Tammany Hall Society. In that capacity, he gained power by gal-
vanizing the immigrant vote, making a fortune through graft,
kickbacks, and general pilfering along the way. Still, he was a
man whose arm-twisting influence earned him a reserved respect
even among the (relatively) more honest politicians like Teddy.
The two men, who had butted heads (figuratively and literally)
over the years, had never enjoyed each other's company.

"Good morning, Mayor Roothevelt," said Tweed, winking at
the mayor.

"Willy boy. Nice to see you," acknowledged Teddy, winking
back.

"My dear Chief," said Tweed. "Johnny-on-the-thpot, I thee,
as always. Good for you!" The big man closed in on Elisabeth,
tipping his fur hat. "Mith Thmith, your radianth fills my thoul
with the therenity of thpringtime."

"Why thank you, Mr. Tweed, or should I say Boss?" Liz giggled
flirtatiously, making sure that Caleb noticed. "However, it's not I
but you who radiates like springtime." Caleb just rolled his eyes.

"I hear he calls himthelf the Thwacker?"

"That's correct," said Caleb, reluctantly. He hated being
watched over by his superiors, and Grand Sachem was as superior
as they came.

"And he writth to Mith Thmith here, care of the *Potht*?"

"That's right."

"How many letters have you retheived, Mith Thmith?"

"Just the one," said Liz.

"Are you quite thure of that?" asked Tweed.

"Yes, I'm quite sure."

"Because it'th important that you let uth know if you've
rethieved any other correthpondenth from thith fiend."

Teddy said, "I guarantee you, Willy, Miss Smith will tell us as soon as she gets another letter from the Thwacker. Now won't you, my hot little Lizzy-wizzy?" Teddy cooed, putting his arm around Elisabeth and squeezing her hard. She squirmed out of his grip, still uncomfortable with the mayor.

"Of course I will," she said.

"That'th jutht fine." Then Tweed turned to Caleb. "Well now, Chief, we at Tammany Hall hear you've been indulging yourthelf in thome conthpirathy theories. Aren't you a little old for these thotth of thecret thothiety theories'?"

It took Caleb a moment to realize what Tweed had said.

"Not that it's your concern, sir, but we seem to have a Mummer connection," he said. "We believe that the killer might in fact be a Mummer or at least affiliated—"

"I athure you, my dear boy, there ith *no* Mummer connection!" interrupted Boss Tweed with authority in his voice. "What you have here ith a lunatic, and that'th all."

"That is odd," said Caleb, "but the last time I checked, I was the investigator here."

"And the latht time *I* checked, Grand Thachemth outranked Polithe Chiefth. It goeth Grand Thachemth, Little Thachemth, mayorth, bookieth, leg-breakers, ithe cream, *then* polithe chiefth."

Caleb had to admit he had him there.

"Chief Thpenther, I am a politithian. A fat, corrupt politithian, and if there's one thing I know, it'th thecret thothietieth. The Mummers are a harmleth bunch of clownth. To accuthe them of murder, well, I find mythelf quethtioning your thentheth."

"With all due respect, Mister Tweed, I believe my thenthes are completely thound . . . sound. . . . My senses are thound." Caleb shook his head; the lisping was contagious.

"Your killer ith clearly a crazed immigrant, who thertainly

hath nothing to do with Coney Island, and thertainly not Midget Thity."

"But the killer mentioned Mummers," Liz began to protest, but Caleb quickly motioned to her to shut up.

Caleb said, "Tweed is right, Liz. There *are* very important people in this city who practice Mummery. We would not want to offend any of them by slinging around unfounded allegations."

"I would lithen to your partner, Mith Thmith. You mutht underthtand that the confuthed mind of the lunatic rarely offerth up the truth. One mutht read between the lineth of hith letter. Perhapth by Mummerth he meant thoth who keep mum. There ith thertainly a virtue in thilenth, ith there not? The mum do tend to live longer, in any cathe." Tweed pulled the latest edition of the penny papers from underneath his arm, and in refolding it, he deliberately displayed its headline to Caleb: *Legendary, Jawless Informant Found Murdered!* Then he cleared his throat and stuffed the newspaper back under his arm.

"I have noticed," said Caleb grimly, throwing a troubled look to Liz.

"The National Organithation of Mummerth donateth heavily to our great Metropolith, and I know for a fact that it is made up of nothing but outthtanding, law-abiding, well-educated, negroid-abominating, white Protethtant gentlemen . . ."

Teddy choked down a laugh.

". . . who could never partake in thuch ghathtly indethenthies. No, my dear duckieth, forget about the Mummerth. It'th a wathte of time." Tweed struck Caleb on the chest with the handle of his cane. "Do I make mythelf clear, Chief Thpenther?"

"As fine crystal, sir."

Liz looked at Caleb, her expression a combination of incredulity and confusion. Caleb stared back at her, his expression

a combination of trepidation, timorousness, perturbation, cold feet, and boiled eggs.

"Eggthellent," said Tweed. "Then I bid you all farewell and wish you the betht of luck! Good day to you."

He spun on his heels, spinning a full turn-and-a-half, and started out of the alley.

Roosevelt called, "Peace out, Willy!" Then he clasped his hands over his mouth like he had just given away the store. "I mean, those of us who labor to bring light to the darkness have become amused . . ."

Liz began "What were you—?"

Caleb put his finger up. "Shhh! . . . Teddy?"

"Yes sir-ree-bob?"

"Will you notify our carriage driver that we won't need him anymore today. We'll take the elevated out to Brooklyn."

"You got it, Chief. We're headed out to Coney Island, then? In spite of what Boss Tweed was saying?"

"Yes, quite definitely. Now hurry along."

"Yeah, yeah, yeah, keep your pants on." Teddy shuffled out, mumbling something about not being Caleb Spencer's house slave.

When he was out of earshot, Liz spoke.

"You think Teddy's involved, then?"

"There's something peculiar going on with him. He seemed a little too friendly with Tweed."

"And he's been acting awfully violent towards me. The things he's been saying. Last night, when you were unconscious, he offered to 'chrome my bumper,' whatever that means."

"Tweed obviously doesn't want us to pursue the Mummer angle. Good—because that convinces me that we're on the right track. He all but warned us not to go out to Coney Island."

"But Teddy was the one who suggested we go out there."

"True."

Liz sighed. "But either way, we have to go, don't we?"

"If only to find out why we shouldn't." Caleb pulled out his .32 caliber six-shot revolver and checked to make sure its barrel was loaded.

"If they're in cahoots, could they be trying to throw us off track? Giving us mixed signals to keep us focused on the wrong course?"

"I hope that's all they're trying to do. I doubt Phossy Phil's murder is just a coincidence."

"What will we do about Teddy?"

"I want to trust him, Liz, but he's being very queer. Still, I don't want to leave him behind."

"Yeah, that's exactly how I feel. If they've gotten to him somehow, I'd rather keep him close by. Maybe we can help him."

"Or at the very least keep an eye on him. But no more sharing clues with him."

"Then before he comes back, you should read this."

She pulled an envelope out of her purse and handed it to him.

"From the Thwacker, then. Why didn't you give this to me earlier?"

"What are you suggesting?"

"I don't know, Liz. Things are getting very complicated. I never would have thought Teddy would have turned against us, but now . . . I don't know who to trust."

"Excuse me, I just received it this morning. Would you have had me hand it over to you in the presence of our unusually behaving mayor?"

Caleb looked her over.

"You can trust me, Caleb. You know that, don't you?"

"I'm sorry, it wasn't that. I was just distracted by how beautiful you are."

"Oh, please." Liz pretended to blush. "I'd kiss you, Chief Spencer, but I'm afraid you'd just faint again."

THE INVESTIGATIVE TEAM MAY HAVE DESPAIRED AT EVER FINDING A PAT-tern, but the fact that the Thwacker had chosen two victims this time clearly indicated to me that there was a significance to that number. The investigative team seemed less interested in that possibility than in that silly Mummer connection, which personally I was beginning to believe was a waste of time—especially when you have an outstanding citizen like Boss Tweed vouching for the organization. No, to me the key here was the number *two*.

As I paced back and forth in my apartment, mulling things over, it suddenly hit me like a ton of bricks: "Go." "Two." "Go to . . . !" The killer was beginning to spell out a message, just as I had suspected. "Go to . . . to . . . *someplace!*" I was proud that I had been able to make the connection, and, just as I always do when I think I deserve it, I gave myself a sensuous kiss on my forearm.

Still, my little "a-ha" moment was overshadowed by the face in the faded daguerreotype marked PRIME SUSPECT that had fallen out of Caleb's diary. What could it possibly mean? The ramifications would certainly boggle the mind if not shake the world's core notions of reality. I dialed and redialed Wendell's cell phone number several times.

"Wendell? Wendell? Can you hear me?"

The connection was not very good.

"You sound like you're in a box," I observed.

"I am. I'm about to be blown up!"

"Oh, sorry, is this a bad time?"

Franny and Emma's bodies were seated at a child's table,
apparently celebrating a birthday party.

"You got thirty seconds."

"How's the crowd?"

"It's half empty. It's that time of year. You know, kids are back in school . . ."

"Sure, sure. Well listen, I won't keep you, but I found something that is really important. It fell out of Caleb's diary. It's a picture of their prime suspect. The guy they thought was the Thwacker. Now I know why the case has never been solved. Can you come over in the morning?"

"Maybe. If you make me pancakes."

"I'm not gonna make you pancakes. Eat breakfast before you come over. I'm not your house slave!"

"If I'm gonna help you with this, the least you can do is make me breakfast!"

"Hey, I don't need your help. I just want to show you this picture. It's got me all weirded out. I know who the guy is, but it's unbelievable. It's. . . ."

Suddenly there was a loud crackling noise from Wendell's side of the connection. Then the line went dead.

"Wendell? Wendell? Oh forget it," I said. "I'll tell you in the morning. Peace out!" I hung up the phone and collapsed back down into my comfy chair. For the next six hours I had a staring contest with the familiar face of the man in the faded daguerreotype. (Needless to say, he won.)

As Roosevelt, Smith, and Spencer boarded the elevated train bound for Coney Island at the Herald Square station, back on Cherry Street, little Runabout, the tough baby gang member, crawled quickly across the boulevard, wearing a clean diaper and clenching the handle of a small bucket in her teeth.

Under the dump on Rivington, the juvenile Mud Tots huddled around the unconscious man. They had wiped some of the crud off his face, but none of them could place him.

"He eats well, that's for sure," said Chickabiddy.

"We're taking a chance keeping him," warned Molly Coddle, still holding her club 'n' spikes. "Let me do him. We can load his pockets up with rocks and sink him."

"Rocks cost money," Chickabiddy said. "And those pockets are worth a fortune."

"But he endangers the tribe," she insisted.

"I say we roast 'im and eat 'im," said Bambino. This suggestion was met with cheers. "We can feed off that blubber fer weeks."

"I said I don't think so."

"But why, boss?" they asked.

At that moment Runabout came crawling up the gravel beach.

"Get the growler," Chickabiddy ordered, and Bambino took the bucket from Runabout and brought it to the chief. He put it up to his lips and drank. Apparently "the growler" was a nickname for a bucket of beer.

"Listen up," he said, addressing the group. "We are the fierce and mighty Mud Tot Tribe. We pillage, we plunder, and we 'rape,' whatever that means, exactly. But if it's bad, we do it! There is no toddler gang more feared then we are and there is not one among you who relishes the taste of a rich man's blood more than I do, but I must warn you, fellow tribesmen, that we are watched by an unseen force. A force that guides us through our victories in battle and provides us with all the luxuries of life that we enjoy." At that point Runabout spit out a disgusting wad of chewing tobacco, picked it up and stuck it in her pipe, and then lit it up.

"This force requires one thing of us," continued Chickabiddy. "To be nice to another human being just once a year—just once

a year!—so that we can then have a clear conscience to go on living the way our ancestors have for generation after generation."

Chickabiddy held the bucket of beer up to the sky.

"And so I say, let this ugly fat load of middle-aged, worthless flesh be our one good-hearted deed for the year. Let us nurse it back to health and send it on its way, and then we will have fulfilled our obligation and can go back to setting hobos on fire and robbing innocent pedestrians. I command this, as your leader and chief. Let it be so."

The Mud Tots cheered in unison.

Bambino said, "And then we can eat 'im?"

Chickabiddy shrugged. "Yeah, I don't see why not."

With that he knelt down and put the growler up to the unconscious man's lips. Bambino held the man's head up and they poured the beer down his throat.

The fat man coughed and then groaned. They poured more in, and after finally swallowing a bit of brew, the man's lids fluttered ever so slightly. A faint smile crossed his lips.

"Weehoo!" he said weakly.

Chapter the Seventh.

In which your humble author exhausts the once copiously unfurled horizons of his much beleaguered thesaurus.

LIZ WAS BEGUILED BY A DUO OF TOWHEADED BOYS WHO BOUNCED AND wriggled in their seats across from her.

"I wanna go on the San Francisco Earthquake Ride, Stink-O-Rama, and the Leapfrog Railroad!"

"I wanna go on the Wild Bucket of Tar, the Earthquake Ride, the Leapfrog Railroad, and the Eccentric Fountain!"

"Let's do the Tempestuous Fish Fry first!"

"And then the Bucket of Tar!"

"There's also the Ill-Boding Electric Seat!"

"Oh yeah, let's do that before Earthquake!"

The little boys could hardly contain their excitement, and Liz smiled at the two; but so consumed in their day's planning were they that they took little notice of her.

"Now, now, children," scolded their mother, "temper your elated spirits with equanimity. Remember, Mamma is taking you to the shore to enjoy the therapeutic benefits of the salt air, and perhaps to promenade with others of our social standing along the boardwalk. It is highly unlikely that we shall partake in any

vulgarian diversions such as the Eccentric Fountain or the San Francisco Earthquake Ride."

"Yes, Mamma," said the disappointed youngsters, the wind in their sails having been winnowed down to a mere wheeze.

"But if you comport yourselves with dignity, I will allow a picture postcard to be purchased with your savings, provided I deem its depiction properly restrained and suitably edifying."

"Yes, Mamma." The boys stopped bouncing and looked forlornly out the train's window at the girders of the new Brooklyn Bridge. Liz made a show of frowning at the stodgy mother, who, catching her glare, countercharged with a repugnant countenance that only the affluent of the day were able to master. Liz, having rubbed elbows with her type before, recognized it as the countenance that said, "Attend to your own trivial affairs, you impertinent, presumably-too-old-to-have-a-child-of-your-own woman; you obviously hail from a lower station and haven't even the right to set eyes upon a matriarch of such high standing as myself!"

"Well, this is more cryptic than the first," whispered Spencer as he folded the second Thwacker letter. Liz and Caleb were being careful not to wake Roosevelt, who lay sprawled across two velvet seats facing them.

"What do you suppose the killer means by the phrase 'two of me'?" queried Caleb.

Liz shook her head and recited:

Jack went out last night to play.
You'll find my work at dawn today.
Follow the clues and you shall see,
Not just one, but two of me.

"And then of course he postscripts it with the customary inflammatory remarks about Roosevelt's weight," added Caleb.

"You don't suppose there are two fiends at work here, do you?" asked Liz.

"Possibly."

Roosevelt shifted and began to babble in his sleep. His traveling companions, now highly suspicious of their friend, listened closely.

"Stop that. No, no! That tickles! Yes, I know it's all the rage, but it's not natural and there's absolutely no way it would fit!"

Liz and Caleb exchanged spent looks and leaned back into their velvety seats. The third day of intense investigation coupled with two sleepless nights had finally caught up with the team, and as the old Chattanooga-Susquehanna-Coney Island line rumbled its way out to Brighton Beach, the ex-lovers relinquished thoughts of murder, mayhem, and Mummers and yielded their senses to a well-deserved slumber.

At this point, dear readers, I must tell you that I have discovered a complex equation that enables one to determine precisely what another dreamt over a hundred years ago on a particular day, at a particular hour, on a particular train headed for Coney Island, and it's really quite simple (at least for me). First you need to know if the subject was breastfed and for how long (the longer the better). Then you take the quotient of a (which is actually b) and multiply it by the finial of the xy factor, and, utilizing a quadratic equation of some kind, you compute the distance between the subject's eyes (color doesn't matter) with the distributive property, $x - 2 = 0$, then you . . . oh, forgive me, I realize that this is probably way over everyone's heads. Suffice it to say that the answer is always correct and it always comes out in the first person, exactly as if delivered from the therapist's couch:

I am standing in front of a horse-drawn carriage. I am only about three years of age. There is a tall man standing over

me, covered in sequins and wearing a brightly colored Indian chief's headdress. "You must go away!" he tells me. "You must never come back!" "But I don't want to go away," I say, and I begin to cry. "You must go! And you will see me no more! Don't try to find me! For I wish not to set eyes upon you ever again." I cry harder. Then someone pulls me into the carriage. I look out the back window as the carriage pulls away. The man who seemed so mean a moment ago now seems sad. He tips his feathered headdress to me and begins to dance, or more like strut, mournfully. The carriage picks up pace, and the man becomes smaller and smaller and smaller. "No, I want to stay!" I scream. "Please no!"

"Daddy! Daddy!"

"Elisabeth!?" She woke to find Caleb shaking her. "Liz, Liz? You were having a bad dream. You're awake now. You were just lost in a terrible 'brown study'! And you were drooling! Are you all right?"

She was sweating and obviously upset. Other passengers turned their heads to see what the commotion was. The stodgy mother with the two boys shot Liz a disgusted look, which clearly said, "How dare you have a bad dream on a public train after Labor Day—and in that dress, my Lord but you look like a lowly provincial chawbacon!"

Liz apologized and then buried her head in Caleb's chest.

Other than the fact that he was a Mummer, Elisabeth admitted knowing very little about her father. She grew up believing he had abandoned her and her mother when she was very young, and she relocated to live with relatives in Maine, where she was raised on a diet primarily of pine cones, seaweed, and fried clams. She was never sure whether her recurring dream was something that had truly happened, or just an invention.

"There there now, all's well," said Caleb. "Take a deep breath and blow it out slowly, just relax."

Comforting Liz was like riding a velocipede, he thought. *Once you learn how, you never forget.* The warmth of her body, the scent of her perfume, her breathing in perfect harmony with his, and the romantic allure of a train ride forced a kaleidoscope of reminiscences to rush through him. How strange it was that fate would bring them back together again under such dark circumstances (if indeed it *was* fate). He recalled William Blake's reflections on love from the poet's "Songs of Experience" and, waxing sentimental, he recited softly, with, incongruously, an affected British accent:

Love seeketh not itself to please,
Nor for itself hath any care;
But for another gives its ease,
And builds a heaven in Hell's despair.

Liz sighed into his chest and the young police chief sighed into her hair, and in a twinkling they had built their own little heaven in hell's despair. (Hey, I just rhymed!) Then Caleb noticed Roosevelt wide awake, lasciviously scrutinizing their every move. He gave Spencer a corrupt smile and a wink, as if to say, *You gotta nice piece of ass there, buddy! Why don't you take her into the bathroom and teach her a thing or two!* The romantic moment broken, Caleb gently pushed Liz back into her seat.

"There now, all better?"

"Yes, yes, quite. Thank you."

The train pulled into the station at the intersection of Ocean Avenue and Grand Cayman Island Boulevard, and Spencer, Smith, and Roosevelt were the first out—one car back, however, a familiar figure stepped onto the platform and walked menacingly

through the billowing steam, shadowing the three from a close distance. It was none other than the mysterious monk-like specter from Kit Burns's Sportsmen's Hall.

NINETEENTH-CENTURY CONEY ISLAND WAS COMPRISED OF THREE GIANT amusement parks: Steeplechase, Luna Park, and Dreamland, each offering a variety of attractions and each connected by a long boardwalk. Steeplechase's centerpiece was a horse race where life-sized mechanical thoroughbreds galloped along a magnetic track. Luna Park came to life after the sun went down, when its two hundred and fifty thousand incandescent light bulbs popped on. But it was Dreamland that drew the most visitors. Offering a look at "the World of Tomorrow," and furnished with the latest futuristic contrivances, Dreamland was the Epcot Center of the pre–consumer safety era. When you entered through its giant arch, you stood in the shadow of the iron Beacon Tower, whose mighty searchlight stretched out, sweeping back and forth over the Atlantic.

"Oh Caleb, doesn't it just bring back so many memories?"

"We're not here for a walk down memory lane, Liz. Let's begin by questioning the wee people."

Dreamland was home to Midget City, an experimental community where three hundred wee people lived and worked under the observing eye of the paying customer. Considering Phil's advice and Boss Tweed's objections, it seemed as good a place as any to begin their investigation.

"And what will we do if it's a trap?" asked Liz.

"We'll just have to try and stay one step ahead," said Caleb.

"Oh, yeah, that reminds me," said Roosevelt. "I've got to—um—get my picture made." He pointed to a tent where a photographer was making daguerreotypes of people with their heads stuck through holes in flats painted with silly bodies. The pictures took fifteen minutes to take, and you could always recognize which patrons had just come from that particular tent by their pained stoops.

"We have a job to do here, Teddy," said Caleb.

"Chill," he said. "It'll just be a minute."

Suddenly, there was a flash of light and a puff of smoke in the center of the boardwalk. Caleb's hand went immediately to his gun. But when the smoke cleared there was nothing but an unimposing old man wearing a cape and brightly colored tights. His shirt was inscribed with LEOPOLD, THE AMAZING EXPLODING HUMAN! The crowd on the boardwalk cheered and applauded.

Roosevelt muttered, "Amateur."

"We're going to interview the Hop-o'-My-Thumbs, Teddy," said Liz. "Why don't you meet us there later, after you're finished?"

"Sure, I'll catch you guys later! Er, I mean, fare thee well, 'til we meet again, pip pip cheerio and all that crap, and remember, nothing needs reforming as much as other people's habits!" With that the mayor bounded off towards the funny daguerreotype tent.

Caleb narrowed his eyes.

"Chill?" said Elisabeth. "What does that even *mean*?"

"Teddy must have sustained an injury to his brain when he fell through the trapdoor. That, added to the damage caused by years of running head-first into a brick wall to demonstrate how thick his skull is to want-wits willing to bet against him, must have finally pushed him over the edge."

"I hope that's all it is."

As they strolled down the boardwalk, heading towards Midget City, they passed the Rolling Rumps family of contortionists, the Good Humor frozen-mayo-on-a-stick carts, and an optigroinagraphic booth, where for a dime a mechanical gypsy would measure a gentleman's inseam. All the while they remained oblivious to the robed figure watching them from the shadows.

"What exactly do we expect to get out of these midgets?" asked Liz.

"Tiddles and Pinch were of an undersized nature. Phil said to look for patterns, even patterns that the killer himself might not see."

"Frankly, I think it's a wild goose chase."

"It may well be," said Caleb, "but we have no choice but to persevere. Besides, if indeed Tweed is involved, at least insofar as protecting the Mummers, then there's a reason he wanted us to come out here, and we're going to find out why."

The killer had put them on a tight schedule, but they could not help indulging themselves by pausing to watch a boatload of screaming vacationers slide down the Shoot-the-Chutes and splash victoriously into the lagoon at its base, where bored carneys fished out the survivors with hooked poles.

They passed the Leapfrog Railroad, a spine-tingling adventure in which two trains faced off in a game of chicken. Just before the moment of collision, one train would shift to a set of upper tracks and literally leapfrog over the other. This dangerous choreography was only successful five out of ten times, but even with a fifty-fifty chance of surviving, people lined up for hours to ride the attraction. Liz hoped the towheaded boys would manage to talk their repellent mother into riding.

Next they passed Fat Moses' Wild Lynch Mob Adventure, which usually resulted in permanent damage to the vertebrae,

but rewarded those who were still conscious at its conclusion with a spectacular panoramic view of all three theme parks.

"Oh Caleb, look!" said Liz, noticing a familiar attraction ahead of them.

"Some things from our past are just too embarrassing for me to remember, Liz."

She was referring to Dr. Courtney's Baby Incubator Barn, a red building topped with a stork holding a bundle in its beak. As they passed, sweet banjo music wafted out of its doors, just as it had back in 1875 when Elisabeth first dragged the uneager young flatfoot named Caleb into the attraction. Despite her independent suffragette exterior, she was always strangely fascinated by the place.

(What follows is another flashback to their love affair, just so you're not confused. The year is 1875.)

"Look at them," she said in awe as they gazed upon hundreds of premature babies displayed in glass enclosures, the little boys with blue ribbons on their heads and the little girls with pink ones. "Look at their tiny hands. They're no bigger than my thumbnail."

"Yes, the babies are quite . . . trivial," said Spencer.

"They're not trivial at all. I think they're just perfect!"

"I didn't mean to say trivial. I meant to say . . . um . . . puny. Repellently helpless. Do you suppose we could go to the Dancing Lederhosen now?"

"I wonder if we'll have a preemie?" Liz mused, her eyes riveted on the little cherubs.

"I should hope not. When and if we ever have children, they should be of a robust and sturdy nature, good fifteen-pounders at birth, I would imagine. I expect my boy to be capable of cleaning and firing a sidearm by the age of two."

"When and if? So you're not sure if you want to have children."

Caleb realized right away that he had opened a can of worms which he would have preferred to remain high on a shelf.

"Well, I simply meant that when and if . . . if and when . . . I mean . . . I'm sure we will . . . I just . . . at present. . . ."

Liz advanced upon him, backing him up against the wall of incubators.

"Don't you want to have children with me, Caleb?" She touched his cheek.

"Of course I do. It's just that . . . not right at the moment."

"No?" said Liz. "Are you so sure?" And with that, she grabbed Spencer, jerked him back behind the wall of incubators and began to feverishly attack the buttons on his uniform.

"Elisabeth, what in the devil . . . this is a family establishment."

"Well then, try to be quiet."

She unbuckled his utility belt, wrenched off his coat, and tossed away his felt hat. In an instant she had his shirt open and was kissing him hard as she slipped her hands down his trousers and squeezed his buns.

"God and country!" Caleb cried, involuntarily saluting.

Suddenly he was flat on his back and Liz, gathering up the massive bundle of fabric that was her dress and pulling down her lead-lined underwear (women wore such undergarments to prevent peeping toms with X-ray glasses from seeing through their underpants) was now vigorously mounting him.

After two minutes, and a climax heard round the world (Caleb's of course) the sweaty and flushed flatfoot appeared from behind the wall, buttoning up his coat, only to find himself face to face with a horrified nanny and her eight young charges in their school uniforms, all staring at him with their mouths open.

"Good day," he said, tipping his hat at the lady.

Liz appeared a moment afterwards, pushing down her dress and straightening her hair.

"Um, he was helping me with my shoe," she said. "It was stuck."

"My goodness," said the nanny. "I seem to have gone suddenly and inexplicably blind."

Liz curtsied, smacked Caleb on his butt, and then dashed out of the barn. "Race you to the Dancing Lederhosen!" she shouted, and Caleb gleefully chased after.

But that was seven years ago. Now, in 1882, their relationship was quite different. (The flashback is over now. You don't have to tax your brain anymore.)

"I don't suppose you wouldn't mind taking a little peek inside for old times' sake, would you?" ventured Liz as they passed the barn.

"We haven't the time."

"From what I remember, it didn't take very long," she said.

Caleb merely grunted. He was busy counting his coins, preparing their five-cent admission fee to Midget City.

Had the police chief glanced behind them at that moment, he would have seen that now, not just one, but three hooded monks were rapidly closing in.

Caleb and Liz ducked as they passed through the portal into the world of the little people. The three monks, however, stopped short of entering the attraction. They were unusually tall men, and they walked stiffly. The door seemed to confound them, as if they were unable to bend properly to fit through. Instead they turned towards P. T. Barnum's Freak Emporium across the way, where a morbidly obese albino named Rob Roy (a famous freak in his day, who had a map showing the oceans and towns where devils lived tattooed on his belly), was enjoying a smoke break.

He noticed the monks going into the Emporium, stamped out his cigarette, and rushed after them.

Inside Midget City, Spencer and Smith were greeted by a gregarious two-foot-tall man in spats and a top hat who, according to historical documents, sounded a lot like Jimmy Cagney.

"Hey, how ya doing, you young lovers? Welcome to Midget City!"

"Oh by golly, you're Tom Thumb! You're Tom Thumb!"

"Calm down, Caleb," said Liz.

"But Liz, this is Tom Thumb! You don't understand, Mr. Thumb. I'm your biggest fan," he gushed, holding out his pad for an autograph. "Would you mind, um . . ."

"Of course not, my dear lad," said Thumb. "Though I'm not sure what you're a fan of, seeing's how all I did was stop growing at age five, endure several decades of abuse, then put on a top hat and start acting cheerful. Who shall I make it out to?"

"The name's Caleb R. Spencer. If you could just write something like 'To the best darn tall person in the world'?"

Liz frowned, pondering her ex-boyfriend's behavior. *No matter how well you think you know somebody* . . . she thought.

"There you go, my boy," said Thumb. "So what brings New York's most famous police chief to our humble little burg? Come to see the basket-weaving today on the town green?"

"Actually, we're looking for information," said Liz.

"Information, huh?" Thumb grabbed his belly and chuckled. "Well, what would a little person like me know about the comings and goings of this great big city? Why, New York is as big to me as all of Africa is to you."

"Please, Mr. Thumb. Could you just tell us if you've noticed anything strange going on lately?"

The three looked around, taking in the full vista of the Lilliputian metropolis: wee firemen were busy dousing the flames

spitting out of a tiny thatch-roofed house, and a miniature suf-fragette parade was making its way up Main Street while a minia-ture throng of offended hooligans chased after them with tiny chains and sticks. A rooster was chasing the mayor in front of Town Hall, a hog rodeo was in progress on the town green, and, above everything, a small man in a model dirigible floated over the square, dropping firecrackers.

"Nothing out of the ordinary," said Thumb with a smirk.

"No. You don't understand," said Liz. "We're serious."

"Why don't you two just take a nice walk around the Bitty River, gawk at us trying to lead normal lives, pay your money, and leave, okay? Midgets have nothing to do with the Mum-mers anymore, you understand? Now, if you don't mind, I'll be on my way."

"We didn't say anything about Mummers, Mr. Thumb," said Caleb.

Thumb, who had just turned his back to them, now clenched his fists in anger. His voice dropped a couple of octaves, and he began to speak with a thick Bronx accent.

"Oh, hell. You went and put your wee foot in it now, didn't ya." He turned around, his placating smile now gone. "My real name's Charley. Charley Stratton," he said, extending his hand. "You two had better come with me."

Stratton's house was large for Midget City, but Caleb and Liz were still forced to kneel by the kitchen table, because the seats were too small for them to sit on without breaking.

"Can I get you two any tea?" he asked. "Personally, I'm having bourbon."

Caleb and Liz asked for drinks, which were served by a diminu-tive black house servant whom Charley referred to as Mammy. When she forgot to put ice in Caleb's drink, Charley yelled at her. Liz noted that he didn't treat her with the sort of sensitivity one

would expect from someone who had lived his whole life as a wee person.

"First, you can just drop all of that hop-o'-my-thumbs bullshit. I'm a dwarf, okay, if you have to call me anything." He downed his bourbon. "Mammy, get in here and freshen my drink, would ya? I'm dyin' out here. Now look, youse two, we don't like to get involved in the affairs of big people. They don't like us, and frankly, we don't like them. There were some who had ambitions—they imagined a world ruled by the little, where the big people were made to do tricks for *us*." He regarded his drink. "Pipe dreams, they turned out to be. But for a while the OHM held some sway in world affairs."

"OHM?" queried Caleb.

"The Organization of Hateful Midgets," clarified Liz.

"We made powerful alliances with the Mummers, and we infiltrated the highest ranks of government. Two or three of us would get on each other's shoulders, put on a trench coat, and run for public office. At night we would sneak up on our enemies and stab them in the knees. Ah, those were the days . . .

"For a while it worked like a dream. Then we were betrayed by the Mummers' new leader, a powerful and ruthless man, the biggest big person of them all. I can't tell you his name, but you know him. He holds high office in this city—and he has a terrible lisp."

"I think we have a pretty good idea who you mean," said Caleb, turning to Liz and mouthing, "Who the hell is he talking about?" His legs were beginning to fall asleep from all the kneeling.

"He wanted to wipe us out, but there were too many of us. The OHM's tiny arm stretched out worldwide back then, and what's more, we knew all their secrets. So in exchange for our silence, they helped us build little communities like these, where

we could live in peace, away from the world, keeping our own customs with dignity and self-respect—"

The mayor of Midget City ran by the kitchen window, screaming, the rooster chasing after him. Several normal-sized children chased after them, cheering and throwing peanuts. Two boys stopped to look in the window.

"Look, Bradley, a hop-o'-my-thumb tea party!"

His companion banged on the glass. "Say something funny, little man."

"Fuck off!" yelled Charley, throwing his tumbler at the window. It hit the sill and shattered. The boys screamed and ran off.

"Mammy, get in here with another glass. And close that curtain, would you?"

Stratton sighed. "But gradually the Mummers stopped being scared of us, and the money dried up, and we had to resort to charging admission. Hence the top hat and the"—his voice shot up an octave—"'How do you do, ma'am! My name is Tom Thumb. I was born when a teacup of golden sunshine got poured into a bucket of lollipops.'"

"So why are you choosing to help us now?" asked Caleb.

"Two words: Tiddles and Pinch." Charley seemed overcome. He dabbed at his eyes with the corner of the tablecloth. "Oh, they were good lasses, once, but they couldn't stand having to perform for their supper, havin' people watch them live their lives, gawkin' and starin'. So they decided to strike out, try to have a bit of a life to call their own, however . . . little."

Liz was touched. She offered Charley her handkerchief. "So they became prostitutes."

"Naw, they were already hookers. They just moved out."

"Can you help us catch the man who did this?" Caleb asked Tom.

"I don't know how much I can tell you. For starters, this

maniac, he's just a patsy. He's a poor sick kid who's doing the Mummers' work for 'em. Ah, my glass is empty. For Pete's sake, Mammy, just bring me the bottle. Second, there's only going to be one more murder before the ceremony. There's no pattern to the murders as far as the Mummers are concerned. As long as there's at least one a night, that's all they need. The killer, he might have his own pattern, but that I can't help you with."

Liz said, "We know when the ceremony is, but we don't know where."

"The Mummers will be sacrificing somebody to the earthly incarnation of their goddess, Erce. That's different than the whore-killing, and probably not nearly as fun. The earth goddess is groomed from birth for the role, and you'll have to figure out who that is before the ceremony, and you'll have to get to her before the Mummers do."

"Do you have any idea who it is?" Caleb asked.

"I know they use astrology or some such mumbo jumbo to pick her, that they set out looking for her on the day of her birth, and once they find her they take her in, but that's all I know."

"So it's possible they haven't even found her yet," said Caleb.

"Possible. The ritual hasn't happened much in my time. The Mummers have been trying to stamp it out for years. The last time, I was only a boy. I don't ever want to see anythin' like that again as long as I live."

"But where?" asked Liz. "Can you tell us where?"

"I'll tell you where, but you gotta do something for me. When the time comes"—he took a bell-mouthed pistol out of his vest pocket—"I want a piece of Tweed. For Tiddles and Pinch—and the glory of the hateful midgets."

"I'm chief of police," Caleb said. "I can't allow that. But . . . if I have my hands full at the scene, I might not be able to stop you."

"That's good enough. All's I need is one clear shot. The ceremony will take place at—"

Suddenly, there was a loud crash outside. Hundreds of tiny voices began to scream.

"What the hell was that?" yelled Caleb.

Liz ripped open the curtain. One of Midget City's outer walls had caved in. Debris was tumbling down all around them. A large chunk of exhibition plaster came through the kitchen ceiling and crashed into the table.

Caleb picked up one of the tiny stools and smashed the window. "Let's get out of here before the roof caves in."

Outside, through the clearing dust, he saw a full-grown African elephant in the process of trampling the citizenry. More of the attraction's walls and ceilings were coming down.

"The whole place is falling apart," declared Caleb. "We'd better get you to safety."

And before Liz could protest, he had her over his shoulder.

"I can walk, Caleb."

"I—" Caleb stumbled to his knees, dropping her on the floor. "I . . . can't. My legs. They're asleep."

Stratton was out in his yard, aiming the pistol at the elephant.

"Ya think you're so big, do you? Well come on. Give it your best shot."

He fired, and the elephant, startled by the tiny but resounding pop, reared up into a cloud of plaster dust. A second later, its feet came down on top of Mr. Tom Thumb.

"Save yourself, Liz!" said Caleb, trying to smack his legs back to life.

Liz huffed. "Hardly."

She threw Caleb over *her* shoulder and rushed blindly through the falling chunks. Finally she was at the boardwalk, a

hundred yards from the structure, which was now only a pile of rubble. Little people were already scavenging through the debris and several carneys had surrounded the elephant and were calming it down.

"Um, you can set me down, now, Liz," said Caleb.

"Are you sure? Maybe I should carry you home."

"Just do it."

She set him down on the boardwalk and brushed a cloud of plaster from the rear of his pants.

"Poor Charley," she said. "He'll never have his revenge."

"And we'll never have our information."

Caleb felt a tap on his rib cage. He turned to find Mammy, the diminutive house servant, proffering a large, old book. Its cover was made of leather and etched with symbols Caleb had never seen before.

"What is this? Does this have something to do with the Mummers?"

Mammy said nothing. She merely held out her hand.

"Thank you, Mammy," said Liz, taking her hand. "If there's anything we can ever do for you—"

Mammy took her hand away and held it out again.

"Um," said Elizabeth.

Mammy said, "You think I rushed in to save that thing for my health? 'Cause of you two, I'm recently homeless. Pay up."

Liz seemed shocked. "I don't see how it's our—"

Caleb emptied his purse into Mammy's hand. "I doubt that elephant got loose without help, Liz," he said.

Suddenly there was another scream. Caleb scanned the boardwalk.

"And it sounds like the fun isn't over yet."

Someone somewhere shouted, "For the love of God, save yourselves. Zip is loose!"

"Women and children first!" demanded the rancorous mother with the two towheaded boys as she flew past Liz and Caleb on her way to the exit.

Spencer and Smith turned to see Zip, a dark-skinned simpleton with a pinhead, strolling down the boardwalk, whistling, with his thumbs tucked in the waistband of his fur trousers. People screamed and ran at his approach. He seemed confused. One lady beat him with her umbrella as she raced by. He appeared dejected. He held out his arms and said, "Hugs?"

Someone yelled, "For God's sake, run! Everyone run! Barnum's wild negrozomoid freakazoid has slipped his fetters."

Zip seemed harmless enough, but the panic he was creating was causing a human stampede. People were trampling one another, knocking over souvenir stands, and setting fires in trash cans, just for the hell of it.

"This way!" cried Caleb, dragging Liz by the arm into the fast-moving crowd.

"Where are we going?" she shouted over the fray.

"Let's try to get out the way we got in!"

Sprinting back towards Beacon Tower, they were forced to navigate through the mad mob hare-footing towards them in the opposite direction. Almost to the exit, they ran smack into a wall of tuxedoed patriarchs of New York's high society: the Vanderbilts, the Astors, and the Carnegies, who, refusing to add their dignified personages to the riot, continued their stately parade along the boardwalk.

"We are dressed in our finest," said Mr. Carnegie, "and we are perfectly willing, if need be, to be trampled like gentlemen." One could almost hear the emotive strains of "Nearer My God to Thee."

"Hurry Liz!" shrieked Caleb.

Emerging from the bedlam, they finally found the exit, but to

their dismay, it was blocked—blocked by three iron thoroughbred horses from Steeplechase. Mounted on top of each faux animal sat one of the three grim reapers who had been following them.

"What sort of hellish miscreations has Old Scratch conjured up for us here?" Spencer catechized, as he pulled out his revolver.

There was a momentary standoff, then the hooded monks put the spurs to the mechanical horses and they began to gallop towards Spencer and Smith.

"Ah, Caleb, I believe they mean to kill us," said Liz.

Spencer dropped to his knee, aimed his .32, and fired. The pathetic report of his weapon sounded like a child's cap pistol, and the bullets traveled so sluggishly slow through the air that one could watch the path of their trajectory as they dropped harmlessly to the boardwalk, far short of their intended targets. He frowned at his gun and looked down its barrel.

"Liz, run for your life!" he ordered, fumbling with more bullets, just as the evil equestrians were upon them. But instead of fleeing, the brave woman put herself between the chief and the iron horses.

"What in the name of Harriet Beecher Stowe do you think you're doing?"

"Saving your life, as usual!" replied Liz, and she pulled out the whistle he had given her the night before and blew hard, discharging an ear-piercing squeal that sliced the air like a razor, provoking an unexpected reaction from the mechanical horses. They neighed sonorously, bucked, and reared back, launching the monks straight up towards the heavens. Caleb watched, dumbfounded, as the horses then stood frozen on their hind legs, as if someone had simply switched them off. *Bam!* The three monks came down hard and then lay motionless.

"What happened?" Caleb queried.

"Behavioral noise modification," Liz explained. "In case of an accident on the Steeplechase, the mechanical horses are designed to immediately shut down when the emergency whistle sounds."

Caleb looked at Liz, bewildered by her never-ending wealth of useless information.

"Bravo," he said, too shaken to conceal how impressed he was. "Well-played. Well-played indeed."

"Osculate my derriere later. We have a bigger problem." They walked to where the three monks lay recumbent and lifeless on the boardwalk. Caleb was still rubbing his butt and limping and praying Liz wouldn't notice.

She pulled back one of the monks' hoods, revealing a kindly-looking white man with a handlebar mustache. Sparks were spitting out of the man's eye sockets and his robe was smoking.

"Curious," she said and removed the other two hoods. She smiled, satisfied with herself. All the faces were identical.

"Just as I suspected. They're Franciscan robots."

Caleb winced as he bent over to get a closer look.

"This is considerably more advanced technology than Boilerplate," Liz said. "Notice how lifelike they are?" She pulled off one of the heads and was studying it.

"That bastard Tweed set us up. The question is why? And what's he doing with these robots?" contemplated Spencer.

"There's only one person who could have built these things. The same man who built Boilerplate."

"Professor Archibald Campion?"

"That's right."

"But you said he went insane."

"That's also right."

"Then how . . ."

"Perhaps he's working out of his cell at Bellevue. Perhaps he created these before he went insane. I don't know. I only know

he's the one person in the world with the kind of knowledge it takes to pull something like this off."

"Then I suppose we're obliged to pay the good professor a visit," said Caleb, not really wanting to see Liz with an ex, no matter how insane he had become.

"You go by yourself. I have no desire to see the man again. I'll try to figure out the significance of this book."

"Liz, it's not safe for us to split up."

"We haven't the time to stay together. The Thwacker will strike again before midnight, and we have only six hours before the Mummers' death ritual." She marched away. "You talk to Campion and I'll meet you back at Delmonico's in two hours. I suspect our strangely behaving mayor is already there enjoying a bowl of hot rear-end pie with . . ." She was almost to the exit when she realized Caleb was not by her side. He was lagging a few yards behind.

"Ow ow ow. I think it's the L4 vertebra, ow ow," he fussed, rubbing the small of his back. Liz huffed, shook her head, looked up to the creator for a little help, and then in one swift move hoisted the police chief over her shoulder and carried him back to the train.

Liz threw Caleb over her shoulder and hurried blindly
through the falling debris.

Chapter the Eighth.

In which a stranger's cranium is revealed to be hairless.

I FIDDLED WITH THE FADED DAGUERROTYPE MARKED PRIME SUSPECT IN THE kitchen of my grand Dakota apartment. The stack of Bisquick pancakes that I had made an hour before was now cold on the plate, and I sat sipping my strawberry Carnation Instant Breakfast opposite an empty chair, wondering what could have possibly happened to my dear friend Wendell. Surely I would have heard had anything gone awry at his performance out at Raceway Park. Or would I? Actually, I probably wouldn't. I mean, who would call *me*? I scanned the newspapers for mention of any New York cabbies with confrontational personalities who may have blown themselves up in New Jersey the night before, but no such luck. So I picked up my Mae West telephone, held her large bosoms to my ear, and quickly dialed.

"Mrs. Pierce? Chris Elliott."

"What do you want? I'm watching Regis."

"Sorry to bother you. But I was wondering if you might know where your son is?"

"Of course, didn't he tell you? He's with the president at Camp David, hashing out a new Israeli-Palestinian peace accord.

He called about an hour ago to say both countries had signed, but now he and the prez were arguing over who gets the scoop, Bill O'Riley or Al Sharpton. How the *hell* am I supposed to know where little Winston is?"

"Wendell."

"What? Look, the kid is like fifty years old, he doesn't have a curfew anymore. Okay?"

"Yes but . . ."

"By the way, I saw you on a rerun of Pyramid. Why the hell would you say 'a sneeze' for 'things that buzz'?"

Wendell's mom was always difficult to talk to. I wasn't quite sure why. I figured she saw me as the great white devil or something, but if she was going bring up my art, then let the heavens be damned—no one debases my *$100,000 Pyramid* performance!

"Because, Mrs. Pierce, I was trying to get the contestant to make the obvious connection between a person with a cold, who sneezes and then puts water on the stove for tea, but falls asleep and the water boils, and the steam ignites the dish towel, and the house catches fire, which causes the smoke alarms to *buzz*. Get it? It was the best clue in the world, except that the contestant was disoriented by the bright lights and by my trying to tap out answers to her in Morse code."

"Smoke alarms don't buzz, you idiot! They . . . make that alarm sound! Anyway, your face looked even fatter on TV than it does in person."

"Mrs. Pierce. I'm worried about Wendell. He was supposed to . . ."

"Look, like I said before. I don't make the kid call his mama every time he wants to wet his dipstick."

"He's making candles?"

"Why don't you try his new girlfriend's place. I gotta go. De-

lightful hearing from you. Hope you get your career off the ground, and never call here again, okay? Bye now."

I hung up the bosoms and staggered—I don't mind saying I was benumbed—into my luxurious living room and collapsed into my love seat. *Wendell has a new girlfriend? A quick-witted, devilish, and altogether eye-appealing one, no doubt.* A little tear rolled down my gee-I-wish-I-had-a-girlfriend-too face. I sighed a lonely sigh. *That sneaky little bugger! Why didn't he tell me?*

"HE'S NOT ONE OF US. HE'S AN OUTSIDER. WHY SHOULD WE BE NICE to him?" fussed Molly Coddle, sharpening the spikes on her shillelagh.

"Because the chief says the hobo will bring us good mojo," Bambino said as he heated up some day-old scrambled eggs.

"If you ask me, its a bunch of malarkey," Runabout chimed in, giving her diaper a sniff as a courtesy to make sure she wasn't reeking. "We've never had to be nice to no one before, and it's worked out all right for us. We're living the life of Riley down here, ain't we?"

"It's just one day, once a year. I think we'll all survive." Bambino stuck his finger into the eggs and stirred them around. Molly Coddle stood and glared at Chickabiddy and the stranger.

"Well, if we must, we must," she said, "but it sets a bad example for the younguns. And we look weak in the eyes of the other tribes."

"Who likes a little maggot-infested blue cheese in their scrambled pigeon eggs?"

Standing in knee-deep water, the hobo, now dressed in the tattered vestments of the Mud Tots, sipped on the growler while

Chickabiddy eyed movements under the water's surface, preparing to launch his spear into an undulating eel.

"You got yourself a sweet setup here, my boy," bellowed the outsider. "Tell me, do you hunt any bigger game? Giraffes, silverbacks, woolly mammoths, that sort of thing?"

"Just woolly homeless people," replied Chickabiddy.

It took the stranger a moment.

"Touché, touché, my good man," he said, bursting into a boisterous guffaw. "A sense of humor is more important than a sense of humility, though I'm a fan of both! I say, would you be so kind as to tell me how far down the river lies the canal?

"The canal?"

"The Panama Canal, my boy! It's urgent I have a word with its foreman. The last time I went through the locks he was a bit chintzy with the water, and I ended up scratching the bottom of my canoe!"

"Uh-huh. My history ain't too good, mister, 'cause I never went to school, an' I don't care, but I'm fairly certain the Panama Canal isn't built until 1914."

"Bully!"

Chickabiddy lunged forward with his spear but missed his elusive prey.

"Bully? . . . Why the *H-E*-double-hockey-sticks did I just say Bully? And . . . there's that strange name again . . . 'Delmo'. It keeps popping into my head. I don't remember anyone named Delmo, and yet the name seems so familiar."

"Here, you try," said the chief of the Mud Tots, handing the outsider the spear. "Take your time, wait till he's right up next to you . . . and then . . ."

"Charge!"

The homeless person fired the spear into the river and impaled a squirming black eel. He hauled it in, took one look at its huge,

wriggling body, and screamed like a banshee in heat. He ran out of the water and his loincloth dropped to his ankles, causing him to trip and fall flat on his face. Bud, the half dog, half porcupine, grabbed the loincloth and ran off with it. Chickabiddy picked up the harpoon and looked at the fine, writhing catch.

"Sustenance for a week," he cried. He regarded the outsider, who was scampering up the beach bare-assed, with renewed approval.

"Outlander!" he called. The fat man stopped scrambling and flailed on the gravel like a beached whale. "Truly you have the spirit of a Mud Tot. Jellyfish!"

"Yes sir!"

"Tattoo him."

Jellyfish, aged six and a half, had been blinded at birth by a humanitarian organization that was devoted to blinding orphans so that they would not become distressed by the lack of windows in their dormitories. He had been kept on by the gang because his lack of vision had heightened his other senses—specifically his senses of irony, outrage, and cruelty to animals, all quintessential Mud Tot virtues. But, most of all, he was an excellent artist, his blind scribblings the nineteenth-century equivalent of a Rothko or a Pollock, and it was he who was called upon to administer the ceremonial Mud Tot abstract impressionist tribal tattoo.

For the next two hours, the outsider's plaintive cries could be heard all the way over to West Cashew Street, as Jellyfish worked on his back with his makeshift tattooing rig, fashioned from a rusted Victrola needle filled with charcoal and tar.

"You're killing me! Please, no more!" pleaded the fat man. "I have no idea when the cavalry will attack, I swear!" His back was nothing but a messy hash of red blood and black ink, vaguely resembling invisible birds peeking through a hallucinated forest.

"I'm just a lowly grunt of the infantry. You ought to be torturing Major Livingston! He's the one you want!"

Molly Coddle, Bambino, and Runabout hovered nearby, getting more than their share of enjoyment out of the outsider's agony. When it was over, Chickabiddy watched as Bambino and Molly Coddle applied a heavy coat of mud to his body and face. Runabout scampered up the fat man's back—eliciting howls of pain—and placed the ceremonial empty kidney bean can on his head, which she then beat repeatedly with the ceremonial prying bar. The transient began to weep, so touched was he at being accepted as one of them, for he knew that without his memory this motley crew would be his only true family from now on. He had resigned himself to living under the dump, happily ever after with the Mud Tots.

"I don't know where to begin," he began, taking a healthy gulp from the growler, and then belching noisily. "This has been the most wonderful day of my life. Of course, I can't remember any of the other days of my life."

There were a few snickers from the tribe. Bambino nudged Molly Coddle in the ribs.

"We're still gonna eat 'im, aren't we?"

Molly shrugged. "It's up to Chickabiddy."

The man continued. "I just think you're all so terrific. Bambino and Molly Coddle, I love you guys, and as the years go by, I'm sure you'll learn to love me, too. Don't you agree? Maybe? Just a little?" He pouted, made the "tiny" sign with his thumb and index finger, and then chuckled, "You two are the best!"

The two exchanged puzzled looks.

". . . and little Runabout, what can I say, I know that underneath that gruff, 'get the hell away from me or I'll beat your fat rump to a bloody unrecognizable pulp' exterior, lies the heart of a true lady, and I thank you for your support."

Runabout wasn't paying any attention, as she was busy trying to light her cigar.

"Finally, Mr. Chickabiddy, I thank you, sir, for pulling me out of the icy waters and giving me shelter, nourishment, and of course these fetching new duds. Don't I look fancy?" He strutted about modeling his rags. "I rather think they flatter my difficult body type. Anyway, in closing, I would like to say to Mud Tots one and all, that even if it takes the rest of my life, I am going to work to earn your respect. It's the least I can do in return for all your gracious generosity. At this moment, on this hallowed ground, I'm reminded of an ancient Chinese proverb. Although short and sweet, it holds more than a little significance to us today." And here the outsider made a series of sounds that were strange to the ears of the Mud Tots but were of course perfectly rendered Cantonese Chinese learned from his Hong Kong nanny. When he finished he explained, ". . . which, translated loosely, means, 'Grow old along with me. The best is yet to be.'"

There was deafening silence from the tribe as the hobo looked around at the befuddled faces of the dirty children and nodded, priggishly displaying an overly self-satisfied expression. "Now, who's making lunch?"

"The outlander has spoken!" announced Chickabiddy. "We have done our good deed for the year, taken in this stranger and nursed him back to health. But now he is one of us and must adhere to the rules of the tribe! Stranger!"

"Yes, El Capitan," he said. "I am prepared."

"We do not know who you are, but you have clearly passed the age of seven, and therefore, as befits a Mud Tot, it is time for you to leave us."

A thunderous cheer rose from the ranks of the Mud Tots.

The bum seemed confused. "What? . . . but . . . I . . ."

"This way out, outlander."

The group ushered him to the top of the dump.

Chickabiddy pointed with his spear. "That way is north, that way is south, that's west and that's east."

"Yeah, but I was under the impression that . . ."

Jellyfish handed him a burlap bag. "The clan all chipped in and put together a little care package for ya . . . nothing much, just some crab shells, a hunk of dried eel, and a wad of chewing tobacco that we all took a turn with, just to get it nice and juicy for ya."

"Well, I thank you, Jelly, but—"

"And as far as this Delmo you seek, there is no one of that name in these parts. If I were you, I'd head north," advised Chickabiddy. "And I hope you find what you're looking for." He handed the man the spear. "This is for you, my fat, confused friend. I've never seen a city slicker spear an eel like that in all my life!"

"You know, I really don't have to go, because—"

"Good-bye, outlander. You will know us no more, and if someday one of us should run into you in a darkened alley, don't be surprised if he sets you on fire, because that is what the Mud Tots do."

"That's comforting."

"But if there ever comes a time when you find yourself in grave danger—from someone other than us—send word, and the Mud Tots will rush to your aid. For we may be nasty, violent, and ill-mannered hoodlums, but we got hearts of gold, and we mostly never forget our own. Fair thee well."

Chickabiddy hugged the man. Each member of the Tots took a turn giving him a friendly punch on the arm as they bid him farewell. Molly Coddle gave him a harsh jab to the stomach using her shillelagh, and Bambino tried to bite a chunk out of his flabby forearm.

A moment later, the Mud Tots had vanished back under the

dump and the fat man was alone on Rivington Street, barefoot, dressed in rags, and holding a burlap bag and spear. Floating inside his big round head was only a vague awareness of the existence of tasty pygmies, the Panama Canal, and someone called Delmo.

"Bully?" he whimpered.

AT THAT VERY MOMENT, IN THE DIM APARTMENT ON THE THIRD FLOOR OF the nondescript brownstone, the tormented killer was holding his head with both hands and literally bouncing off the walls.

"No! No! No! Make it stop! Mother, make it stop! Why? Why? This isn't me! This isn't what I do! I'm a good boy! People like me! They think I'm cute! Why must I do these horrible deeds? I don't want to kill! I want to sing! And dance!"

He pushed over his stack of taunting mail and took from his bag of tools a top hat and cane.

"Gotta dance, I gotta dance! Make room world, 'cause I gotta dance!"

With that, the killer began to hoof it around his dark chamber à la Fred Astaire, leaping from one piece of furniture to the next. He stood on his messy bed and sang as fast as he could:

Sweet Rosie O'Grady,
My dear little rose.
She's my steady lady,
Most everyone knows
And when we are married
How happy we'll be!
I love sweet Rosie O'Grady,
And Rosie O'Grady loves me!

He bowed to an imaginary audience and then collapsed on his bed, sweaty and winded. He lay there staring up, his imagination creating animals out of the cracks in the plaster on the ceiling. "There was a hippo, and there a tiger, and there a pair of happy prostitutes strolling down a lane . . . but what was that behind them . . .

"No!" he cried, the rhythmic pounding of his pulse resounding in his head like a bass drum. "No no no! Don't run away! Come back and sing with me! We'll sing a jolly little ditty."

Softly, with increasing speed, he began to recite:

There was a little girl, who had a little curl
Right in the middle of her forehead.
And when she was good, she was very, very good.
But when she was bad, she was horrid . . .

"All of them so horrid, those little girls. Walking the street in their filthy curls, hawking their wet biggles and burlap sandies. But at least they know they're bad, so bad, so horrid. Not like those society ladies in their clean clean very goods. Like Emily Dickinson and Harriet Beecher Stowe. And that distasteful Liz Smith, no, my dear Liz, you haven't been very, very good. In fact, you've been very, very horrid. What shall jolly Jackie do about that?"

Knock, knock, knock.

"Not while I'm singing!"

"Did ya want me then, Doctor? I thought sure I heard ya call my name, I did," said Mrs O'Leary.

"No, Mrs. O'Leary," replied the killer from his bed, "I was singing a delightful little ditty about a Mrs. O'*Grady*. Not a Mrs. O'Leary! Thank you just the same. You may go now."

"Another murder last night, there was," Mrs. O'Leary continued. "Two more, in fact, it is. That makes it three all told, it does!"

"We could make it four right now if you like, Mrs. O'Leary!" murmured the killer.

"What was that, now?"

She was met with a surly silence.

"Well, you best be tellin' Miss O'Grady to stay offa the streets tonight, if she be caring about her vitals and tenders and such. They say these two were missing their clavicles, their uvulas, and their aortas, they do! What kind of demented lunatic would run away with a lady's clavicle, I ask you, I do!"

"Probably an immigrant!" replied the maniac. "Many of them enter our fine country with barely a clavicle to their name, and then they have the unconscionable nerve to go out and steal ours!"

"My thoughts exactly, Doctor!"

Ring!

The killer picked up his phone and Mrs. O'Leary pressed her ear to the door. She heard the doctor speaking softly in a deeper and darker voice.

"Yes, I understand. Erce walks among us."

There was a pause, and the boardinghouse-keeper strained to hear more. She bent down and tried to peer through the keyhole.

Suddenly the chamber door swung open, and the killer stood before her, stark naked.

"Oh my, taking a bath, are we, Doctor?"

"Time, Mrs. O'Leary. Pray tell me the time."

"Half past five, it is," she replied. "Sunset is upon us and they say the butcher is sure to strike again tonight, they do!"

"Have these quickly cleaned and pressed for me, Mrs. O'Leary. For I will need them later, this evening." The monster handed her a bundle of blood-soaked clothing. "And no starch this time."

"As you wish, Doctor."

"Oh, and Mrs. O'Leary, kindly drop this in the mail for me."

He handed her a box addressed to Elisabeth Smith, care of the *Evening Post,* and on it was emblazoned in bright red letters, WARNING: BIOLOGICAL WASTE, DO TAKE CARE.

"Right away, Doctor!" The killer closed the door and Mrs. O'Leary waddled back down the stairs, regarding the blood-soaked clothing.

"Tsch, tsch, tsch. I do wish the doctor wouldn't wear his suit when he paints, I do."

LIZ SAT IN A CORNER BOOTH SURROUNDED BY STACKS OF REFERENCE BOOKS she had picked up at the library. Delmonico's had a strict ordinance preventing women from dining by themselves, and an even stricter ordinance preventing women from reading. Although Lorenzo Delmonico could overlook the latter for the brash lady reporter from the *Post,* he could not allow her to dine unescorted, and so he provided Liz with a surrogate dinner partner, a middle-aged gentleman in an ill-fitting tuxedo.

"Good evening, my name is Tex, but everyone calls me Beanie."

"Okay, fine. Just sit down and be quiet, I'm in the middle of something here."

"Fwooo, it's much cooler up here. I've been stuck in the boiler room for hours," he said, fanning himself with the menu. "Slow night for spouseless ladies, I suppose. Ooooh lookie, they've got mincemeat and turtle egg beignets tonight!"

"Shh," Liz admonished, her head stuck in a book of hieroglyphics.

"Sorry, so sorry, yes, I know you're working on something."

The waiter approached.

"Madame, may I start you off with a cocktail?"

"I would love a sloe gin fizz, waiter," said the man, licking his lips.

"One glass of water for the gentleman," said the waiter gruffly. "And the lady?"

"I'll have a God's Own Enema."

"Perhaps the lady would like something a bit more, um, delicate?"

Liz gave the waiter a glare that told him what she thought of delicacy.

"Do you mind me asking what you're working on there, miss?" inquired Tex.

"Look, I don't mean to be curt, but I'm on a bit of a deadline here and—" When she looked up, she saw that her comrade was rather desperately cramming his pockets full of raw veggies.

"Um, are you all right?" she asked.

"Yes, quite so. These crudités are just so exquisite, I thought I'd take some home . . ." Liz gave him her skeptical look. He hung his head plaintively.

"That is, if I—er—had one. The management have been kind enough to loan me the use of a pallet beneath the boiler while I work off a little—er—financial unpleasantness between myself and the establishment by washing dishes and feeding the furnace, and providing the occasional—er—companionship to unescorted ladies. But of course I'm disturbing you. I'm sorry."

Liz's heart softened. She shut her book and gave the man her full attention.

"I'm sorry, what did you say your name was?"

"Tex. But everyone calls me Beanie."

"Okay, first off, why Tex?"

The man held his finger up while he masticated a mouthful of bread and then swallowed.

"Pardon me. I'm just a tad ravenous. I haven't eaten in two

days. Tex is short for my Christian name, Terrence Xanderthorp III."

"That sounds rather regal."

"No such luck. My parents gave me the name hoping it would enable me to gain entrance to a higher station in society, but it is just a name, and no matter how hard one tries, one can't conceal one's Mulberry Bend heritage, can one?"

"And why do they call you Beanie?"

"Oh, that's easy."

Tex put down his rolls and wiped his hands. He reached into his hair and, with a series of snaps, removed it from his scalp, revealing a billiard ball of a bald head.

"Oh." Liz covered her mouth, attempting to conceal her amusement.

"That's okay, madam. You may laugh. I do. It is rather funny."

"Pardon me for asking, but do those snaps hurt?"

"Nay, not anymore," he said, reflecting on the rug he held in his hands. "You see, I went bald when I was very young, due to the sodium chloride in our sheets. We lived next door to a saltpeter foundry. So, before I left home, my parents scraped together all their savings and bought me this wig. They paid extra for the snap-on model so I wouldn't be embarrassed in a big wind."

"Sounds like your parents were very thoughtful people."

"Oh, they were indeed, miss. They were the salt of the earth. No pun intended."

"Please, call me Elisabeth," she said, extending her hand for Tex to shake.

"Your—ahem—*enema,* madam." The waiter handed Liz her umbrella-laden frappe.

"Don't suppose there's a sloe gin fizz there for me, is there?"

"And your *water,* Beanie." He slammed the glass down on the

table in front of Liz's new friend. Tex gulped it down. "And for heaven's sake, do snap your hair back onto that frightful head of yours, Beanie, or Mister Delmonico shall have to return you to the bellows chamber." The waiter started to leave.

"Excuse me, waiter. Just a moment. Apologize to Mr. Xanderthorp, right this instant."

"Madam . . . he's just a pretend—"

"Apologize!"

"Miss, it's really not necessary," said Tex, embarrassed. "He's only doing his job. I'm just supposed to sit here and pretend to be a scandalously wealthy riverboat gambler."

"Nonsense, Terrence! This man was disrespectful to you and I expect him to apologize. Otherwise I may be forced to consult with Lorenzo Delmonico himself." She directed the last part of her sentence to the waiter.

He stiffened, gritted his teeth together, and then bowed his head to Terrence.

"My deepest apologies, sir. I meant no disrespect."

"Fine," said Liz. "Now, my friend requested a sloe gin fizz. Go and fetch it, post-haste."

"Yes, madam." The humiliated waiter scuttled off.

"Thank you, miss . . ."

"It's Elisabeth."

". . . but I have no means of repaying you."

"Don't you worry Terrence, I'll just put it on my expense account."

Not being used to smiles from pretty ladies, Tex quickly diverted his hungry eyes away from Liz and back to the basket of dinner rolls. Liz returned to her work deciphering the tome that Mammy had given them, while Tex stuffed his face.

"Some hieroglyphics, is it? You're an archaeologist, then?"

"Something like that. I have been trying to decipher this book

all evening, but it almost seems as if it were written in a hundred different languages at once."

Tex glanced over her notes.

"Perhaps there *is* a way I could repay you."

"Terrence, that's sweet of you. But this is way over your head. . . ."

He casually pointed to a symbol.

"That sign there means 'heavy feline' or 'fat cat.' Though in the ancient tongue of the Celtics, it's 'morganna.'"

"Well, yes that's right, but I can't put together—"

"The preceding signs, 'ya pa,' might look like nonsense, unless you think of them as initials. 'Ya pa,' or in the Java Applet, *JP*. Put it all together and you have 'ya-pa-morganna' or 'J. P. Morgan.'"

Liz's mouth dropped.

"Good lord, how did you do that?"

"When I left home, I lived for a long time in the catacombs beneath the public library. At night, I used to sneak up and devour anything and everything that I could possibly read. I was especially intrigued by our language. Its origins and its interconnective history. For all the good it's done me, huh?"

"Terrence, I know a bit about hieroglyphics myself," said Liz, "but I would not have translated that as J. P. Morgan. I thought it meant 'one-eyed paper sock with a bad case of herpes.'"

"And that's absolutely correct, if you were deciphering it as a purely Egyptian/Greek Ptolemaic script, like that found on the Rosetta stone, but what you have here is far more complicated. You're looking at a very ancient, obscure language, my dear. A language created out of many others and refined over centuries for one purpose only—to conceal secrets. It combines the earliest forms of hieratic script with the Semitic alphabet and primitive pagan ideogrammatic glyphs. It's still used today by many

of the more antediluvian secret societies, like for instance the Knights Templar . . . and . . ."

". . . and the Mummers?"

"Yes. The Mummers, certainly."

"Your sloe gin fizz, your majesty," said the waiter.

"Keep 'em coming," ordered Liz.

"Would madam and the, ahem, gentleman care for dinner?"

"Bring us the chef's taster's menu," she said, not even looking at the waiter.

"But, madam, that's a ten course banquet . . ."

"Then you had better get started. Hurry along."

"Yes, madam."

Liz shoved the big book in front of Terrence, who was savoring every sip of his cocktail, and scooted next to him.

"What about this one, Terrence? What does this one mean?"

"Well, let's see. Oh my goodness. It's rather naughty isn't it? The phallus represents sturdiness, or 'that which is straight,' pronounced 'stanfa.' The snowflake symbol is a non-color."

"White?"

"That's correct, 'stanfa-white'."

"Stanford White."

"The famous architect, isn't it?"

"Terrence, if this book is what I think it is . . ."

Liz was starting to get flushed as Terrence deciphered more and more names.

"Let's see," he continued, "here we have the symbol for 'that which is too powerful for the groin,' or 'hernia,' and then the sign for 'wet dirt' adjacent to 'quick,' which is represented by a female lover obviously disappointed by her male mate. So we have 'hernia-wet dirt-quick,' or more precisely, 'Henry Clay Frick,' the great industrialist."

"But here's one that really stumps me," said Terrence, pushing the book over to Liz. "Together it's 'the bottom of the foot,' 'the clean sphere,' and 'the one who roughs it in nature.' I have no idea what it could mean."

"That's simple," said Liz. "The bottom of the foot is the 'arch.' A 'clean sphere' is 'bald'"—she tapped Terrence on his noggin—"and 'one who roughs it in nature' is a 'camper' so it's, 'arch-bald-camper' or Archibald Campion."

"Oh yes, the infamous professor who went insane."

Liz paused for a moment. *"Non compos mentis,"* she said again, softly.

"And this," continued Tex, "is strange. It stops being a list of names and there's a poem of some sort. And it's in a phonetic English, as if its meant to be read aloud:

By De Temporum Ratione we pray to
those who celebrate with us Imbolce, Beitane,
Lugnasda, Lammas, and Samhain.
We pray to Hezmonas and
all the Valkyries to bring forth
our true virgin goddess, for she walks
the earth even now . . ."

Liz touched her forehead and seemed about to faint. She nearly fell out of her seat, but Terrence caught her.

"Elisabeth, what's wrong?"

"I don't know what came over me. I was thinking of my—of Archibald, and I had a sudden sense of déjà vu! I was in a small room, maybe a cupboard. It smelled of old cheese. Someone was reading those words. I knew I was supposed to hide, but the words, they made me want to—to *dance*."

Nearly involuntarily she stood up, her arms outstretched.

"Yes, to dance! I feel it all over my body."

"I think that this is the program for some kind of ceremony," said Terrence. "Maybe you've been involved in one like it before, since you've clearly had some past dealings with the Mummers."

Still bobbing a little, twisting her hands, Liz said, "What, was it in the paper or something? Is there anybody who doesn't know?"

"Well, a) you have this book, which is clearly not available at your local library, or at least none that I've ever lived under; b) in this list of names, there's a lizard from a Siberian picture script, a blue 4-H ribbon from the ancient Iowan, and a man with a hammer. Lizard, Best, smith."

Liz stopped in her tracks. "Elizabeth Smith."

"Yo, Liz!" cried a familiar voice across the dining room.

Terrence said, "It seems you have an admirer."

Teddy yelled from the lobby of Delmonico's. "I've been looking all over for you guys. Where the hell you vanish to? I nearly got trampled by that pinhead thing."

"Friend of yours?"

"I used to think so." Liz shoved the book under a placemat. "Do me a favor," she whispered to Tex. "You know nothing about what we've just been talking about, all right?"

"My lips were already sealed. Living in basements, elevator shafts, and men's washrooms has taught me the value of discretion."

Teddy came up behind her, putting his hands on her shoulders.

"Hey good lookin'. I mean, er, Dame Smith. We got to go meet Caleb at my—whaddayacallit back now—my abode. He awaits us. Tallyho!"

"Didn't you just say you'd been looking all over for *us*?" Liz asked, carefully.

"I, um, I was talking about the two of those," he said, giving her a shake. "Now come on, we have to go now, get it? There's a carriage outside with our names on it."

Just out the front window, behind each potted palm that flanked the entrance, she saw a pair of black-robed figures doing their best to hide behind the skinny trunks. Say what you will of their nefariousness, they weren't the cleverest evil goons Liz had ever encountered.

"Ah, yes, I see. Shall we, then?"

The waiter brought the first course of the chef's taster's menu, a platter of nacho chips with gooey melted cheese on top. Liz pulled him aside.

"The bill is to be put entirely on my account, and there is an extra tip in it for you if you treat this man like a king. Do you understand?"

"Yes, madam."

"It is a shame that I must depart, Terrence. I don't know how to thank you enough. Here's my card." She set it down on the placemat and tapped it emphatically. "If you ever do come up with a solution to that delightful riddle we were discussing, you would do well to send the answer to me, here—or, if I am for some reason unavailable, to Caleb Spencer of the NCNYPD." With that she leaned over and gave him a gentle kiss on his bald head.

"And by the way," she said sadly, "you don't need that silly wig. I think you're dashing just the way you are."

Terrence was overcome with emotion as he watched the kind spouseless lady take her leave, and he might even have cried had not his youthful exposure to the salt refinery desiccated his tear ducts.

"Thank *you*, Elisabeth," he said softly.

The homeless man fired the spear and impaled a squirming black eel.

He watched her step out onto the rain-soaked street, where several men hastened her into a carriage, which pulled away.

And beyond that, concealed by the shadows, a tall man with thin fingers and battered hands watched as the buggy disappeared down the street.

The two aging combatants were now the best of friends, and upon reading the newspaper accounts of the grisly murders, Grant looked to Lee with that Yankee twinkle in his eye—a twinkle that was remarkably boyish for his age—and in his vulpine way said to Lee, "It must be the work of a rebel," whereupon Lee put out his cigar and stiffened in his chair and remarked, "Sir, if it were the work of a rebel, it would be work that I would be deeply proud of," and with that they each shared a laugh . . . I've always enjoyed that story.

—Shelby Foote

Chapter the Ninth.

In which an innocent, if corpulent, damsel is lamentably slaughtered and a bedlamite takes flight.

AT APPROXIMATELY 7:45 PM, THE "BLUE WHALE," AS THIS LADY OF THE night was known, had just executed a perfect double belly-smacker with an extra raspberry-dip top on a drunken sailor in a dumpster on Eighth Avenue. Now, having received her two ducats for services rendered, the hefty lass crossed Forty-third Street and began to shuffle east.

Nowhere in any of the genealogical archives or census reports from 1882 was her real name recorded, but my research has revealed an old-world custom of naming homely children after the animals they most closely resembled, which would support the notion that Blue Whale was the harlot's true baptismal name. Although I have found no Blue Whale recorded in any birth records, I did find, sadly, a Fat Cow listed. The cruelty of nineteenth-century parents is not to be underestimated. It is possible that she was uncomfortable with such an abasing moniker and changed her name to the more august-sounding Blue Whale. (But that seems unlikely, doesn't it, unless she were as small-brained as she was big-boned.)

She was forty-five years old and weighed a robust three

hundred and fifty pounds (or nigh on twenty-five stone for my readers 'cross the pond), presenting a daunting enough countenance to dissuade any rumdum intent on getting his ya-yas off by bashing a sporting girl. Blue Whale was unquestionably the most successful working girl in New York City— that she would accept payment in the form of plankton and other small marine life made her particularly popular with the fishmongers—and everyone in the Bend knew her and knew of the numerous brothels on the Upper East Side to which she played madam.

Catering to the more discriminating palate, she welcomed a well-to-do clientele who paid handsomely for a higher standard of personal attention, as well as a proficiency in the sometimes bizarre proclivities of the affluent. Well acquainted with their latest fetishistic trends, Blue Whale equipped her whorehouses with private rooms for "mud thumb-wrestling," "hanky chewing," "oriental-carpet sniffing," and in one frequently raided bordello on Sixty-fourth Street, she offered a "Would the lady care for a Cuban cigar?" room, a "Hey, this pork loin tastes foul" room, and the most popular of all, the "Pretend you're my mother-in-law having tea and cucumber sandwiches with her ladies' group whilst I bugger your bum from behind" room.

But despite Blue Whale's success, she never forgot where she came from. Tonight, as she made her rounds checking in on her various cathouses, she pocketed extra coinage by consummating a snatch of "quick Idaho hash browns" behind dumpsters or in darkened doorways.

She had just stepped off the curb on Twenty-fifth and Lexington when the clangorous vibration of wooden wheels on cobblestones startled her and a black buggy came barreling around the corner, splashing up foul, lice-ridden gutter water and causing her to fall back onto the sidewalk. The dark carriage skidded to a halt.

"A pox on ya! Ya cross-eyed, catch-colt inbred!" bellowed the madam, shaking her fist. She rocked on her hands, attempting to hoist herself up.

She watched as the buggy's folding steps flipped down and its door opened ever so slowly. A mysterious man descended. He turned towards Blue Whale, and, taking large strides, approached her.

"Are you injured?" he asked, as he pulled her to her feet.

"Just my pride," she said, "and my fur coat."

"Oh my, it's all wet, isn't it? I'm so terribly sorry. My cab driver doesn't speak a lick of the Queen's English. I suspect he's right off the boat and must have just received his hack license this very day."

"That's all right. No harm done . . . Chief Spencer." (See, it's our hero Caleb, not the Thwacker. I bet I had you going there for a bit.)

"I assure you, the department will pick up the tab for the cost of the dry cleaning, if you'll just . . . I'm sorry, do we know each other?"

"You don't remember? You put the collar on me about a year ago."

"But of course, Blue Whale! I was trying to place you. Your size seemed so familiar to me. I thought perhaps you were my old high school gym teacher!"

Blue Whale let out a jolly chortle. "No, no. You won't find me near any gym. Unless of course it's a house call."

"Quite so. So, how *are* tricks?" Caleb grinned, amused by her droll quip.

"You know me, always busy. I just can't seem to find the time to take a break. I'm what they call a work-a-binger. Anyway, I s'pose you'll be wanting to arrest me, seeing's how I'm out enjoying a bit of the old 'night-walking' again, eh?"

"I should, if only for your own protection, but I haven't the time."

"My own protection?"

"I would advise you to stick to the bawdy-houses tonight, Blue. The streets are not safe. Especially for one of your vocation."

"Why, my dear Chief Spencer, take a good look at me. Do you honestly suppose that some crack-brained immigrant armed with a mere bag of apples could do any harm to the mighty Blue Whale?"

"Even so, I would consider it a personal favor if you would stay indoors and alert your sisters-in-arms to do the same."

"Well, as it so happens, I'm on my way to Club 64 as we speak." She moved close to Caleb and ran her chubby fingers down his lapels. "Perhaps you'd care to drop off the fee for the dry cleaning there? Shall we say around 10:30?"

Caleb curled his mouth and gave her a little wink. "Although I'm flattered, dear lady, I'm not that sort of man."

"I'm quite certain I don't understand. I would simply appreciate it if you or someone else in your department could drop off the boodle for the dry cleaning *later on*, like around ten or ten thirty."

"Oh, I thought . . . just send the bill to the nineteenth. Now then, please allow me to give you a lift up to Sixty-fourth Street. I'd feel better if I could."

"Fancy that, the Blue Whale riding uptown with the chief of police!" she said, hooking her arm in his. "Well sir, what *would* the gossip hounds think?"

Across the street, there was a pop and a billow of smoke, and, emerging from the shadow of a mango tree, a low-set man with muttonchops and oily hair, whose name has been lost to history (actually it hasn't been, I'm just too lazy to look it up right now), watched as the chief of police and the prostitute boarded

Caleb's carriage and rattled away, heading north towards the Upper East Side.

The man quickly jotted something down on his pad, threw his camera and tripod over his shoulder, and climbed atop his own carriage. Whipping his horse mercilessly, he flew off at a breakneck pace. The fancy Victorian lettering became a blur on the side of his buggy as he raced downtown, making it nearly impossible to read J. R. BENNETT'S SENSATIONAL PENNY PAPERS! ALL THE NEWS NO ONE ELSE WILL PRINT! WITH SPECIAL ATTENTION GIVEN TO ANY SALACIOUS INTRIGUES INVOLVING OUR FINE CITY'S DASHING YOUNG POLICE CHIEF, CALEB R. SPENCER!

BELLEVUE MADHOUSE AND GIFT SHOP, ON THIRTY-SIXTH AND SECOND, was the first asylum devoted to the rehabilitation of the "Feeble-Minded and the Demonically Possessed." It was established in New Amsterdam in 1658, when, just like today, feeble minded-ness and demonic possession were traits enjoyed by most New Yorkers. Dr. Jacob Verrenvargonhoff was Bellevue's esteemed founder and the man credited with the first comprehensive treatment for those afflicted with psychotic disorders, as well as pioneering the revolutionary "Pinch, Pull, and Pray" method for those afflicted with bothersome anal fistulas.

Verrenvargonhoff believed that the most promising treatment for the mentally ill—or "de idiots," as he called them—was to be kept in chains, locked away in damp, vermin-infested dungeons, forced to eat his wife's spaghetti, and compelled to endure nightly torture sessions overseen by his staff of demonically possessed psychiatrists and happily administered by the asylum's mad jailers.

Bellevue's reception center was a dimly lit room with several

wooden pews and a large, ornately carved podium behind which stood the hospital administrator. He was a bald, officious man with a frozen smile.

"Good evening. May I help you?"

"NCNYPD. I'd like to speak with one of your patients, please," Caleb said, flashing his leather-bound gold shield.

"All right. Have you visited with us in the past?"

"Ah, not recently."

"Then you're probably not in our files anymore. If you'd just take a seat and fill out these forms, the doctor will be with you momentarily." He handed Caleb a clipboard and motioned to the pews. Amongst the hopeless specters awaiting treatment, Spencer noticed a familiar face smiling behind her needlework, though it took him a moment to place her.

"Mary Todd Lincoln!" he cried.

"Hiya Abe," she said and blew Caleb a kiss.

The man addressed Caleb again. "Do you have your insurance card with you? We accept everything except HIP."

"No, you don't understand. I'm not a patient, I need to *speak* with a patient."

"Uh-huh. I see. And who exactly is it that you 'need' to 'speak' with?"

"A Professor Archibald Campion."

"Oooh, the professor, huh?" The man rubbed his chin and looked Caleb up and down. "Difficult . . . but not impossible. It's gonna cost ya."

"What? I'm not paying you anything, you charlatan!"

"Fine. If that's how you want to play it. I'll take you to Campion, but first you have to prove yourself worthy."

"Worthy?"

"I will set you a series of tasks, each more insidious than the

last. First, bring me the broomstick of the Wicked Witch of the West, and I'll consider granting your wish."

"What? That movie isn't even released until 1939, well after the invention of motion pictures, which also hasn't happened yet."

"Just bring me the broomstick!"

Dr. Jacob Verrenvargonhoff IV opened his office door and ushered out an abomination. It was the famous tap dancer and comedian, John Merrick, the "Elephant Funny-Man."

"We made real progress today John, yes?"

"Oh yes, Doctor, I believe my head is getting smaller and smaller with each session as I rid myself of these damn dreams that are so crowded inside it." He covered his bulbous head with the filthy pillowcase that audiences loved to see him wearing.

"Make sure we drink our sulfuric acid tonics twice a day and use plenty of moisturizer, and we'll see you next week, yes? Come right in Mr. Baum, and we wear our straitjackets when we're not in our cells! Yes?" Mr. Baum, the bald man behind the podium, scampered into Verrenvargonhoff's office.

"May we help you, sir?"

"Caleb Spencer, chief of police."

"Oh, yes, of course you are. Just a moment please. Mrs. Lincoln? We're a little backed up tonight, its going to be at least another hour. Yes?"

"That's fine, Dr. V," said the former first lady. "I'll just run out and do a little shopping."

"Now then, how can we be of service to you, Chief Spencer?"

"Well," Caleb began, a clear tone of frustration in his words, "as I told your next *patient* in there, I need to speak with your Professor Campion about a matter of great importance. It regards an ongoing investigation."

"I see. Well, first you'll have to prove yourself worthy, yes?"

"Oh for Christ's sake."

"Just a little madhouse humor, Chief. We can't spell funny farm without 'funny,' now can we? Now, we *do* realize the professor is extremely dangerous, yes. Last week, he beaned one of our guards with a five-pound homemade flatiron. Ingenious work, really. He fashioned it entirely out of thin strips of water-closet paper, woven so tightly together you'd swear it was made out of iron. We can't be responsible for your safety, yes?"

"*We* can take care of ourselves, *yes*?" said Caleb, brandishing his nightstick—which, often during fits of brandishing, he felt compelled to polish vigorously with a chamois cloth. He had just got it good and going when the doctor interrupted him.

"Very well, then. I'll have my turnkey accompany you. But you'll also need this, yes?"

The doctor handed him a square wooden birdcage. Caleb frowned, befogged.

"You put it over your head, Chief Spencer. It's for your own safety. Madhouse regulations, yes? Even we loonies have to follow a rule or two from time to time."

MR. FINNEGAN, THE ASYLUM TURNKEY AND FORMER SOUTHERN PRISONER of war, was dressed in his old Confederate uniform. Around his generous waist he wore a thick utility belt with hundreds of keys dangling from it, as well as various implements of attack: clubs, brass knuckles, hammers, boxing gloves, and the new experimental Edison stunner gun, which had the unfortunate habit of setting the asylum on fire whenever it was used.

The big man had tied a ragged piece of old beef jerky (left over from his days with Stonewall Jackson's brigade) to the bars

of his birdcage, so that it remained at all times within convenient reach of his tongue.

"Let's take a shortcut through the operating theayder," he said, choosing a big key and unlocking a door.

While the two quietly made their way around the upper tier, Caleb was intrigued by the medical demonstration in progress below. Old men with big mustaches leaned over the bleachers, endeavoring to get a clear view of the man tied to a Windsor chair. He was presided over by a surgeon in a chef's hat, who was preparing to operate. (It's a common misconception that surgeons were also barbers; in point of fact they were actually French chefs who had been deemed too slipshod in manner to prepare an adequate créme bruleé, and had to make a go of it somehow.)

"This patient is cursed by what is known today as sleeplessness, or *insomnia-protemtia, n'est-ce pas*? It is beholden on us as curers of the sick to rectify this dreadful and life-threatening affliction, *oui*?" He lectured while deciding on which of the two jagged-toothed saws he held would be appropriate for the procedure.

"Really, it's not all that bad!" the patient protested. "It just takes me a little longer to get to sleep than my wife. That's all!"

The French cook nodded to a crew of wards who converged on the man and covered his face with a cloth. They held it firmly over his mouth and nose. Within a minute he stopped jerking about and fell asleep with a slaphappy grin pasted across his face.

"Would that everyone afflicted with *insomnia-protemtia* had a bottle of the chloroform in their pantry. We wouldn't be forced to do these ghastly operations any more, *n'est-ce pas*?" Then, with a click of his heels, the chef began to saw open the crown of the man's skull. Caleb buckled and gagged, not so much at the nauseating sight—he had seen worse in his tenure as police chief—as at the obscene sound of saw on bone. Retrieving his handkerchief

and covering his mouth with it, he tried to put the image out of his head by thinking of nice things like pretty flowers, yellow butterflies, and fluffy omelets with Jimmy Dean sausage.

"What you are seeing here is the heavy cream and truffle sauce that is drizzled over the rare sweetbreads, *n'est-ce pas?*" Caleb diverted his eyes and kept moving. The turnkey, however, found the gory happenings delightful.

"I enjoy it when the brains come out. Hee-hee-hee, kind of reminds me of the battle for Antietam. But don't you worry, Yankee boy, I'll have ya out of here in a jiffy."

He opened another door and led Caleb down a set of stairs.

"That chloroform is sure fancy stuff," he said, trying to make conversation while chewing on his old beef jerky. "It's another Southern invention, you know. Like pulled pork, square dancing, and inbreedin' for genetic supremacy. Before chloroform, they had to hold the poor soul down while they carved 'im up. Now, with just a couple of whiffs you're out for two days!" *Out for two days? That's good stuff indeed,* thought Caleb. The two meandered down a hall and then, oddly, into a supply closet, where the ex-sergeant lit an oil lamp and tried to locate a secret door.

"It's in here, somewhere."

Caleb had swallowed a little spew before it could expel itself, and now, getting his sea legs back, he began to feel like himself again.

"Oh, here it is! Through this secret door into the snake pit, and then to the professor's cell."

While the veteran searched his belt for the right key, Spencer glanced about the room. Shelves of blankets, surgical instruments, musical instruments, instruments of torture, and canned oatmeal graced the walls. Then his eyes fell upon a shelf with lots of bottles marked CHLOROFORM. *I bet that would add a kick to*

a laudanum ether frappe! he thought, and slipped a bottle into his pocket.

"Stay close," warned the turnkey, pulling out his stunner gun and cranking it several times to get a charge. "And keep a sharp eye out for snakes."

"Snakes?" cried Caleb. "What kind of asylum is this?"

"Dr. Verrenvargonhoff's idea. Most people here are so crazy they see snakes, so if they *actually* see the snakes, they ain't crazy. It's called homeopathy."

"That's ridic—" began Caleb, only to be interrupted by a hiss and the sound of something scaly striking the cage around his head.

"What the—" he began again.

"Just act natural," said Finnegan.

They had arrived at the epicenter of the asylum. The grim place was filled with every conceivable variety of brainsick unfortunate. Some wandered about giggling to themselves, some were embroiled in debates with invisible partners, some were confined to small cages on the floor, and still others were bound in the latest in archaic fetters from the *Inquisition's Surplus Torture Paraphernalia and Swimwear* catalogue. A number of uniformed jailers with birdcages on their heads wandered about the room, periodically giving an unsuspecting bedlamite a whack on the cranium while dodging the occasional spitting pit viper.

Caleb thought to himself, *Why am I putting myself through this? Campion is probably just another wild goose chase.*

An old, crazed Italian woman scampered up to him and tugged hard on his sleeve. "Dami, why you do this to me? Dami, please!" she implored before the turnkey gave her a powerful *zap* from the stunner, sending her flying backwards into a peaceful game of cribbage between a mumbling old man and a pile of dung. Her rag-doll body jittered like the jittering jitter-bug do!

"D-d-d-d-d-d-dami, wh-wh-wh-wh-why, y-y-y-y-y-y-you . . . d-d-d-d-d-d . . ."

"You gotta teach 'em who's boss!" the rebel said, oblivious to the now burning straw on the floor. The noise in the place was deafening, and he had to shout over the ruckus so Caleb could hear him.

"Campion's a sly Yankee, the kind of yellow-bellied bastard who would sneak up on ya in the dead of night by way of Telegraph Road, and then attack ya mercilessly, while ya slept in your wet bedrolls atop muddy old Pea Ridge!"

"I heard about the flatiron incident," Spencer yelled.

"I've had my own dealings with him. That's why he's in solitary. He wove a wad of johnny-paper into a bag a apples and thwacked me upside the head with it!"

"What?" shouted Caleb, trying to fend off the gaggle of loons pulling on his clothes and yanking on his cage.

"The monster is down this hall," directed the turnkey as they entered a slightly quieter section of the place, passing row after row of incarcerated maniacs. In a way, the maximum-security ward at Bellevue was a metaphor for the multiethnic boiling pot that New York City was rapidly becoming. Though, in yet another way, it was a big cage full of minorities. In one cell, an Italian man sat on his cot and bobbed his head back and forth, while in another a Russian woman hummed softly and danced like a ballerina, and in still another cell a German shepherd wearing a straitjacket gnawed happily on a human bone.

"You keep Campion in solitary?"

"Have to . . . he's daffy, you know! But we got him in a straitjacket, chains, and heavy shackles, so don't you worry, he'll be as meek as a Union prisoner of war with a bad case of diarrhea! Hee-hee-hee-hee. By the by, I hate to remind you, but the straitjacket is another great Southern invention."

They stood in front of a thick iron door, and the turnkey banged on it three times.

"Coming in, professor! You got a visitor! Be nice now! We don't want no trouble."

He put the key into the hole, undid several latches, and then heaved the heavy door open.

"Chief Spencer, allow me to introduce you to Professor Archibald Campi . . . what the hell?"

The cell was empty!

Campion's manacles and straitjacket were in a big pile on the floor. The turnkey pulled out his whistle and blew hard.

"Excape! Excape! Lock down!!" he hollered. "Lunatic loose! Jailers grab your cups!" A succession of whistles could be heard as the alarm spread from ward to ward. The confused turnkey picked up the restraints and shook his head.

"Now how in the hell did that slippery blue devil do that?"

Caleb was already working to solve the conundrum, his eyes intensely scanning the dank chamber. The walls, floor, and ceiling were covered with insane scribblings, doodles, algebra calculations, diagrams of Boilerplate, and numerous drawings of a giant sphere encased in a glass square structure.

It seemed the brilliant professor was still inventing, but inventing what? And for whom?

No windows! thought Caleb. *Only one door locked from the outside . . . chains and straitjackets. It's just impossible! Unless . . . unless . . . No! That's ridiculous. It just couldn't be so.* His mind raced to find another solution, but he couldn't. *Unless . . . you were Houdini?*

"Houdini!" whispered Caleb. Then he turned to the Southerner. "What was it you said just now? Something about apples?"

"I said Campion fashioned a bag of apples out of a roll of johnny-paper and thwacked me over the head with it."

At that very moment Caleb's eyes zeroed in on something scratched on the wall. He read,

**da mummers are da wonz dat don't get
blamed and wees da wonz dat get thwacked**

"Good Lord!" he exclaimed, his eyes going wide. *It's him!* He shot a look down at three bowls of uneaten oatmeal sitting on the floor. "How often is he fed?"

"Just once a day . . . we slide it under the door."

Three bowls of uneaten oatmeal. The murders began exactly three days ago!

Caleb's body rushed with adrenaline. He had his man (or men)! He yanked out his mobile phone, dropped to one knee, started up the little furnace in the back, and began to dial Liz's number.

"Hey, that's one of those new talky things, right? We sure could have used those at the battle for Bacon Grease Hill. We gave you guys a hell of a lickin', but we had terrible communications. We tried writin' messages on cannonballs and shootin' 'em at each other. It didn't work as well as you might thi—"

"Shhh!"

One ring. Two rings. Three . . .

"Come on, Liz, pick up. Pick up!"

"Glad tidings to you, it's Dizzy Lizzy. I'm not available to receive your call at present. I'm probably out dining and dancing with some extremely handsome and extravagantly rich young gentleman who fancies me for who I am and doesn't expect me to abide by society's contemporary expectancies and stay home like all the other ladies, baking yeast rings."

Caleb rolled his eyes. "Okay, okay, come on. Come on!"

"If you'd like to leave me a short communiqué, please be so kind as to do so after the pretty chimes, and I shall return your call posthaste. That is, unless my young gentleman friend has other plans. Tootles." Then came the pretty chimes.

"Elisabeth, it's Caleb, listen to me. Professor Archibald Campion *is* the Thwacker! There is no doubt in my mind. He escaped Bellevue sanitarium three days ago, exactly when the murder spree began. I also believe that he kills his victims by thwacking them from behind with a burlap bag of apples fashioned out of strips of privy paper woven tightly together. But hold on to your socks, that's not all. I'm certain that he's being aided by a magician . . . the famous Harry Houdini! I know it sounds mad. I know Houdini doesn't even start performing for another twenty years. But the Spanish-American War hasn't happened yet, either, and *The Wizard of Oz* . . . well, maybe I have been a little crazy, a little too starched-collar literal about the actual course of historical events. But that's going to change. From now on you're dealing with a whole new police chief. A wilder, more impulsive Caleb Spencer, who can pick out his own ties and choose his own evening's entertainment. And you want to know something else about this new Caleb Spencer, Liz? This is a Caleb Spencer who is head over heels in l—"

Caleb turned to see that Finnegan had picked up a bowl of oatmeal, stuck his finger in, pulled up a gooey dollop, and was now struggling to get it through the bars of his bird cage and into his mouth.

"Don't touch that! It's evidence!" ordered Caleb, dropping the phone.

"Damn Yankees, think they're the boss, ever since the war. Well, mark my words, the South shall rise again! For in this land . . ."

"Now listen very carefully, Liz," Caleb continued, pacing the cell, no longer bothering to talk into the phone, "we can't notify the precinct. Tweed has everyone in his pocket. We are going to have to do this ourselves. You and Roosevelt can sit tight. I'm going to the Lyceum Theater to arrest Houdini. It all fits, Liz! We did it. We solved it. Jack the Thwacker is Campion and Houdini! They are possibly even the same man! And I'll bet you ten to one, they're both Mummers!"

Elisabeth heard Caleb's faint voice emanating out of the large cornucopia-shaped speaker attached to her princess mobile phone, but, at the moment, she was disinclined to pick it up. She thought Caleb's choice of words, *sit tight,* was highly ironic, considering the predicament in which she found herself. For she was bound hand and foot, gagged, and locked in the Yahi Indian's cage in Roosevelt's conservatory. Her muffled appeals for rescue elicited nothing but odd stares from the birds, alligators, and Komodo dragons populating the menagerie.

From her spot on Ishi's stool, she could see that someone had defaced the nude portrait of Roosevelt, scrawling "Hi, my name is fatty! And I stink!" in a balloon over the mayor's head. Liz had been tied up now for over an hour, and as she strained against her bonds, she could just make out the sound of two male voices whispering in the parlor. She immediately stopped squirming and pressed her ear against the bars.

"Did she put up a thtruggle?"

"Hell yes, she did. She nailed me a couple of times in the nuts! Look, this was not part of my deal. I was just supposed to come down here, spy on the investigation, and then go back. Maybe feed them a couple of red herrings. In and out, that's it!"

"We all make our own deals. Quite frankly, I don't know what your deal is and I don't care. But while you're here, you'll play by nineteenth-century rules, and right now that means

you're working for me. Underthtood? Now where'th the book of nameth?

"Don't worry. It's, uh, safe."

"I want that book."

"And you'll have it. After I'm safely back in the contraption and not a moment sooner. You see, it's my insurance policy. I wouldn't want anyone thwacking *me*."

"Do you realisth that if that book geth out, the *whole* plan would be ruined, and that includes whatever your cut ith, my friend?"

"It won't get out as long as everyone plays nice. I've heard about your ruffians, and your cutthroats and plug-uglies. I despise your so-called Gilded Age. Gilded if you're rich, white, own property, and don't, like, have typhoid or something. You'll get your book as soon as I get the hell out of this stinking world."

Liz heard a few bars of music. "The Holly and the Ivy," she thought.

"Hello? . . . really? I'll be right there. That was J. R. Bennett. It theemth that one of his reporterth, a Lony Boil"—that was the guy's name I was trying to think of! And I didn't even have to look it up! I'm gonna give my elbow a smooch for that one— "hath uncovered an interethting development regarding our Chief Thpenther. You thtay here and watch the dame. I'll let you know when to bring her to Vithta Crag."

"Hey, screw you."

"Thcrew *me*? Thcrew *me*?"

"No, I said *s*crew you, lardy. With an *essss*."

"We'll thee who's *thcrewed* when you dithcover the thecret of the Marvelouth Time-Jaunting Contraption."

"What are you talking about?"

"Didn't your girlfriend tell you?

"Tell me what?"

"Friend, she played you for a thucker. She gave you a one-way ticket, boy. Thith ith your home now, and you ain't going back anywhere! Tho if I were you, I would thtart getting uthed to wearing a top hat and cummerbund! Good evening to you, thir, or should I say . . . peath out?"

Liz heard the man laugh. A door slammed shut.

" 'Bye now," cried the animatronic gorilla cheerfully. "Teddy was sure happy you dropped in. Come on back and see us again real soon now, ya hear?"

CALEB SLUNG HIS PHONE OVER HIS SHOULDER. "THANKS FOR THE TOUR OF your maximum-security ward, Sergeant," he cracked. "If you could just keep your patients from escaping, it would be perfect." He started to leave, then stopped and turned back to the rebel, "By the by, I hate to remind you, but the North won!"

And with that he left.

The turnkey looked as if steam were about to blast from his ears. Balancing on the edge of Southern pride over the deep abyss of out-and-out witlessness, he fell to his knees and vociferated a sorrowful *no-o-o!!!* Its depleted resonance was a mere echo when it arrived outside, but it still elicited a smile from Caleb as he boarded his carriage and headed across town to the Lyceum Theater and his date with Houdini.

Although Caleb's astute eye had caught the inscription scrawled on the wall, he passed over something very important. On the floor, in the corner of the cell, there was another inscription—one of a different sort altogether, one that would have profound consequences for Elisabeth, and for Caleb, and for Roosevelt—and for yours truly as well.

The inscription read:

I'm not *non compos mentis*! But I feel I've been a dunce, a beetlehead, and a boob! (Also, a clodpoll.) I'm so sorry, little Erce. Please do forgive me.

THE FIVE-STORY GOTHIC MANSION AT 121 EAST SIXTY-FOURTH STREET IS today one of the city's most cherished landmarks. But, back in 1882, it was simply one of the many opulent houses erected on the fashionable block between Park Avenue and Lexington. Although its imported stained glass and steeple roof resembled that of a church and distinguished it from the other estates, it was, by comparison, not considered particularly impressive at all.

The building itself has a fascinating history worth mentioning here: at one point it was home to the great urban developer Robert Moses, the man who came up with the notion that you could halt African-Americans from using public pools in the city's white neighborhoods by simply keeping the water temperature *really* cold.[3] In the 1960s Bob (or Ray; I get the two confused)— of the popular comedy team Bob and Ray—ran the underground railroad, or "el railroad undergroundo," for illegal Mexican immigrants out of the mansion. His idea was that if they made it to his home then they could work their way up the East Coast via a series of safe houses to Canada, and, finally, to freedom. Unfortunately most of them were stopped at the border in California before they could even attempt the four-thousand-mile cross-country trek to "Bob's Safe House," and so, alas, the se-

---

3. Not to cast any aspersions on the many other useful facts presented in this book, but this one is actually true.—Ed.

cret railroad folded and has since been lost to history. Still, it was a noble effort, and we send our heartfelt kudos out to Bob (or Ray, or whomever) for at least trying. As of this printing, the beloved actress Brigitte Nielsen, her betrothed, bartender Matia Dessi, and rapper Flavor Flav reside at 121, and I think you'll join me in wishing them all the best.

In 1882, however, the building's uncanny likeness to a house of worship made it the ideal location for Blue Whale's most frequented house of whoreship.

"You got a customer in the Once Around the Park room," said Lilly, a perky *fille de joie,* as Blue Whale finished up with a gentleman in the Thighs or Pies room.

"Regular, is he?" asked Blue.

"Officer of the law. Says he's the chief of police, no less."

"Ah yes, dropping off the swag for the damage to my fur, I suspect."

The dark walls of the Once Around the Park room were decorated with horrible paintings on velvet, mostly depicting the Four Horsemen of the Apocalypse, as well as a few representing a variety of dogs in bowler hats playing card games, but the unmistakable impression one got in the chamber was that of being enclosed within a warm, nurturing, pay-by-the-quarter-hour womb. This palpable sensation was heightened by the red glass globe of the oil lamp, which gave a rouge-tinted illumination to the whole womb—I mean room. Scattered here and there was a sundry array of equestrian necessities: jodhpurs, horse whips, riding boots, blinders, buckets, and feed bags.

"Tsch, tsch, tsch. I do wish the girls would straighten up after a derby," muttered Blue to herself, picking up some sugar cubes and half-eaten carrots.

"Hello? Chief Spencer, are you in here?"

There was a deathly silent pause before a man in a top hat and tails stepped from behind a gaudy oriental screen.

"Good evening," he said.

"You're not Chief Spencer."

"I'm afraid not."

"One of his lackeys then, are we? Fine. It'll be twenty quid. But I warn ya, it'll be more if I can't get the chiggers out of my fur!"

"My, my, but we're in such a haste. No snappy repartee? No flirtatious confabulations to break the ice? Just straight to the dirty deed and have done with it? Is that how it goes?!"

"Look, copper, it's a busy night. I have to get back to . . ."

The man dropped a huge wad of money in the center of the messy iron bed and Blue Whale's eyes lit up.

"I see . . ." she said, assuming what she assumed was the obvious assumption, ". . . we're here for a bit more, aren't we? I'll get me harpoon."

"Don't bother," said the man, smiling a smile that wasn't really a smile at all, but rather an earnest appeal to the prostitute's better senses, a plea to pick up and leave, to run, to birth herself of this womb before it was too late. But, unfortunately for Blue Whale, she read his expression as nothing more than a simple pervert's smile, and so, in one of her last acts on earth, she began to pull off her dress and lead-lined girdle.

"You can try on the jodhpurs behind the screen," she offered, revealing her flabby body covered with hundreds of whale tattoos. "You look to be about a 34 inseam. Or if you'd like to Ahab it, there's also a pegleg under the bureau, I think, where the last gentleman kicked it."

"That won't be necessary," said the man, retrieving a little box from his carpetbag and placing it on top of the night table. He opened it ever so gently and an agreeable ditty—a melodious melody—"Sweet Rosie O'Grady," floated out.

"Oh, a music box! Isn't that nice. Sets the mood, doesn't it? Now then, what shall we call you . . . besides 'good-looking'?"

"That's a very good question. But I don't know the answer to it. You see, I go by many names." He extinguished the oil lamp, its red glow giving way to the flickering amber light from the fireplace.

"Uh—huh . . . okay," said Blue, assuming this was some sort of new bourgeois game they were playing. "Well then . . . shall I guess?"

"Yes. Do guess! That would be . . . quite . . . sigh . . . jolly, I suppose."

"All right. Let's see, is it Frederic? No, not Frederic. Um . . . Ferdinand? Wolfgang? Werner? Malachy? No, those don't fit you. I know, it's John! You are most *certainly* a John! From now on, whenever I think of you, I'm going to think of a John."

"How very perceptive you are. And just for that, you may call me by my nickname. I'm quite sure . . . sigh . . . you've heard—oh, bother, what's the point?"

"What's the matter, mister? Spirit willin' but not the body, is it?"

"I'm afraid—I'm afraid all the joy has gone out of it for me."

"Oh, we got just the thing for that, we do. Salts of mercury, down in the kitchen cupboard. One little pill, and half an hour later you're as stiff as the mast that bore our forefathers hither, you are."

"Don't you ever wish, my dear gargantuan one, that there were more to life than just a quick *penny in the old zoetrope,* or whatever you ladies are calling it these days? Do you not ever dream?"

"Ah, sure John, every young gal has dreams. But like my mamma said, put dreams in one hand and manure in the other, and see which one gets filled up first!" With that she laughed and slapped her thighs, sending a ripple along her lap.

"As for myself," sighed the man, "I always dreamed of becoming a dancer."

"Ah, is that all?" laughed Blue Whale. "Well then, why don't you dance?"

"If it were only that simple. I am afraid my life has taken dark turns, down dark alleys, into even darker alleys from which no man can return."

"Ah, you men. There ain't no law against it, like there is against just about everythin' else. Just dance, if you want to. And if afterward, you want a romp through the rosy den with a sportin' gal, then that's fine, too. Who says you can't do both?"

"Why, my mammoth matron, I do believe you're right! There's no reason at all why I can't have *both* my dreams."

"There you go, that's more like it. Now what do you say, shall I get me harpoon?"

"Oh, but first, my dear sweet angel, you must guess my nickname. I'm quite sure you've heard it . . ." The customer's spirits seemed to rise suddenly. A note of near hysteria crept into his voice. "Many times, no doubt. Perhaps . . . you've even grown . . . to dread it."

"Uh-huh. Okay, and what might *that* be?"

He reached into his carpetbag . . .

"Nothing too saucy, my dear lady. Just a little old humble name that will soon be known around the world—Jack the Jolly Thwacker!"

Blue Whale's scream was lost in the orgiastic howls and squeals of ecstasy emanating from the other rooms. It happened so quickly—a wallop from a burlap bag marked MCINTOSH, a *thud*, a sneeze, a burp, and then it was all over. Despite the whale's brassbound insistence that she could protect herself, the chubby harlot proved no match for the 'doctor' and his bag of fruit.

Wanting no interruptions, the Thwacker locked the door, took

a moment to stoke the crackling fire, and then retrieved his tools from his trusty carpetbag. Now, unlike with the other murders, he was free to take his time and quietly indulge in his hellish art. Working in the challenging medium of human intestines, he allowed his hands to be steered by their evil muse. When he was all done he stood back admiring his work, and he realized that on this night he had created his one and only, his true masterpiece. It was the most loathsome, macabre, and sheerly *icky* death tableau you could possibly imagine. (Imagine the most disgusting death tableau and then multiply it by ten. Nope, not even close.)

And all the while, he danced.

THE NINETEENTH PRECINCT WAS ABUZZ WITH ACTIVITY—UNUSUAL FOR the late hour—when Mrs. O'Leary waddled in and meekly asked the desk sergeant to whom she could speak about her tenant, who had just returned home covered in blood yet again. The desk sergeant told her to go home, because the Thwacker had already been identified by an eyewitness to the latest murder.

"Yes, but I really think I should speak with Chief Spencer, I do, you see . . ."

"Chief Spencer is no longer in charge of the investigation, Madame," said a voice behind her. "I am."

Mrs. O'Leary's orbs widened, and she gulped hard and then curtsied deeply to the dapper man in the detective's suit.

"Oh, Mr. Byrnes, you are. A pleasure to make your acquaintance, it is," she said, nervously fluffing up the back of her hair. "But you see, I've been following the investigation in the penny papers, and I believe that the man you're looking for resides in my home."

"My dear woman," said Caleb's longtime rival, taking her

"Hiya Abe!"

hand gallantly in his. "We at this precint appreciate everything our citizens have done to help us pursue this and other cases. Undoubtedly our jobs, as hard as we work at them, would be impossible without the input of fine citizens like yourself, whose concern for civic morality and the pursuit of justice exceeds that of many of the men history chooses to enshrine."

"Oh, well, I just wanted him to stop bleedin' on me linens, I did, but if you say—"

"But if you take a moment to peruse this advance copy of the morning's penny papers, you will see that your concern, though laudable, is misplaced." Byrnes held up the front page of the morning edition. Mrs. O'Leary gasped.

"Good gracious no! says I. I do, I did!"

BLUE WHALE HACKED
Caleb Spencer / Jack!
Entire City on Lookout for Maniac,
Police Chief THWACKER!

And underneath the headline was the photo Lony Boil took of Caleb and the Blue Whale boarding the police chief's carriage.

"So you see, dear citizen, you may rest easy, for we know *exactly* who the Thwacker is. And it's only a matter of time before he's captured . . . dead or alive."

Chapter the Tenth.

In which the Marquise de Merteuil plots revenge on the Vicomte de Valmont (played by John Malkovich) as Madame de Tourvel takes a powder.

"GO GO—TWO—BLUE WHALE?"

Was that the sum and substance of the Thwacker's message? "Go to the blue whale?" If so, what the hell did it mean? It may as well have been another language to me. What the hell is "the"? I decided to reexamine the recent grisly photogravures to determine exactly what the killer was really trying to say.

This time, the psychotic post-mortem tableau was more disturbing than anything previously attempted. The weighty Blue Whale had been affixed to the ceiling of the Once Around the Park Room. Her intestines lay coiled like rope on the floor, the end threaded through a heavy pulley tied securely around the woman's waist—apparently the means by which she was hoisted up.

As soon as I saw the image my brain clicked louder than ever before. *Click, click, click, click!* went my brain until the neighbors began to pound on the wall. "Go go two blue whale . . . once around the park—" Or, as it finally hit me like a ton of ever-loving bricks, "Go go two the blue whale, once around the park!"

Now I got it! (But I still wasn't sure how the "the" fit into the whole thing.)

Anyway, today, just as back then, there was only one "blue whale" to "go go to" "around the park," and that was the 75-foot leviathan mounted on the ceiling of the Milstein Hall of Ocean Life at the Museum of Natural History on Eighty-first Street and Central Park West.

My mind clicked ear-splittingly loud now. CLICK, CLICK, CLICK, CLICK, CLICK, etc. Why didn't the investigative team in 1882 come up with the same assumption? But of course, I knew exactly why, didn't I? (I'm asking you. *Didn't I?* . . . Okay, forget it. Last time I ask you anything.) It was because they were too hung up on romancing, kidnapping, and arresting each other to realize what was really happening, that's why! (I guess.)

I tucked all green-eyed indignation with respect to Wendell and his new hot girlfriend into the faux-onyx keepsake box in my overworked and loudly clicking noodle and hastened to supply my rucksack with a camera, laptop, hair thickener, résumé, photos, and pepper spray (just in case I indulged in some tasteless museum cafeteria food—I don't get why they don't come out with a salt-and-paprika spray). For safety purposes, I pinned onto my slicker my personal information tag, which includes my name, blood type, and the person to contact if I get lost—in my case, Wendell's mom, as my parents always pretend not to know me around strangers (for tax reasons, according to my dad). Then I headed out for a fun day at the museum.

I also brought along the faded daguerreotype that had fallen out of Caleb's diary. Had I only known how much trouble that thing was about to cause me, I would have gladly left it behind, if not shredded it, torched it, and flushed it down the potty bowl.

THE TEN O'CLOCK SHOW AT THE LYCEUM THEATER WAS JAM-PACKED. Houdini's performances tended to be, and Caleb was forced to stand next to a naked bronze statue of an elderly Greek man, his shriveled protuberance perfectly level with Caleb's eyes.

Onstage, Houdini, a short, muscular man with a high-pitched voice, was in the midst of his famous Curdled-Milk Canister Escape act. He had performed the illusion hundreds of times without incident, but tonight something was terribly amiss. He had been sealed inside the small container of chunky, sour milk for over twenty minutes now, and the audience was getting restless. The orchestra vamped as Houdini's beautiful assistant, Bess, smiled sweetly and strutted back and forth in front of the can, which was rocking violently in response to Houdini's desperate agitations within.

Bess looked at her watch, and, resolving that it had been long enough, signaled the orchestra to hit a crescendo. She unlocked and opened the canister's lid, and it immediately toppled over, splashing its twenty gallons of stinking unpasteurized milk all over the stage and finally belching out a small bundle of gagging flesh. Houdini was still bound in heavy chains from his neck to his ankles. He struggled to get himself up on all fours, vomiting curdled milk in front of the disgusted audience. His cheery assistant encouraged the crowd to applaud, and, although they were a bit confused, they eventually did.

"What the hell are you doing to me here?" Houdini spluttered in his pip-squeak voice.

"That's for last night," said Bess through her frozen smile as she continued to sashay back and forth in front of the retching illusionist.

"I told you it's not my fault . . . it's my fat-assed brother's fault!"

His brother Hardeen was one of the leading specialists in X-rays, and Houdini had volunteered several times to be a guinea pig for his experiments. Apparently the frequent exposure had left him incapable of getting a solid red rocket on, and although Bess cherished him despite his shortcomings, occasionally (depending on the cycle of the full moon), it really pissed her off.

Caleb folded his arms and leaned against the statue of the Greek elder so that its protuberance nestled firmly within his ear. "This is the great Houdini?" he asked the statue, but it couldn't answer because it wasn't real, and even if it were real, it would not have spoken English.

Helpers from backstage arrived and undid the magician's bindings, and Houdini, great showman that he was, took a deep bow, after which he vomited again.

Next, Bess sidestepped across the stage like a Vegas showgirl carrying a big sign that read THE GREAT CHALLENGE ACT.

"And now, ladies and gentlemen," announced Houdini. "I challenge any man to come up and punch me in the stomach. For my iron girth is capable of withstanding any . . ."

Bwowmp!

Bess hauled off and delivered a powerful wallop to the little man's sternum. Houdini buckled over, grimaced, and coughed up an eclectic assortment of glass shards, sewing needles, razor blades, and five Oscar Mayer wieners he had wolfed down on his twenty-minute supper break.

"I wasn't ready yet," he hissed out of the corner of his mouth.

The orchestra gave him a ta-da! and he winced as he took another deep bow.

"Finally, ladies and gentlemen," he said, shoving Bess into the

wings, "if there is any member of law enforcement in our audience who would care to handcuff me, I'll be happy to demonstrate how easily I can escape any such contraption."

"I'll do it," said Caleb, marching up to the footlights.

"Why, ladies and gentlemen, it's none other than our own chief of police, Caleb R. Spencer!"

The crowd applauded, unaware of the headlines in the latest penny papers now being circulated out on the streets. Spencer mounted the boards and pulled out a set of iron manacles.

"Break his index fingers, then he can't get out," whispered Bess from the wings.

"Now, Chief Spencer, to what do we owe this unexpected visit?"

"Well, if truth be told, I'm here to arrest you, Mr. Houdini."

The audience laughed.

"Oh, arrest *me*, is it? Well, I hope you won't need *this*!" Houdini produced the police chief's nightstick. The audience applauded. Caleb, genuinely impressed, prepared to handcuff the slippery prestidigitator.

"Or this!" Houdini now held up his pistol. Caleb immediately felt his holster for the sidearm, but it wasn't there. The audience guffawed and applauded.

"How in the name of Emily Dickinson in heat did you do that?"

". . . and I *certainly* hope you won't need *these,* now will you?" Houdini displayed a pair of pink frilly underpants with an unfortunate brown streak on them, and the audience roared with laughter as the embarrassed chief of police frantically groped his butt and turned purple realizing that he was out there onstage sans his underpants.

"Where the hell? How the hell?"

"Magic, my dear constable, magic! But don't ask me to make

that naughty stain disappear! I'm not *that* good, sir!" and before Caleb could respond he found his wrists securely bound by his own restraints. Houdini smugly dangled the keys in front of him. The crowd went crazy, rising to its feet and applauding stentoriously. Bess just rolled her eyes.

"So you see, Chief Spencer, it is not I who is under arrest, but rather you!"

The public cheered, the band did another *ta-da!,* and Houdini bowed deeply.

Suddenly the house lights came up and a voice from the back of the theater announced, "I couldn't have said it better myself, Mr. Houdini."

Detective Thomas Byrnes entered in the company of a legion of uniformed officers and plainclothes roundsmen, who quickly mounted the stage and surrounded Caleb. A hush fell over the crowd.

"By the power vested in me by the honorable and esteemed Ice Cream and by the greatly beloved association of Tammany, I hereby place Police Chief Spencer under arrest!"

"Good heavens, no! On what charge, Byrnes?" demanded Houdini.

"Homicide, my dear wizard. For the murders of Old Toothless Sally Jenkins, Emma May Pinch, Franny Rose Tiddles, and the corpulent whore known fondly to the common folk as Blue Whale. Ladies and gentlemen, though it might astonish you to know this—it has certainly flabbergasted myself—the seemingly humble civil servant you see before you is none other than the infamous Jack the Jolly Thwacker!"

The audience stared dumbly, confused by the long speech.

"Spencer is the Thwacker," he clarified. "And I'm here to arrest him."

The crowd applauded and cheered, but then realized they were

applauding and cheering a homicidal maniac, so they quickly began to boo and throw rotten tomatoes.

"Hang the lunatic!"

"Burn the witch!"

"Spank the monkey!"

"Bang the drum slowly!"

"Byrnes, you bastard!" shouted Caleb over the mob's raucous roar. "What's your involvement in all of this? Who's paying you? You, you, you . . . Mummer-lover you!"

"It saddens me to do this to you, Caleb. Your years of service have been invaluable to this city, but that does not in any way excuse the making of artsy dioramas from the flesh of ladies of the night. Take him away, men," ordered Byrnes. The cops pulled Caleb off the stage and out to a waiting paddy wagon, with orders to imprison him downtown at the dreaded "Tombs."

Back inside, the crowd was going wild. As the curtain closed, Bess came out of the wings and draped a towel over Houdini's shoulders.

"So I assume we'll be going to rescue him, then?" she asked.

"Of course. We cannot in good conscience stay out of this . . . though I'm afraid it means this will be a long night . . . we'll be bound to come home exhausted and I doubt I'll be able to—"

Bwowmp! Bess punched him squarely in the stomach again.

"Dammit, woman, I said wait until I'm ready!"

ON TWENTY-SECOND STREET, A HOMELESS MAN COVERED IN DRIED MUD, wearing a loincloth, carrying a spear, and chomping on a wad of pre-chewed tobacco shuffled somewhat aimlessly uptown.

"Delmo?" he beseeched with pathetic intent to every passerby, but his petition was met with only strange looks. The self-absorbed

pedestrians gave him a wide berth as they passed him. (The sensible routine of giving crazy homeless people a wide berth was initially established in the 1800s in New York City, and I'm happy to report that it is one of those rare traditions from the Gilded Age that has survived the ravages of time and is still practiced with great aplomb by most city-dwellers today, including a handful of levelheaded, slightly less crazy homeless people themselves.)

The hobo traipsed past the Eden Musée on Twenty-third Street. Its façade was ornamented with an amalgam of overdone French moldings along with twelve plaster reliefs representing the rear ends of the founding fathers (a little folly added by the French architect for his own amusement). The Musée was New York City's answer to the famous Madame Tussaud's of London and housed a collection of imaginative wax tableaux with historical and mythical[4] motifs. The chamber of horrors was a particularly popular attraction and indulged the Victorians' fascination with all things Egyptian—the rotting mummy display was considered most de rigueur. But the tattooed wanderer's attention was grabbed by a window spectacle entitled "The Zulu's Favorite Pastime, as Far as We Can Tell," which depicted a naked African woman mounting a naked African man.

"Why, I've witnessed this celebration before!" he bellowed, feeling a slight awakening in his loins. "But when I saw it, they were bouncing up and down—and rather energetically, I might add."

He pulled open the door and entered the Musée. Wandering around the place, he felt that it all seemed very familiar to him—the wax figure of little George Washington hacking down

---

4. Pornographic.

a cherry tree, Lizzy Borden hacking down her mother, and Peter Stuyvesant hacking down Native Americans. The Musée was on the 'hacking' edge of waxery and already offered a timely diorama of Old Toothless Sally Jenkins with her wig of intestines, about to be thwacked by a shadowy figure lurking in the background, whose face was obscured by a mask. "Will the 'Old Gooseberry' Ever Be Caught?" was the title of the scene, but because of the evening's events at the Lyceum, artisans were already hard at work on a Police Chief Spencer wax head to plop on top of the killer's body.

The overgrown Mud Tot turned around and was met with an eerily lifelike figure of none other than Mayor Teddy Roosevelt. If the man had felt a slight awakening in his loins before, now he felt an all-out eruption. *Who was this familiar, devastatingly handsome man with the marble eyes?* He knew not. He only knew that no matter how much it weighed, he had to have it. Mostly because the man's suit was simply to die for.

He fathomed it was now or never, and in one swift move wrenched the mannequin off its stand and vaulted towards the door. Whistles blew as guards took off in pursuit. At the entrance, the burly sentry held out his hands, "Stop! Thief! Stop!"

But the derelict shouted "Charge!" and rushed straight into the guard, sending him sailing into the diorama of Booker T. Washington surrounded by a gang of hooded klansmen holding chains, whips, and ropes, entitled "A Klansman's Christmas Wish." The vagabond bolted the Eden Musée and made his escape down a narrow alleyway, all the while with the stiff mayor bobbing along with him under the clutch of his muddy arm.

I WAS TWO STEPS OUT THE FRONT DOOR WHEN IT OCCURRED TO ME THAT I might enjoy something sweet to eat at the Museum of Natural History. So I went back into my kitchen and retrieved a 3 Musketeers bar. On my way I cut through the living room and paused atop the massive pile of Thwacker research material scattered all over the floor. *If something should happen to me at the Museum, something dreadful, something unspeakable, who could make any sense out of all this stuff?* I thought. *Certainly not my friend Wendell, who's too busy with his new girlfriend to even return my calls!*

It seemed a wise time to put the material in order, considering the complexity of the investigation thus far. (This part will also be a useful recap for any of our more "challenged" readers. But just so you more-advanced kids don't get bored, I've included some foreshadowing as well.)

At this point in my research, Caleb had been arrested by Detective Thomas Byrnes, accused of being the Thwacker, and sent downtown to sit in his own filth in a cell in the dreaded Tombs. (Caleb was a very clean man, so they had to import filth from outside counties for his cell.)

Liz had been kidnapped, presumably by the odd-acting Roosevelt and Boss Tweed, and was at present bound and gagged behind the bars of Ishi's cage in the conservatory at Roosevelt's house.

The odd-acting Roosevelt had told Tweed that he was in possession of the Book of Names, but also warned him that he was not about to give it up until he was safely back in the "contraption," whatever the hell the contraption was. But I knew he was bluffing, because Liz had the forethought to leave the book in the trustworthy hands of Tex at Delmonico's.

Meanwhile Tex was enjoying a ten-course banquet on Elisabeth's account, continuing to decipher the prominent names of New York City's high society listed as Mummers in the book.

Who was this handsome man with the marble eyes?

The mud-covered hobo with amnesia (who could he possibly be?) was scampering around the streets of Manhattan with the stolen wax figure of Mayor Teddy Roosevelt under his arm.

As for the Thwacker himself, he was probably back in his dark chamber in the nondescript brownstone having another battle with his conscience (or just beating off). For a homicidal maniac, he seemed to feel pretty bad about what he was doing, though still he apparently couldn't help himself. However, his usefulness would soon run its course and he himself would become a murderer's target—in fact, he would become his *own* target (foreshadowing!).

I was still not sure why Harry Houdini and Bess were on their way to help Caleb, but I presumed Houdini was indeed in cahoots with the insane professor Archibald Campion and that I would discover their true connection to all these events shortly.

My floor was so cluttered, in fact, that as I left I stepped over a letter that someone had slid under my door. I would never get the chance to read it (more foreshadowing!), but I would learn enough later to get the gist of its contents:

Mr. Elliott:
Meet me at the Museum of Natural History at Eighty-first Street and Central Park West. I have information for you regarding the Thwacker case. Come alone.

not the villain, I swear

Fortunately, as if by some incredible coincidence, that was exactly where I was going! Phossy Phil must have been right after all about there being patterns in everything. Whatever the reason, I was on my way to face with selfless determination and unwavering audacity (and, as backup, a secure set of adult undergarments) whatever dangers surely awaited me in the dark Hall of Ocean Life.

Chapter the Eleventh.

I have no idea what this chapter is about.

FOR ME, THE AMERICAN MUSEUM OF NATURAL HISTORY HAS ALWAYS BEEN a magical world filled with dark corners, dinosaur bones, mysterious crystals, and the occasional flash of cavewoman flesh in the dioramas. A place to truly lose oneself. In fact, I got lost every time my parents brought me there. Sometimes they got lost, too, sometimes so lost they ended up at home without me. It taught me a good lesson, though, because now you cannot get me near the place sans my personal information tag, savvy?

The museum, situated between Seventy-seventh and Eighty-first streets, was erected the same year the Dakota was built, and for a long time they were essentially the only structures of any significance on the Upper West Side (besides, of course, the Shim Si delicatessen and Laundromat, which still stands on Eighty-fifth and Columbus). If I had lived back in the Thwacker's day, my bedroom window would not have looked out on the apartments across the way, where the large-breasted woman who insists on undressing in front of her bathroom window every night at exactly ten-thirty is beginning to look like she could stand to lose a couple of pounds, but rather I would have had a direct

view of the Natural History Museum and probably some crabby old curator prancing around, doing some sort of half-assed voodoo dance after hours in the Hall of Eskimos or some bullshit. I'm sorry, I shouldn't talk that way. Curators and fat women are people, too. I'm just still really mad at Wendell.

And had I been in the nineteenth century, there would have been few places for my "shadow" to hide in. As it was I didn't notice him for a while. At first he was just one of those sounds that might be your own feet but also might be someone timing their steps to yours so that they won't be heard, but then he started to wheeze. I walked faster. By the time I got to the museum stairs, he was panting and muttering under his breath about "why won't he slow down, he's so fast!" I turned to confront him.

"So, I've been meaning to ask you, if you're a talent scout, why do you always go around dressed like the guy from Monopoly?"

"Don't go in the museum!" he wheezed. His voice was all gravelly, like some kind of talking rock tumbler. "You don't understand. The people are horrible! The food is nasty! They're going to have like nineteen wars, and nothing's ever going to make any sense!"

"Look, I'm in kind of a hurry here. The museum's about to close. So maybe you could just give me your card?"

"I'm not a talent scout. No, no, no, it's me! I'm me!"

The man took off his top hat and I finally got a good look at . . . the most disgustingly old human being I've ever seen. He had to be over 150. His totally hairless head had shriveled up to the size of a raccoon's.

"Man, you're gross."

"Don't you recognize me? Am I that old? I used to be so . . . debonair. Just like you are now."

I squinted. "Don Imus?"

"No, not Don Imus. Idiot. I'm *you!* and I'm here to . . . oh, now I can't even remember why I'm here. I'm so tired!"

"Look whoever you are, I'm really sorry you're down on your luck. Here's a quarter. I got to go." (I didn't really hand him a quarter. It was just a button. I figured he was so old he wouldn't be able to tell the difference.)

"I tried to scare you at the audition, but that didn't work," he said. "So I thought I'd get the diaries . . . you see, I thought if I could stop you, it would keep all this from happening. But then I got really confused and ended up just smelling that bra for four hours, and the clerk threw me out! He wouldn't even let me keep my mask and gloves."

"Ha! I got to keep mine."

"Do you still have it? The bra! I know you took it. Give it to me!" he began to paw my person with his old-man hands, which were like scabby old sticks of butter. "I would kill our mother for one last sniff."

"Eew, get away!"

"Please! You have to believe me! If you go in there, I'll end up—I mean—oh Lord, it's too confusing! One hundred and twenty-three years!"

"Stranger! Stranger!" I cried, batting him away with my elbows. Old as he was, he went down easy. "Stranger, stranger, stranger!" I continued as I ran into the museum. I ran right past the ticket counter and didn't stop until I was inside the cavernous Hall of Ocean Life, gazing up at the colossal blue whale hanging from the ceiling. I couldn't help but be comforted by its serene majesty. *Boy, what I wouldn't give to be a colossal blue whale!* I thought—the same ambition I had when I was a child. I sighed. After a few minutes of deep breathing and about ten imaginary showers, I felt much better.

"*Balaenoptera musculus,*" said a short, wrinkly woman.

"I'm sorry. I don't speak Budapest."

The woman giggled heartily. "No, no. That's the actual name of the species. 'Blue whale' is just its common name."

"Oh, I see. And what makes you the big expert?"

"I'm the museum curator, Ellen Flutter," she said, extending her hand for me to shake.

"Oh, I'm so terribly sorry, Madam Flutter," I said, bowing and genuflecting. "I should have known I was in the presence of someone with a rack of brains on her and not just someone who spends her nights dancing around the Hall of Eskimos!" I giggled nervously, because I had no idea what the hell I was saying.

"Ah . . . right." Clearly, neither did she.

"So, um, how much does it weigh, anyway?" I asked.

"A whale this size weighs about four hundred thousand pounds."

"No, I meant the Hall of Eskimos. But that's okay, you shouldn't be required to know every little fact about the place just because you're the curator. I'm sure I can find it in a pamphlet somewhere."

"Uh-huh."

"Four hundred thousand pounds, huh? *Tsch, tsch, tsch.* That's heavy," I observed. "What do they eat?"

"Believe it or not, just little shrimplike krill."

"I believe it. That's my favorite, too. Whenever I go to Red Lobster, it's the fried shrimplike krill platter for *moi!* And I don't need any of those imitation crabmeat hush puppies for starters either! Just the krill, a bib, and it's bon voyage, see ya in the men's room in an hour!"

"Well, that's a lovely thought. You know, you look rather familiar to me," the woman said, studying my finely buffed body parts with an appreciative eye.

"Possibly. I'm a celebrated performer. You may have seen my work. I had a little show called *Get a Life?*"

"Oh right, that abomination. But that's not what I was thinking about . . ."

"I portrayed Mark Hamill in a made-for-TV movie. Ah, and I also created the role of the tempestuous Donkey Number Three in *Equus* . . . I'll be appearing soon in *The Phantom Toll Booth* as the . . ."

"You're the guy from *Home Alone,* right!?"

"No . . . no. That wasn't me. That's another actor, named Daniel Stern."

"Oh . . . he's good. So what else have you played in?"

"Oh, well, as I just said, you may have seen *The Mark Hamill Story* on TNT . . . and . . ."

"Wait, I know . . . you were in *Frankenstein!* Right?"

"Huh? . . . no . . . I mean . . . well, which *Frankenstein* are you . . ."

Suddenly a bell rang.

"Oh, I'm sorry, we're closing," she said.

"Great, this was a bust. I was hoping to solve an old murder mystery today. See, I'm writing this book, and I thought all the clues pointed to the blue whale. But I guess I was wrong. There's nothing unusual going on here . . . so . . . peace out and thanks for the whale info, Miss Footer."

"Flutter."

"Yes, I know, I'm hurrying. Jeez!"

"Mr. Stern," she said, grabbing my elbow. "You know, it's not often that we have a celebrity of your caliber visit us here in our little museum. How would you like a private showing of 'The Search for E. T.' in our new Rose Center planetarium?"

"Okay, what's the catch? How much? And I'll tell you right

now, I'm not gonna have sex with you just so I can watch some cheap 'a-whora-boring-alices' flash on and off as the nebula of Ortega implodes into a million galaxies. Been there done that, savvy?"

"No, no. The planetarium is far more sophisticated now and it would be absolutely free. My treat. Of course, if you enjoy it, perhaps you could spread the word amongst your Hollywood friends, like your costars in *Home Alone*? We rely heavily on private donations from the likes of Joe Pesci and such."

"I see. I think we're speaking the same language here, lady."

"I sincerely doubt it."

"Payola is alive and well and living in the Museum of Natural History, am I right?"

"Ah, yeah, something like that. Plus no one's been in for the show lately, and we have to run the thing at least once a day to keep the dust off the light bulbs. So what do you say? Would you like to go?"

I scratched my whiskers. "Well, I haven't been to the planetarium in years, and I make a habit of not turning down any freebies." (That was obvious because I was dressed in my freebie wardrobe: *Get a Life* baseball cap, *Late Show* T-shirt, and *Cabin Boy* slicker.) "Plus the handicap van doesn't leave for another hour . . . so what the hell?"

"Wonderful."

Mrs. Fluffer held my hand, pulling me along to the Rose Center, and I found myself becoming more and more excited about the E. T. show and babbling uncontrollably like a silly schoolboy.

"The last time I went to the planetarium it was called the Hayden Planetarium. Do they still call it the Hayden Planetarium? Or is it just called the Rose Center now? It was for the Christmas show in 1967. But I guess you people don't do the

Christmas show anymore right? On account of it not being politically correct and all? Because not everyone celebrates Christmas. Some people celebrate Hachchnika and some people celebrate Koala and we should respect all traditions, right? My mom brought me to the Christmas show but she got lost and I had to take a taxi home and then she had accidentally changed the locks. Wait, no! Scratch that! What am I saying?"

Mrs. Flutter sighed, cocked her head, and cracked her neck.

". . . No, my mistake, the last time I went to the planetarium was in the twelfth grade with a bunch of friends. We went to experience the awe and wonder that was 'Laserium.' Man, was that cool! Bing, bang, bong, lasers shooting every which way, Pink Floyd music blaring. It blew my mind, lady. It. Blew. My. Mind." I felt my slicker to make sure I hadn't forgotten my 3 Musketeers bar. "As a matter of fact, if I remember correctly, I think my friends got lost that night . . ."

Miss. Flutter waved off the security guard as we plowed through the entrance of the futuristic Rose Center for Earth and Space. It was incredible—like something out of a James Bond movie. The gargantuan white ball representing earth sat encased in a colossal glass box, which allowed one to circumvent the sphere while offering the public outside on Eighty-first Street a view. Other planets hung around the giant ball as steam poured out of its base. It resembled a huge alien spacecraft readying itself for blastoff. Although I'm not one for progress, and I would have preferred the city to remain as it was in the Age of Innocence, I had to admit that the new planetarium was quite an improvement over the old one with its dark brick exterior, dwarfish green dome, and clockwork African-American manservants.

"Have a safe journey, Mr. Elliott, I mean . . . enjoy the experience, which will be, um, like a journey, metaphorically speaking."

"This is awfully kind of you."

"It's my pleasure. Just remember, when you feel like throwing up, swallow hard! Our custodial staff takes a dim view of spectator puke, and you wouldn't want to arrive at your destination all smelly. They take an even dimmer view of it there."

"No problem. I'll just throw up into my sleeve. But what do you mean by destination?"

"Well, I mean your, um, metaphoric—oh, just get in the machine, you monkey."

And with that the little woman shoved me into the planetarium and slammed its door, leaving me unaccompanied in the dark, round room.

I found a large and extra-cushy seat—*just for VIPs,* I surmised—and while unwrapping my 3 Musketeers bar, I was startled by Mrs. Flutter's angry voice emanating from the loudspeaker.

"There is no eating or drinking allowed in the Rose Center! Also:

No flash photography!

No talking!

No sleeping!

And, absolutely no whacking off, Mr. Elliott!"

Well at least she's finally getting my name right, I thought.

Suddenly the dome above me was alive with billions of stars darting across the galaxy and all at once I was one with the universe. A man's voice narrated while cool techno music thumped in the background.

"Hello, *que pasa?* I'm Harrison Ford. When I'm out at my ranch in Jackson Hole, Wyoming, I often like to spend the nights sitting on my porch, looking up at the vast cosmos which surrounds and dwarfs our petty little human selves, and thinking to myself about how these property taxes are *eating me alive.* I mean, I'm rich, but nobody's *that* rich. Thus, barring a restructuring

of our nation's tax laws, I'll be picking up a little extra change serving as your narrator on this and several other planetarium presentations. But don't expect me to like it. So, anyway, it's a lovely evening, isn't it? A long long time ago, in a galaxy *not* so far away, wonderful things were about to happen."

The dome exploded in a blast of brilliant white light and then, through a cheap champagne-bubble effect, the earth came into focus. "Radical," I said, which is a secret code I have with myself that means "crappy."

"The Big Bang!" continued Ford "And now behold—Earth! In this context, 'behold' is just a verb, and any association between what follows and, say, the Bible, should be deemed purely coincidental—because, let's face it, what happens in the Old Testament is simply not plausible. But to truly comprehend the possibility of life on other planets, we must first comprehend the earliest beginnings of life here on Earth."

I readied myself, anticipating that the show might actually be really, really . . . dull. Harrison continued, "In the beginning, the world was in the grip of constant cataclysmic eruptions. It was bombarded daily by giant meteorites, and was covered in a stale shroud of sulfuric oxide which made the whole place smell like a hunk of old butt-ass limburger cheese. It would be another billion years before the seeds of life would take hold and the first tiny microorganisms, called pollypoggywaps, would slither from the steamy bogs. There is absolutely no way it could have happened in just seven days, like your precious Bible claims. But let us now explore these early times. . . ."

I slumped in my seat and my lids began droop, but the techno music was quickly replaced with the opening chords of "Free Bird." I sat back up to enjoy the tune. Harrison stopped talking, and on the ceiling, strange pictures mixed in with seemingly

disordered words started to pop on and off. Was I dreaming? What the hell did this have to do with E. T.?

Mother.

Country.

Father.

Jerk.

Each word was separated by a string of disturbing images; war, hurricanes, earthquakes, and the *Dallas* twentieth anniversary cast reunion show, all rapidly flashing above and around me. The images were so snappy that I could barely identify them before they disappeared.

The montage grew more and more frantic as the volume of the music grew louder and louder. *If I leave here tomorrow, will you still remember me?*

"What the hell kind of spaced-out space show is this supposed to be? Some artsy-fartsy Gene Roddenberry crap?" I shouted to no one in particular, because no one in particular was there except for me.

I was beginning to feel sick. So I swallowed hard, but I knew whatever I swallowed wasn't staying in my tummy for very long. I tucked my hand into my sleeve, in order to make a receptacle.

The images now included a mix of color and black-and-white photos, creating an annoying strobe effect as their contents—a kaleidoscope of fast-moving decades—whirled around me and raced across the dome above me.

I felt a deep rumbling in my seat and thought perhaps I had indigestion, but suddenly I experienced the sensation of a

powerful explosion of gas—too powerful to be me. Gravity glued me to my seat. It was as if the planetarium itself pulled away from its anchors and lifted off its foundation and was now hovering like a flying saucer. It wobbled and yawed from side to side. It began to revolve, slowly at first, then gradually picking up speed and gyrating faster and faster—spinning and spinning—whirling and twirling—racing out of control, creating a violent maelstrom of intense pigments, distorted imagery, and otherworldly sounds and languages—its vortex was swallowing me up and making me the center of the mass of confusion. My face jiggled like rubber—my cheeks warped under the weight of the mighty g-forces pushing against them, and my baby-fine wisps of blond hair were standing on end, magnetically charged.

"Good God, I'm being torn limb from limb!" I screamed—but it was so way cooler than Laserium!

I couldn't hold it in anymore and I barfed into the galaxy. The universe spun around me, and I was hit smack in the face by my own disgorge. I heard someone laughing, and turned to see John F. Kennedy standing beside me.

"That's what I call a whirly-twirly-bird," he said, the Kennedy wit not being as adroit as I'd always imagined. "Holy shit, run for your life!" he added, and he screamed and bounded across the planetarium, chased by Lee Harvey Oswald, who was impersonating Groucho Marx. "Say the secret word," said Oswald, "and a duck will come down and reward you each with a sexy Marilyn Monroe."

"I think that crossed the fine line of good taste, don't you, Chris?" said Marilyn Monroe, standing next to me stark naked, washing down a handful of pills with a glass of champagne while Bobby Kennedy humped her from behind.

"The only thing we have to fear is Marilyn herself!"

commented Franklin Roosevelt, as he wheeled across the dome's ceiling. "Whee," he added.

"What's happening?" I shouted.

"Over there, over there, send the word over there. That the Yanks are coming. The Yanks are coming . . ." A brigade of Pillsbury Doughboys in World War II helmets was marching straight for me. I screamed and hid under my seat.

Time didn't seem to exist anymore, and yet I felt as though I had been traveling for hours and hours. I crouched under my seat, too scared to open my eyes. I had to pee really badly and I hoped we would stop at a gas station soon.

"It's okay, don't be afraid, no one's going to hurt you."

I opened my eyes and a giant vanilla ice-cream cone was in my face. It was female, I presumed, because of its bright red lipstick and long blond hair. It batted its voluptuous eyelashes at me.

I screamed again.

"Now now, calm down, sweetheart," she said, comforting me. "You're almost home. Just remember, my husband runs the place, so, word to the wise, don't cross him, and don't say anything about his sprinkles. He's sensitve, and he can be a mean bugger when he wants to be. I think maybe he has a few loose vanilla beans, if you get my drift." Then she kissed me, winked, and flew away.

I'm dying! I thought. *Somebody must have slipped me a mickey in my Carnation Instant Breakfast!*

I was hyperventilating. I was sweating. My mind was a wash, susceptible to any ludicrous suggestion. I was about to pass out, or perhaps pass on, when the au courant, histrionic bel cantos of Mozart's Symphony Number 35 in D Major persuaded me to live a little longer. How I knew it was Mozart's Symphony Number 35 in D Major I can't tell you—I just knew.

On the ceiling old photos—*daguerrotypes?*—materialized and

dematerialized in rapid succession. What were they? They were speeding by so fast. I furrowed my brow, squinted, and allowed the remaining mushy bits of my brain to recognize them as photogravures of old New York City: the Flatiron Building, the Nabisco Pork Fat and Hardtack Foundry, Madame Stuart's French chateau, *Le Turkey Mound,* and the giant statue of Nathan Bedford Forrest holding high his glorious burning cross. It all felt so familiar to me, and along with the images there now appeared a new series of words:

YOU

. . . Pictures of: the Mulberry Bend, Bandits' Roost, half-eaten pies and disoriented sea lions, Old Toothless Sally Jenkins, the nondescript brownstone . . .

ARE

Mozart's thrilling symphony building to a crescendo . . . multiple angles of Mrs. O'Leary from the killer's point of view . . . the dark alley with little Franny Rose Tiddles and Emma May Pinch . . . the killer's hands—*or were they mine?*—decorating the alley with streamers made of intestines.

HIM!

My senses were being bombarded by the loud music and the overwhelming imagery: hoisting Blue Whale's humongous body to the ceiling of the Once Around the Park room, a Mummer parade, Boss Tweed, Roosevelt, Spencer, and the beautiful Liz Smith.

The round room was now falling—falling—falling—falling . . .

YOU ARE

falling—falling—falling . . .

Now, on the ceiling, quick shots of black top hats, carpet-bags, apples, Vincent Price, Christopher Lee, Peter Cushing, Oliver Reed, and snippets of every Jack the Thwacker movie ever made, and then just as the music reached its thunderous finale, the planetarium crashed down with a deafening boom and I bounced in my seat. "Oh!" I exclaimed.

All was quiet. All was calm. All was right with the world.

On the dome I watched as the final word evaporated amidst the stars. . . .

THE THWACKER!

I gasped—*You are the Thwacker!* Somehow, despite the fact that it made no sense, I already knew I had to at least be related to the monster. I pulled out the daguerrotype marked PRIME SUS-PECT, and I stared at the bearded face, whom I was sure was a distant relative. The face I had been pondering ever since it fell out of Caleb's diary. The face I so desperately wanted to share with my friend Wendell. It was, of course—*me?*

"I wish not to hurry you, my good sir. But it *is* closing time."

My pupils dilated at the light coming from the opened door of the planetarium. I squinted at the silhouetted figure who was entreating me to exit.

I rose to my feet and stumbled towards the door, my head still a whirling dervish, an eternity of vertiginous merry-go-rounds.

"Your hat and coat, sir," said the man, who was dressed in a burgundy bellhop's uniform complete with pillbox hat.

I didn't remember bringing a coat, and certainly not a top hat, with me. I glanced down to make sure I was still wearing

my *Late Show with David Letterman* T-shirt and my *Cabin Boy* rain slicker.

"Your cane, sir." he handed me a silver-tipped walking stick.

"And your carpetbag."

"All of this is mine? Are you positive?"

"But what vexes you, my dear sir? You surely checked these articles with me when you entered." He helped me on with the coat, which fit snugly over my slicker. "I do pray you found our little celestial photoplay suitably edifying? As for myself, I feel the most laudable sections are those relating to our star of Bethlehem and the current relevance of our blessed Holy Bible even amidst the present tumultuous times in which we live." He brushed my shoulders vigorously with a short whisk broom and placed the top hat right over my *Get a Life* baseball cap. "Do you not agree, sir?"

"Huh? . . . yeah, sure. Um, hey, how do I get out of here?"

"Eighty-first is straight up the stairs and to your right. Shall I call you a hansom?"

"You can, but 'boyishly charming' is probably more accurate." I gave him my most comely smile, but he looked back at me a little fearfully and gave me a wide berth as I stumbled up the steps and out the door.

I pushed open the heavy wrought-iron gates and stepped outside. It didn't occur to me that the façade of the planetarium was no longer glass, but rather the old dark brick and iron, and there was no white sphere anymore, just the small green dome and an incidental sign welcoming visitors to "The New Hayden Celestial Conservatory."

The first thing I noticed was the rain. It was pouring. Negative ions charged the air, and my senses revived a bit amidst the breeze that rustled the leaves in the park across the street.

I stood on the corner of Eighty-first and Central Park West

receiving the full impact of the downpour, trying to decide whether or not to hail a cab to the Dakota or just to walk home, but the decision was quickly made for me, as there were no cabs to be had. Cabs always go off-duty when it rains—a phenomenon celebrated with a wink and an all-knowing smile by my good friend Wendell—but the truth is, I didn't see *any* cars on Central Park West. *Maybe they're shooting another episode of* Law & Order *tonight,* I thought.

Still a tad unstable, I began to foot it south. Right away something struck me as odd and altogether disconcerting. It was not the generous number of horse-and-buggies stationed outside the Museum of Natural History—they always congregated where tourists showed up—nor was it the pedestrians dressed in period costumes dashing for the nearest dry shelter—there could have been a turn of the century theme party in progress at Tavern on the Green—nor was it the strange fact that I was unable to discern any true colors around me—the whole city seemed tinted with a brownish-yellowish haze, as if it existed in a wash of sepia, like a living daguerrotype. Perhaps the intense E. T. show was still playing tricks on my peepers. No, my friends, it was none of those things that struck me as odd.

What was disturbing me greatly was the fact that I could see clearly all the way down to the Dakota. There were no buildings in between—nothing in the way. Where had they all gone? Where was the apartment building that blocked my view of the museum, with the big-breasted woman undressing in front of her bathroom window? To my astonishment, there were no city blocks laid out at all—only muddy rain-drenched mounds lay between my apartment and the museum.

I felt faint. Could the unimaginable have happened? Did the terrorists drop a "go back in time" dirty bomb? My knees buckled

out from underneath me, but I caught myself with the help of a lamppost.

"Do you require assistance?"

I tried to focus on the uniformed anatomy half-hidden under the black umbrella.

"I say again, sir. Do you require assistance?"

"Where's the party?" I asked, sounding a bit polluted.

"I beg your pardon?"

"The costume party!" I was trying to convince myself that I was speaking with a reveler dressed up as a Keystone Kop, but deep down I was starting to realize the truth.

"What do we have here, O'Halloran?" asked another officer approaching in the rain.

"Just a guzzler who's quaffed more than his share of the old firewater, Sergeant. Whew, he's covered in keck, that's for sure."

"Well, set him in the paddy wagon and truck 'im to the Tombs. We'll let the rich bastard sleep it off in style."

"Yessir."

"Wait a tick," said the sergeant. "Let's take a look-see in his pouch."

The officers grabbed my carpetbag.

"Hey," I said.

"Quiet now. Be still." The sergeant rifled through the satchel, ignoring my rucksack and retrieving instead a burlap bag marked MCINTOSH APPLES and stained with dried blood.

"St. Dybbuk in a blue dress! What have we here?" exclaimed the sergeant. "Check his papers."

Officer O'Halloran retrieved a wallet from the long black coat.

"Name's Chris Elliott. Resides at the nondescript brownstone at 240 East Nineteenth."

"Hey, that's not true. I live at the Dakota." I fumbled for my

personal I.D. card, but it was gone! That damned hobo must have butter-pawed it off me.

"Sergeant, before Detective Byrnes arrested Chief Spencer, was there not a housekeeper claiming the Thwacker rents a flat at that very same address?"

"If you say so."

"And what do you make of this, sir?" O'Halloran handed the sergeant the daguerrotype marked PRIME SUSPECT.

The two officers slowly turned their faces towards me.

"But you see, it can't be. I'm not from here. I live in the year 2005!"

"For crow's sake! And all the while the good chief wallows away amidst his own excrement in the Tombs, and we have the real Thwacker, right here and in our very own grip, no less. Mind you, O'Halloran, I never cared for the chief, and he's welcome to spend the rest of his life sitting in his or someone else's excrement as far as I'm concerned, but right now, the gods have seen fit to land this unfortunate in my hands. Don't you see? He's my ticket to a gold shield. Imagine it—a good one for the penny papers it is: Byrnes arrests the wrong man, and I apprehend the real Thwacker. I'm sure to get a promotion now, regardless of how much I drink and mercilessly torture handcuffed perpetrators who don't speak a lick of the Queen's English."

"Man, you really got issues, fella," I quipped.

"Cuff him and let's book him at the nineteenth."

"The hell you will," I said, and I pulled out my pepper spray and shot a blast at both cops. The flatfoots screamed and covered their eyes, and I made a dash for it, sprinting west as fast as my manly legs would carry me.

"Good God, I'm being torn from limb to limb!"
I screamed—but it was so way cooler than 'Laserium'!

Chapter the Twelfth.

In which, condemned to the past, your humble scribe encounters an up-and-coming young Larry King.

I COULD HEAR POLICE WHISTLES BEHIND ME AS I RAN AND RAN AND RAN. It would have made more sense for me to try to get back to the museum, though, knowing what I know now as I steal a few precious minutes to write amidst the clatter and confusion of the filthy basement establishment I call home, I see that it would have been futile. As it was, I was in a panic, and I instinctively sprinted toward my apartment in the Dakota.

All the while my brain was clicking resoundingly in my head (not with the usual *click click click,* but with a decidedly nineteenth-century articulation, a kind of *clanckety, clanckety, clanckety, clack*). *Had I actually gone back in time? Was the planetarium some sort of time machine? Was Mrs. Flutter setting me up to be Jack the Thwacker? Or was I really him?*

My sprinting grew more and more laborious, as with every tromp my corrective Wallabies sunk deeper and deeper into the mud and the manure. No amount of research could have prepared me for the way the city smelled. It was awful. The air was so foul as to appear brown. I have since realized that the sepia prints we refer to as daguerrotypes are in fact a form of crude

color photograph. (Maybe that's why they called it the Gilded Age?) I caught sight of a strange object growing larger in the distance—a cart with a big umbrella on top. *It was a hot dog stand!*

Pulling my collar closed, I approached the vendor cautiously. I had to find out if my fears were warranted or if I was simply mad.

"Excuse me, what year is it?" I shouted over the deluge.

"I pray, good sir, repeat yourself, for the tempest rages too clangorously to allow me to hearken to your needs satisfactorily," replied the hot dog vendor in pretty much the way any hot dog vendor in New York City would reply today. So that told me nothing.

"The year?" I shouted again, "what year is it?"

"Why, it's the year of our Lord 1882! It is. Welcome to America, my friend. You've been on the boat so long, you don't know the year? Quite daffy are you, then? You poor immigrant."

"Then it's true," I moaned.

"What is true, my good man?"

"I've traveled back in time."

The conclusion was at once horrifying as well as astounding. How did it happen? Is it possible that I was merely hallucinating? Some scientists hold that time is nothing more than an existential state of mind. Had I been toiling away so unremittingly on this book—living each day in the pages of the past—that my subconscious simply expatriated (hey, that's kind of a brilliant idea for a book, isn't it?)? I felt dizzy and I felt hungry, too.

"Um, give me one with just mustard and sauerkraut, please."

"My apologies, friend, we haven't any mustard, but that's a grand idea. I'll be certain to wise up old man Hellmann to the notion."

Then he handed me a sugar cone filled to the brim with

thick mayonnaise and topped with a dollop of steaming saur-kraut.

"That'll be two bits."

I really wanted a wiener, but I have to admit I was a tad curi-ous about the whole mayo craze, having read so much about it for so long. So I shrugged. *What the hell, you only go back in time once,* I thought, and pulled out my Diner's Club.

"Oh, did they not change your currency on Ellis Island?" the vendor asked.

Of course! He couldn't possibly know what a credit card was.

"What is it? A kluge or a geld?"

I suddenly eyed the paddy wagon wheeling its way down Cen-tral Park West. Officer O'Halloran and the sergeant were on top, whipping the horses furiously.

"I'll tell you what," said the vendor, "let this be my treat. God bless ya, friend, and remember, we were all immigrants once, but I'd lose the accent if I were you. *Arrivaderci!*" I thanked the kind man and asked his name so that I might send him a gift at a later date.

"Larry King," he replied.

I attempted to lick the mayo as I ran, but alas, I was only able to swallow one complete mouthful before the rain washed it away—but I'm happy to report that it was a mouthful of sheer oily delight!

Even as my body quivered with adrenaline, I was willfully en-thralled by my new incogitable environment. After all, this was the period in New York City history that captivated me the most. The majestic architecture, the cultivated manners, the simplicity of life, the disregard for one's fellow man, the plagues, the ram-pant corruption, the unmitigated racism, and the uncontrollable violence—all the things our grandparents called "the good old

days"—and all the things that pressed my imagination into over-time when I would sit in my ex-wife's clothing and daydream about what it might be like to actually stroll down a street in nine-teenth-century New York. It was all now an exciting reality that was trying to kill me. Lucky for me, I was an expert on the era.

For instance, as I ran, I noticed teepees dotting the sur-rounding landscape. This was no surprise, because although in time this territory would grow to be the fashionable Upper West Side, in 1882 it was still populated by a handful of Dakota Indi-ans (hence the name of the building I lived in. I bet you didn't know *that,* did you?). The Dakotas carved out a meager exis-tence producing souvenirs for the tourists, like "I Simply Adore NY" top hats made out of dried corn husks, or "I Am Quite Fond of NY" snuffboxes made out of dried corncobs, or statues of Nathan Bedford Forrest made out of dried cornbread, and, of course, pig-bladder condoms embossed with the mayor's endur-ing toothy smile, and, along the side, the famous Teddy truism: "In this country we have no place for hyphenated Americans."

"Damn it all to hell in a handbasket—plus five!" I bewailed as the muck swallowed up one of my Wallabies—the one with the extra-thick gum heel. Too bad, for there was no time to waste.

Henry J. Hardenbergh designed the Dakota as well as the Plaza Hotel, the University Club, and a radical new restaurant plan that would become the Popeye's Fried Chicken in Times Square. To describe the ten-story masterpiece simply as grand would be like calling a Roman aqueduct "just another water park." Its gothic edifice was, and still is, accentuated by a giant arched entryway, which opens onto a central courtyard. Hard-enbergh garnished the building with a fanfare of niches, nooks, crannies, alcoves, recesses, and cubbyholes. Its myriad of bay windows played host to the best views of Central Park, and in 1882, if one stood on its upper balconies and looked north, one

might catch a glimpse of the bombastic, lockjawed wildlife that grazed freely in the open meadows that would one day become Greenwich, Connecticut.

The rain had let up a bit when I finally rounded the corner on Seventy-second Street, and I stealthily ducked into either a crevice or a cranny, I can't remember which. Peering out, I observed a legion of hansom cabs discharging elegantly apparelled ladies and gentlemen. Costumed porters stood on the curbside checking each arriving guest's invitation. I resolved to gain entrance to the Dakota by blending in amongst them. So I bundled up my coat, adjusted my top hat, and did my very best not to hobble, as I was missing my right shoe.

"Hold on there, fella. What can we do for you?" Two burly doormen were standing in my way.

"Why, I'm just going up to my apartment, gentlemen," I bluffed.

"And what apartment would that be, sir?"

"That would be apartment 8S, as if it's any concern of yours. Are you new?"

"Oh, 8S, is it? Then you're attending Madame August Belmont's black tie dinner, are you?"

"Huh? But of course! Madame August Belmont's black tie dinner in apartment 8S. Where else would I be going? Are you . . . daffy?"

"My apologies, sir. May we see your invite card?"

"My invite card?"

"Yes sir."

"Well, you see, my invite card is not with me. It's with my wife. Perhaps you've heard of her, a certain . . . Mistress Randolph P. . . . Wendle . . . bopper III . . . Ltd. And she's already upstairs. So if you'll excuse me . . ."

"That would make you *Mr.* Wendlebopper then?"

"Yes . . . *Lord* Wendlebopper, that's correct. That's me."

The two doormen exchanged smirks and looked down at my shoeless foot.

"All right, Lord Wendlebopper, why don't you just turn around and bop back from whence you came. Eh!?"

They took me by the arms and ushered me away from the entrance.

"Wait, you don't understand. I really do live here. I just don't live here right now, but I am gonna live here in the year 2005 . . . I just stopped by to see if the super had painted the living room yet!"

The doormen shared a hearty laugh at my expense, and I limped dolefully back down Seventy-second Street.

Denied entrance to my own building! How humiliating!

My apartment had been in our family for many years, but I didn't remember a Madame Belmont in the family tree.

At a side entrance, boys in white aprons were unloading boxes of champagne from a buggy and carrying them down to the Dakota's freight elevator. I could hear police whistles and the rattle of the paddy wagon approaching, and I realized I had no choice. So I gathered up my nerve, tightened my buttcheeks, picked up a box, and confidently carried it into the basement.

I put my box on top of the others in a dumbwaiter and, when no one was looking, climbed into the back of the lift. The door slid shut and I could feel the elevator going up.

"Make haste, Mary," said a man's voice. "They're requesting more Blanc de Blanc."

The dumbwaiter door opened and a craggy little old lady in a maid's uniform began to haul the boxes out.

"Yeah, yeah, I know. Hold on to your wet willies," she said. "They've been downing the bubbly all night. They can take a little break."

The feisty hag looked to be about twice my age. Her voice was shrill, and she was not particularly attractive—in fact, you might even say she was repugnant looking, like something out of a Fellini movie, and yet there was something about her that seemed almost . . . human. Or at least like something that was raised by humans. When she pulled the last box away, she found me cowering in the back of the lift.

"Hey! What's this shit? Who the hell are you?"

"Ma'am, I'm an actor," I whispered. "I used to live here. I mean I do live here. . . . I mean I *will* live here . . . look, I'm in terrible trouble. The police think I've done something that I swear I'm innocent of. I need a place to hide. Just for a little bit, so that I can figure out what to do. Please help me."

She sized me up. Planting her hands on her hips, she ogled me up and down, weighing the pros and cons of abetting a fugitive. There really wasn't anything in it for her. (At least that's what I thought at the time.) But I sensed that she understood the panic and helplessness consuming me. Either that, or she was just a horny old chambermaid from 1882.

In later years, penning her memoirs from her isolation cell on North Brother Island in the East River, she wrote of our encounter:

His face possessed the doltish countenance
of a dead blowfish.
His head appeared oddly small for his
porcine body, which was the consistency of wet dough or
perhaps semirigid porridge, and his words, for the most
part, comprised in their totality a treasure
trove of unmitigated twaddle.
Still there was something about the
beef-witted saphead that kind of got the

old juices going again if you know what I mean
and I wanted nothing more than to pop
his cherry right then and there!

"Okay, handsome, at ease," she said. "I won't give ya up. Just put this on and help me with this shit." She tossed me a white apron, which I tied around my overcoat. I began to unpack the bottles of champagne with her.

"Mary, who in the blazes is this ragamuffin?" inquired another domestic.

"Shut your big trapper, Claudine, and mind you're own *P*'s and *Q*'s. The kid's with me, got it?"

Claudine backed away, and the old maid leaned in close to me. "They won't bother ya now—not now that they know you belongs to me!" She cracked open a yellow, rotten-toothed smile and I nearly fainted at the smell of her nineteenth-century breath.

I glanced around my kitchen. It was indeed *my* kitchen! It looked almost exactly the same except for the cabinets; they weren't painted my happy purple anymore—they were the original ugly polished hazelwood with inlaid mahogany. And in place of my jocular Mae West was a gaudy Sarah Bernhardt phone—her false wooden leg being the receiver. (There's just no accounting for taste.) Chefs, butlers, and maids were scurrying all around and orders were flying:

"More caviar!"

"More poached salmon!"

"More corn dogs!"

"Madame Rutherford requests a brushman to cleanse her palette before the next course!"

"Does anyone know how to administer the Herr Heimlich?

Commodore Wells is choking most egregiously on a squirrel claw."

"Here, sexy, take this to the mixologist in the butler's pantry," the old gorgon said, batting her goopy eyelashes at me and handing me a bottle of champagne.

"Yes, ma'am."

"'Ma'am?' 'Ma'am' is my mother. The name's Mary."

She gave me a wink and a smack on my ass, which I have to admit made me feel dirty, like a cheap dime-store male hooker (which, by the way, is not the worst feeling in the world). *If Mary is in her eighties,* I thought as I proceeded to the pantry, *how the hell old is her mother?*

The mixologist took the bottle from me with a puzzled look and carried it into *my* dining room! I peered through the opening in the swinging door and got a look at the excessive affair.

I was immediately pissed off at the re-, or should I say *pre-*, decorating Ms. Belmont had done to my dining room, even though I knew this was in the past, long before I was even born and before the apartment was ever mine. (Figure that one out.) My avocado-colored wall-to-wall shag carpeting was gone, exposing the actual wood floor, and the giant mural depicting me as Percival in a suit of shiny armor astride a white two-headed horse was also missing, as was my Sharper Image air purifier— and believe me, they really could have used it. The place stank like whatever they're always cooking down at Tad's.

On either side of a long table elegantly set with fine china and Baccarat crystal sat at least thirty prominent and powerful New Yorkers from 1882. I recognized them immediately from my research: John Jacob Astor, William L. Shermerhorn, J. P. Morgan, Cornelius Vanderbilt, Archibald King, W. C. Rhinelander, and Robert Goulet, among others. The women were all beautifully

attired in satin and chintz gowns with diamond brooches and wristlets that dazzled so that they blinded the eye, while the gentlemen were clad in tuxedos and wore on their heads laurels of woven olive branches. (Okay, what*ever,* fellas.) Above the table, an ethereal woman, costumed like an angel, swung back and forth on a trapeze, plucking a lute and singing "I Dream of Jeannie with the Light Brown Hair."

As the butler made his rounds dilatorily, refilling their champagne glasses, I couldn't resist eavesdropping on some genuine nineteenth-century high-society repartee.

Ward McAlester commented on how "languid and flatulent" this year's Fourth of July fireworks display was, and Mrs. William Duncan, always one to agree, concurred, adding that she felt the display to have been quite "jejeune." Old Henry J. Clews observed that "one day, the horrid rabble of uneducated mongoloids would rise up again to protest the draft!" This elicited a tempered titter from the table, compelling his young wife, Lucy Worthington Clews, to lean over and gently remind him that there was no draft in place at present, and that the Civil War had been over for almost twenty years. "Quite so," he said, "quite so. Well played, my dear, well played!" At that, Madame Belmont discreetly signaled the mixologist to cut off Mr. Clews's Blanc de Blanc supply. Newly received New York socialite Sallie Hargous relayed in minute detail her arduous recovery in Newport after being overcome with the vapors upon witnessing a homeless man urinating on the flowers in front of her Fifth Avenue mansion.

I had just about fallen asleep standing up when suddenly Cornelius Vanderbilt and John Jacob Astor rose from the table to stretch their legs conveniently close to the pantry door.

"Is everything in place?" asked Vanderbilt in a low voice.

"According to Tweed, it is," replied Astor.

"Everyone has their headdresses and their banjos?"

"As far as I know."

"Is it true that the earth goddess has been located?"

"She has."

"And the Book of Names?"

"Safe."

"Then this shall be a true Saturnalia," said Vanderbilt, and the two clanked their champagne glasses.

"To midnight and the castle on Vista Crag," toasted Astor.

"To the death of the earth goddess," added Vanderbilt, "and to the rise of the Fancy Brigade!"

Astor smirked and said sarcastically, "Hail to Erce."

Vanderbilt chuckled.

"Yes indeed, 'hail to Erce,' . . . shall we say . . . for the last time?"

The two threw back their champagne and returned to the table. I felt a icy chill run down my spine and a tingling at the base of my neck, as well as a fluttering in my stomach—all signs which usually indicated that I was about to have diarrhea. But I tried not to think about that, and would advise you to do the same.

I was raised in New York City, so I knew exactly what the castle on Vista Crag was—it was Belvedere Castle in Central Park. That was where the death ritual would take place at midnight. Suddenly I realized why the fickle finger of fate had ferried me back to 1882—it was to deliver that very message to my friends Caleb and Liz. I began to rush out of the pantry—

"Hey, where's the fire? Besides down in my bloomers?" cracked Mary, grabbing my wrist.

"Nowhere, but I have to get out of here. I have to go help some people."

"Hey, hold the phone, pretty boy!"

She was quite strong for a crusty old crone, and she yanked me into the back stairwell.

"I'm on a five, Claudine, if anyone asks," she shrieked and then closed the door behind us.

She stood staring at me for an awkward moment. *What the hell does she want from me?* I wondered. Then she leaned up against the wrought-iron banister, pulled out her pouch of tobacco, and rolled herself a fag.

"Listen Mary, I want to thank you for not screaming when you saw me, but I really have to get going."

"You know," she said, licking the edge of her cigarette in a deliberate manner, "I've seen some pretty ungrateful shit in my day, but you take the cake."

"What? No! I'm very grateful—didn't you just hear me say thank you? But I have to hurry."

She struck a match on her butt and then lit her cigerette.

"Did you ever hear me ask why you were running from the coppers?"

"Um, I don't think so."

"S'pose it's 'cause I's already seen this?"

She handed me a piece of paper with a crude drawing of a bearded, bald man with lots of pimples on his face that bore a striking resemblance to yours truly. The caption read:

Imbecile Wanted in Connection to Thwacker Murders! Chief Spencer may not be the killer!

"Wow, they sure get these out fast," I said. "It's almost as if they were expecting me. It's Kafkaesque . . . or burlesque, I'm not sure which."

Mary took a long pull off her cig and then blew the smoke in my face.

"I wonder if I should turn you in now or later? Mr. *Thwacker* man."

"You wouldn't do that, would you? I'm innocent."

"Ah honey, we're all innocent. Who knows? Maybe I've already notified them. Maybe I haven't. Maybe they're on their way . . . or then again, maybe they're not."

"What do you want?"

"Oh, I think you know, kiddo. It may have been a long time, but the old dog-eared oven mitt never forgets."

"Eeew!"

She tossed her cigarette down and stamped it out.

"Now you're going to give me a proper thank-you, understand?"

She forcefully pulled me to her and planted a slobbering kiss on my lips. I tried to pull away but she was too strong for me. I thought about that movie where Demi Moore rapes Michael Douglas—but somehow this wasn't the same. Probably because this chick was way old. She took a breath and coughed in my face and then dove into my mouth again. Then she pushed me against the wall and hiked up her dress.

"Okay cowboy, drop them trou!"

I felt woozy and nauseated. I began to gag.

"You gotta be jollying me!" she spewed.

"It's just a dry heave, I'm okay, I'm okay. I think I'm okay . . . wait . . . no, it's not dry! It's Mr. 3 Musketeers, with a dollop of mayo and sauerkraut!"

"Oh Christ!"

I was about to vomit when suddenly a commotion broke out in the kitchen—lots of boisterous, angry voices bellowing on

top of each other: "What is the meaning of this?" . . . "Why, this is an outrage!". . . "Police! Everyone stay where you are!". . . "But we haven't had our créme brulée yet!" . . . "I was just about to try the Egyptian quail." . . . "Don't worry, citizens, we're just making a quick arrest!"

"Thanks a *lot,* Mary!" I said wrathfully as I sprinted for the back stairs.

"I've got some spirits of camphor if you need 'em, Thwacker man," she shouted after me. The back door burst open and a battery of policemen rushed the rear stairwell. Mary pulled out a long kitchen knife and started swinging it to and fro.

"Hold it right there!" shouted a cop.

"Up your ass, flatfoot!" shrieked Mary, and she flung her body into the wall of blue uniforms. I stopped on a lower landing and watched the skirmish from a safe vantage point. I didn't like the old crone, but I didn't want her to get hurt on my account.

"You're under arrest, for knowingly spreading a communicable disease, Mallon," announced another officer as he took hold of Mary's wart-covered arm. It was only then that I realized the cops weren't there for me.

"The hell I am, you piece of shit!" she yowled, and then she squealed like a pig. "I'm innocent. I've never been sick a day in my life! I ain't going back to isolation."

It took five husky officers to finally subdue the foul-mouthed old biddy, and as she was dragged away kicking and screaming, she called down to the stairwell where I was hiding, "Welcome to the world of typhoid fever, Mr. Thwacker Man!"

The back door slammed shut and the echoes of the violent arrest reverberated down the marble stairwell. I stood alone breathing heavily beneath a flickering gas lamp. *What the hell just happened?*

"Mary Mallon?!" I said to myself. "Good God! Typhoid Mary!" And then, as if on cue, I began to cough.

"Oh, no, no, no, tell me it's not true!"

I coughed and spit and furiously tried to wipe her gross slaver from out of my mouth. After a moment of sheer hysteria, in which I lost complete control and pounded my head against the wall, danced a jig, and spoke in Appalachian tongues, it suddenly occurred to me that I may have brought my amoxicillin—the powerful antibiotic that I took whenever my plantar warts flared up. I patted down my slicker and quickly located the vial. So grateful was I to find it that I gave it a long and sensuous kiss.

"Oh thank you, thank you, thank you," I lovingly repeated over and over and then popped a few tablets.

I felt better immediately. I may have been lost in a new and strange world with only one shoe to my name, but now I had one up on the Victorians—*Bring on your diseases, your plagues, and your pestilence, you unwashed masses you, 'cause I got twenty-first-century miracle drugs! And ain't nothin' gonna hurt me now!*

Then I skipped happily down the back stairs and slipped out the Dakota's side door. Before I knew it, I had footed it all the way down to Columbus Circle, and I stopped at the base of the explorer's statue to catch my breath. It was quite calm and quite peaceful there. I was amazed by how quiet the night was. If not for the occasional clomping of a horse, or the mooing of a cow, or the screaming of a battered wife, you could almost hear a pin drop. Gradually I became aware of faint piano music washing melodiously over me. It was a familiar ragtime tune. I recognized it as "Solace" by Scott Joplin, because I've seen *The Sting* like a gazillion times. It's one of my favorite movies. (But I still don't get why the F.B.I. was so happy at the end.)

I knew there used to be a popular dance club somewhere on Columbus Circle, and at that very moment, prompted by a bit

of nineteenth-century indigenous wisdom, I turned to my right, and there directly across the street was Resnick's Happy Jangle-Bangle and Mince-About Hall. My heart leaped. Time was of the essence, but I might never have another opportunity to experience the excitement and electricity that the celebrated Resnick's was famous for. *Don't I deserve to indulge in just a little sightseeing while I'm here in 1882?* I thought.

Resnick's was the legendary establishment that made stars out of the likes of Sophie Tucker, Al Jolson, and Charlie Chaplin (not them, but the likes of them). It was 1882's Studio 54, and there is absolutely no current-day equivalent to it except for maybe the Roxy, or the China Club, or Crobar, or Club New York, Drinkland, Plaid (formerly Spa), Club Capitale, and My Momma's Hatbox.

I also felt an incredible urge to move—nay, to dance!—because I'm really a dancer at heart. That's what I love to do the most—to dance! (Sound familiar?) *What a thrill it would be to boogie down with some nineteenth-century babes,* I thought. Checking my watch, which had automatically switched over to 1882 time, I saw that it was only ten o'clock—two hours before the death ritual. I had time.

What I didn't have was money. For certain, Resnick's wouldn't accept my Diners Club, and I had to have some bling on hand in case I got lucky with the historically accurate ladies, so I resolved that there was only one thing to do—beseech my ever-loving ass off!

This was going to be very difficult for me because I'd never asked anybody for anything in my life, so I wasn't exactly sure how one begs.

"Father, can you spare a quarter for an old altar boy? I'm a Catholic. I'm also a vet."

"Are you indeed, sir?" asked the kindly old priest who stopped to aid the recumbent unfortunate in the single shoe. "I pray then,

tell me what regiment you were in? And who was your commanding officer? And in what great battles where you victorious? As a matter of fact, what side where you on? North or South? I'm quite curious."

I sensed a bit more than curiosity in the old holy man's 'tude.

"Um . . . no, see, I'm a veterinarian," I said. "Just a few ha'pennies would do, if you please."

"It would not 'please,'" snapped the kindly priest, now turning into a meanly priest. "You, sir, are a scoundrel! There are many without means these days. But one needn't prey on the generosity of others. One must learn to pull one's own boots up by one's own straps. It is your kind of scourge that is ruining this grand city. You will be accorded nothing from me but a fine good evening to you, sir!" And he stamped off.

How could I be ruining the city? I just got here! I decided to try a different tactic.

"Spare some change?" I pleaded to an approaching couple. "I'm a hungry little orphan waif." I extended my palm.

"Hold your nose, Lucretia," advised the man. "The odors of the lower class are made up of tiny spores that, once embedded in the nostrils, can cause great damage to a woman's reproductive system."

"Obadiah, heavens no!" exclaimed Lucretia, pinching her nose with her fingers.

"A fine good evening to you, sir," was all Obadiah proffered as he tipped his hat and blinked away my plea.

This pattern continued as New Yorker after New Yorker either overlooked me altogether or fired off some virulent commentary as they passed by. I suddenly understood this was how it felt to be poor and homeless like so many of the indigent people I used to give a wide berth to on the streets back home, and I determined right then and there that when I returned to the twenty-first

century, I was going to make a real concerted effort to at least smile and nod before giving them a wide berth.

Of course I knew my next idea was probably morally wrong, but having lived in the nineteenth century for no more than an hour—and already being a suspected serial killer—I thought, *How could a little insignificant mugging make things worse?* I was getting nowhere with this begging ploy. Once I got back to the present it would all be history. ("It would all be history," I like that one.)

I desperately needed money, not just to buy a dance card to Resnick's but also to buy another shoe, and to eat, and for cab fare, and for the essentials, and . . . well, I could go on and on justifying it, the point is that I was well within my rights as a novice time-traveler, and I have a clear conscience.

I pulled my *Late Show* T-shirt over my mouth, pushed down the two hats I was wearing, and then waited, lurking in the shadows. It felt naughty, but it was also kind of sexy acting out everyone's secret fantasy of being a New York City mugger. That is everyone's secret fantasy, isn't it? It's not just mine, right?

It didn't take long before a well-heeled older couple strolled by. I waited for the opportune moment and then leaped out and promptly slipped and fell.

"Okay, hold it right there!" I said in a gruff voice.

"Yes, of course. Are you in need of assistance, sir?" asked the man.

"What? No! What's with you Victorians? No, I don't need assistance, I need your money!" (I was pretending that I had a gun in my pocket.)

The man grew perplexed.

"My money, sir? Why, my monies, if that is what you are referring to, are invested in the soon-to-arrive coal-powered buggy,

the steam-powered toaster, and the newfangled kerosene-powered home washer machine."

"Take a bit of advice from someone who knows: you might want to check out General Electric's portfolio. I wouldn't steer you wrong, friend." I smirked, trying not to betray how pleased I was with my rapier wit.

"Sir, you insult me! I favor not the 'within trading,' and I would think you wise to go peddle your motley-fool tips to some other unscrupulous pigeon. Now if you will excuse us, we bid you a very fine good evening, sir."

I rolled my eyes.

"Yeah, yeah, but before you go, let me have your money!"

"Phineas," said the lady, "I do believe this gentlemen means to filch us!"

"Not filch you, lady. *Mug* you! The term is 'to mug.' You don't filch somebody, you mug them. Remember that!"

"I only have two bits," said the man, his hands shaking as he passed me the change.

"That will do fine, Phineas," I said. "Now, this never happened, understand? It was just a dream. Believe me, I wouldn't have done this unless I had to. I'm a nice guy and when I get situated in . . . a sweatshop or a street gang or something . . . I'll send it back to you. Now be on your way . . . and . . . and . . . a fine good evening to you both."

The couple hurried off, but before they were gone, Phineas turned back and tipped his hat. "And a fine good evening to you as well, sir," he reaffirmed.

It would be recorded that at 10:00 PM on August 26th, 1882, Phineas T. Titinger and his wife, Obedience "Beebee" Titinger, were robbed at point of pistol by a new breed of criminal—and I'm proud to report that on that very date, thanks to me, the

newfangled term "mugger" entered the New York City vernacular for the very first time in history. Actually, as no one had ever robbed anyone in quite that fashion before, it's possible that I even started the whole mugging craze.

That went so well that I thought, *One more couldn't hurt. I mean, just to have something left over to try to get a good honest start on. I mean, since I've already gone and become a mugger and everything, I might as well make a night of it.* I crouched in the bushes again, waiting for another hapless passerby. It wasn't long before a man came along, walking rather nervously, wearing a cloak and top hat, and carrying a cane and a bag. I could not make out his features, but I knew immediately who it was. Even his characteristic don't-mind-me-just-stealthily-avoiding-the-cops creep was like mine. Then I saw his bag—his carpetbag—and I was sure.

Did we resemble each other? Perhaps he was bald with a beard and had pimples as well. I only knew that if I were to prove my innocence, I would certainly have to produce the real Thwacker, so I resolved to follow the mysterious man in the top hat to whatever sinister end awaited us.

I resolved to follow the mysterious man to
whatever sinister end awaited us.

Chapter the Thirteenth.

*In which our hero escapes, a parley
is set, an ally is murdered,
and a tree grows in Brooklyn.*

A BLOCK NORTH OF CITY HALL SAT THE HALL OF JUSTICE—OR, AS IT WAS more commonly known, the Tombs. Built to house no more than one hundred prisoners at a time, by 1882 it held over five hundred thousand inmates, most of whom were compelled to spend their days stacked naked (as there was no room for clothing) like pancakes, one on top of the other, in commodious six-by-six cells. The design of the exterior of the stone structure was based on a steel engraving of an actual Egyptian tomb, and the interior was inspired by a steel engraving of Oscar Wilde's bachelor pad in the fashionable bailiwick of East London.

The inmates were assigned cells befitting their crimes. For instance, the top tier hosted those suspected of "asshead misdeeds," such as laundering someone else's clothes, card counting at tarot tables, making cross-eyes at a fancy lady, and not washing one's hands after "tossing the raw pork." The second tier was reserved for far more serious transgressions, such as not moving up in line at the bank, finger-brushing one's teeth, and voting consistently for the Green Party. Finally, the bottom tier incarcerated those accused of practicing Christian improvisational comedy, unlicensed

gynecologists, and Jack the Jolly Thwacker suspects (of which there was only one). It was there in a private little cell that Caleb sat on his bunk reflecting on the strange events that had deposited him into such a dismal predicament.

Poof!

Suddenly there was a puff of smoke. Out of it stepped Harry Houdini and Bess. All three tiers of inmates commenced to cheer and applaud.

"What in the Jack be nimble, Jack be quick, is going on?" asked Caleb, grasping the cold bars of his cell.

"Never fear, my good man. I've come to release you! For if any mortal walking terra firma today could render your deliverance from the unassailable Hall of Justice, it is I, the great Houdini!"

Again cheers issued from every cell in the block as the prisoners craned their necks to get a good view of the show through their bars. They were used to more mediocre entertainment, like perhaps a hymn or two from the Sisters of Mercy, or a second-rate Punch and Judy act, or at best a convict rodeo. So to have Houdini perform for them was a particularly uncommon treat.

"You're going to rescue me? Why? I know that you and Professor Archibald Campion are most assuredly the Thwacker! I have no doubt of it."

"You are wrong, sir," blustered Houdini, as he theatrically doffed his shiny robe and handed it to his lovely assistant Bess. Then he leaned into Spencer's bars, cupped his hands around his mouth, and whispered, "Archie just designs my illusions. That's all. But keep that under your hat."

He stepped back, again the unabashed showman.

"And now ladies and gentlemen . . . oh, excuse me, I mean . . . and now gentlemen and gentlemen, I will perform for you my first miraculous effectuation, if I may. Bess?"

Bess held a sign reading THE GREAT NEEDLEPOINT ILLUSION and the convicts all clapped.

"If he's gonna get me out of here, why doesn't he just do it?" Spencer whispered through the bars to Bess.

"This is the only way he knows how. He can't perform without an audience." Caleb gave her a puzzled look. "I know, I know, you don't have to tell me—it's crazy! Try having sex with the guy. Sorry, but you're not up until the big finale."

Houdini took a long gulp of water and then cleared his throat.

"Bess, may I have a needle, some thread, a piece of fabric, and some stuffing, if you please!" She handed him the items he requested and slowly, one by one, he swallowed the objects, making a buffoonish show of how each one tasted. Then he buckled over and started gagging and retching so violently as to alarm even Caleb. After ten seconds, he regurgitated a small throw pillow which had on its front an exquisitely rendered needlepoint portrait of a certain young police chief.

The incarcerated rabble went crazy, clanking their tin cups on their bars as Houndini took a bow.

"This should afford your summer house a trifle more betterment, Chief!" he said, flashing his gleaming white smile and tossing the pillow through the bars to Caleb.

"Yeah, that's sensational . . . but . . ."

"And now, I shall need a volunteer." He walked to the cell directly adjacent to Caleb's, laid his hands on the padlock, and without any effort whatsoever, unlocked the door. A bewildered unlicensed gynecologist shuffled out.

"Hey, I'm right here! Open *my* cell!" complained Spencer. "I have lives to save, you know."

"Patience, patience, my dear Chief. I'm getting to you."

"Now sir, will you be so kind as to bind me in this regulation

crazed person's straitjacket please." The inmate accommodated the athletic magician.

"And now please anchor my ankles to the chain that you see on the floor there, if you will be so kind." Again the inmate obliged him.

"Come on, come on," moaned Caleb.

"My friends, you are all fortunate enough to witness, for the very first time anywhere, the amalgamation of two of my most perilous and conspicuous feats—the Straitjacket Escape and the Metamorphosis!"

Caleb clapped his palms flaccidly. "Okay, okay, wheee! You're gonna escape from a straitjacket . . . blasé, blasé, blasé. Please, I implore you, hurry up. There are lives in peril."

Bess began to tug hard on a rope and the magician slowly rose about twenty feet into the air. There he hung, suspended upside down in the center of the cell block.

His captive audience whistled and stamped their feet.

Houdini wiggled and writhed, contorting his sinewy body in an exhaustive battle against the stubborn straitjacket when suddenly . . .

Poof! A puff of smoke and he vanished.

"Lord, how did he do that?" "Where did he go, Lord?" "Lordy, what just happened?" "Good Lord, I must be seeing visions!" "Lordy Almighty, maybe Houdini is the good Lordy himself!" etc. etc.

Poof! He reappeared, now on the main floor in front of Caleb's cell, still struggling in the confines of the constricting jacket.

"Damn thing may have licked me this time, Chiefy," said Houdini. Before Caleb could respond . . .

Poof! He dematerialized again. Then . . .

Poof! He was back! His head was now sticking out of the drain in Caleb's cell.

"Forget the straitjacket, how the hell do I get out of this?"

Poof! Another puff of smoke and "Where did he go? Where is he? What the? Who the? When the?"

"Up there!" shouted a convict, and everyone looked up to see Caleb, now in the straitjacket, dangling from the chain twenty feet above the floor. Then . . .

Poof! Caleb was back in his cell.

"Do you purchase them by the pack or roll them yourself, Chief Spencer?" Houdini was now sitting nonchalantly cross-legged on the table in Caleb's cell. He was wearing a silk smoking jacket and ascot and was puffing away on a cigarette.

"I prefer to roll them myself," the magician commented as he regarded his cigarette with curiosity. "Saves money, and improves concentration." Caleb stepped towards him.

"Mister Houdini, I am in a terrible hurry. The Thwacker could strike again at any—"

Poof! Houdini evaporated in a billow of smoke.

And now Houdini reappeared, back dangling from the chain in midair, squirming once more to jerk free from his tenacious bindings.

"I'm dreadfully sorry, gentlemen," he said. "I don't believe I can get out of it this time!" And then he winked slyly.

The convicts all laughed uproariously and applauded.

"Ta-da!" voiced Bess—not a very convincing stand-in for an orchestra.

The whole cell block rocked with boisterous excitement.

Caleb just shook his head in frustration, picked up the burning cigarette left behind by the sorcerer, and sighed. He plopped back down on his cot and smoked. It was undoubtedly going to be a long while before Houdini got to the "big finale."

He dozed off, sleeping fitfully as Houdini sawed Bess in half, escaped from a tank full of piranhas, and swallowed and

regurgitated an entire safe. Caleb was just about to lose his mind, when suddenly his cell door popped open.

"Ta-da," said Bess.

"Ta-da? That's it?" After all the fanfare, Caleb was exasperated. "That's the whole finale?"

Houdini said, "It *is* just a simple lock, Caleb. I'm surpised you couldn't pick it yourself."

"Why you—" But Caleb collected himself, remembering his mission. "I'll be on my way now, then. Thank you both kindly for your 'assistance.'"

Suddenly the iron doors to the cell block opened and in marched Detective Thomas Byrnes. Houdini and Bess vanished in a puff of smoke before Byrnes could even register their presence. The place burst out in whistles, hoots, and catcalls, as if a naked woman had just walked in. The officious Byrnes halted and peered coldly about with an expression that clearly registered "Quiet down or I'll have you all put on half rations of creamed suet," and the jail hushed to a dead silence.

"What on earth is going on here, Caleb? Why is your cell door open?"

"I'm leaving, Byrnes. I've got a crime to solve."

"I should think not. I know what you're up to with this other Thwacker business. The Ice Cream was in my office with one of those posters they've been putting up everywhere. He wanted me to release you, but I didn't agree. It all seems too convenient, if you ask me."

"What seemed too convenient? What posters?"

"As if you did not know already. Moments after I made a move to arrest you, they appeared everywhere, as if they had been prepared in a warehouse for just such an occasion." Byrnes handed one to Caleb. "It's clearly fake. No one's head could possibly be that small."

"I haven't seen these. Who is putting them up?"

"Why, your associates, of course. The enemies of the 'secret or-ganization' that you kept refering to in your letters to the *Evening Post*. Quite ingenious, to fabricate a criminal in order to instigate a takeover of this fair city's philanthropic society of Mummers."

"What on earth are you talking about?"

"It took me a long time to put the pieces together. I followed the trail to one Phossy Phil, an informant with a most particu-lar deformity—"

"Yes, yes, I know all about the jaw."

"Ha! I knew you did. That was a test. For, you see, there the trail grew cold—cold as the clammy hand of death, I might say. For it seemed you had already taken care of him. You might have gotten away with it, too, if you had not, in the madness brought on by your bloodthirsty rage, been so careless as to leave this be-hind." He handed Caleb a small, white, sticky piece of paper:

HI MY NAME IS
Police Chief Caleb Spencer

"Byrnes, you idiot."

"I still might not have been able to put it all together, but for-tunately I received a visit from the esteemed boss of Tammany Hall."

"Tweed."

"Yes, he put it all together for me. The Fancy Brigade, you see, is a radical faction of the Mummers, which is planning to take them over and transform them from a force of good into a force of greed and domination. Fortunately, however, I have their leader right here."

"Byrnes, you've been tricked. I don't have the time to explain now, but if you just let me—"

Byrnes drew his pistol. "You're not going anywhere, Spencer. You've defiled the good name of this department and of good detectives everywhere. You have dragged the hem of the good lady Decency's dress through the muck of—"

"Oh for heaven's sake," said Houdini's voice. A puff of smoke exploded in Byrnes's hand, and suddenly Caleb was holding his pistol.

"What manner of devilry?"

There was another puff of smoke and Byrnes was suddenly gagged. The cell erupted with applause and catcalls. Then another puff of smoke found Byrnes hanging upside down from the ceiling of Caleb's cell, secured in the straitjacket.

"Thank you, sir," called Caleb to the disembodied voice. "Now, if I only had my mobile phone—"

Another puff of smoke found the mobile phone in Caleb's hand. A final puff produced his nightstick and .32.

"Perhaps Liz has left me a message."

Caleb pulled out a long ticker tape communiqué and began to read it. But it wasn't from Liz.

Hello? Chief Spencer? Oh . . . I hate these damned machines . . . um . . . I am unable to reach Miss Smith, so as per her request, I am contacting you instead. My name is Tex—I'm a friend. Miss Smith entrusted me with the Book of Names and I have been doing much deciphering of it. It seems that all of New York's influential patriarchs belong to one brigade or another of the secret society of Mummers and they are involved in a deadly business. The book tells where the death ritual will take place. It is to happen at midnight at . . . errrr, ahhhh . . . something . . . in my back . . . a knife . . . I think . . . maybe a fork . . . definately not a spoon! . . . . possibly a hatchet. . . . I'm dying, I am . . . Chief

Spencer, I fear Miss Smith is to be made the sacrifice at the death ceremony . . . ow . . . bullet in my head . . . I'm going fast . . . please save Liz Smith! . . . and tell her thank you from me. Those were the best darn nachos I ever had!

And then the message abruptly ended.

"I'm sorry about this, Byrnes," Caleb said as he left. "But it's for your own good."

Outside on the Tombs's steps, Caleb found Houdini and Bess standing by the street. He quickly loaded his pistol. "Okay, I don't have time to play games. I need answers and I need them now!"

"I can't tell you much," said Houdini. "Campion designs my tricks and in return I visit him and keep him apprised of any Mummer activities . . . parades, conventions, that sort of thing."

"Why? What does he care what they do?"

"I don't know. He's a strange man, not the most pleasant person in the world, but a brillliant thinker. He has me over a barrel because he knows the secrets to all my tricks. So I do what he asks me. But if he's the Thwacker, I assure you he's been getting no assistance from me. On that I give you my word, sir."

"Well, I didn't really believe that you could be involved," said Caleb. "I mean, you're a celebrity, and everyone knows that celebrities don't kill people. But I was hoping that if I put pressure on you, you would tell me where I could find Campion."

"I swear, I don't know. But he wanted me to deliver this to you." Houdini handed Caleb an envelope. "Best of luck to you, Chief Spencer, and I hope you can save Liz Smith—I enjoy her column. I would help, but we have a midnight show. So until we meet again . . ."

Then he took hold of Bess and theatrically twirled her around, and with a *poof!* and a puff of smoke, they were gone. Actually,

there was no puff of smoke and they weren't gone at all—they were still there.

"Bess, what's the problem?"

"Don't ask me. Maybe you used up all your liquid smoke? You've been blowing it out your ass all night!"

"Oh for Christ's sake. Okay, let's grab a cab."

Their contentious voices faded away as they walked down Centre Street in search of a checkered hansom cab. Meanwhile Caleb tore open the correspondence that Houdini had delivered to him:

Dear Chief Spencer,

There is much for us to discuss and it is time we do so. If you value Elisabeth's life, meet me immediately at Mayor Roosevelt's house. All shall be explained.

Yours,

Professor Archibald Campion

"Never fear, my good man, it is I, the great Houdini!"

Chapter the Fourteenth.

In which your amiable author pursues the dastardly butcher and is appalled by his unexpected activities with a certain inebriated harlot.

ELUDING THE POLICE PROVED EASIER THAN KEEPING UP WITH THE MYSTERIous man in the top hat. By his actions, he was obviously trying to evade the authorities as well. Every so often he would take cover in a doorway, prompting me to do the same just a few yards behind him. Then, when he felt the coast was clear, he would continue his hastened traipse, changing directions often and with no discernable pattern other than a zig-zag route which was generally taking us south, then to the east, or "back and to the left." He alternated his style of walk as well, sometimes taking exaggeratedly long strides, sometimes rapid itsy bitsy little ones, sometimes skipping like a little schoolboy, and sometimes dancing along singing "Sweet Rosie O'Grady" as he went. Each time he changed his style of walk, I did the same. I was determined not to lose him.

I followed him through the red light district, the Tenderloin district, and the District of Columbia before we reached Herald Square, at which point he hiked up his trousers and began to wade through the manure. Begrudgingly, I did the same.

On the other side of the square, he turned abruptly left. This put us on a dark deserted side street between Seventh and Eighth avenues on Twenty-first. I knew right away where we were—this was the Thwacker's favorite hunting grounds. The original Original Ray's Pizzeria was only a block away.

His footsteps scuffled rhythmically on the wet cobblestones while mine limped like a one-legged man's (because I was missing my right shoe, remember?). Occasionally he would stop and look behind him, as if he knew he was being followed, and I would have to dive into a doorway or a Dumpster, or a pothole full of excrement, so as not to be discovered.

Twenty feet from the end of the block a shabbily dressed, drunken prostitute scuffled out of an alley and fell smack into the arms of the man. I froze and hid behind a trash can, watching.

"Oh, pardon me, sir. I didn't see ya there!" chirped the woman, and then she belched. "Care for a quick blow job?"

"A what?" asked the man incredulously.

"Sorry gov'nor, just a new bit a slang the ladies are passing round. You know, a quick windy-work on the old peter pipesies!'"

"Oh, now I understand," he said. "Blow job just sounded so—indiscreet."

The times, just like the skyline of the great metropolis, were definitely a-changing, and it would be recorded that at 10:45 PM, on the night of August 26th, 1882, the vile idiom 'blow job' entered the New York City vernacular for the first time (which is a shame, because I was really hoping to coin that one myself). After that, prostitution, as well as married life and teenage puppy love, would never be the same.

"What do you say? Only cost ya a ha'penny or two."

"That's very kind," said the strange man, "but I'm not used to such generosity. You see, I'm not particularly kind myself."

I stood up. I knew what was about to happen, and I knew I

had to stop it. But at the same time I was seized by my paralyzing native–New Yorker instinct not to ever get involved.

"Oh?" giggled the harlot, as she played with the buttons on the man's coat and curled up against his chest. "Are you naughty, then?"

"Not naughty, my dear. Just jolly."

I slowly began to approach, whispering, "No, no, don't do it. No, no. Lady, run, run."

"What shall we do now?" asked the man.

"Whatever pops your cork, laddie boy," said the looped whore, as she popped the cork off her rum bottle and took a long swig.

I began to pick up my pace. "No no no! Enough is enough. . . ."

"I want you to have something. It's something I never go anywhere without," said the man, and he slowly began to reach into his carpetbag. And then . . .

I was running as fast as I could, but I misjudged how far behind them I was. I wasn't going to make it in time!

. . . and then . . .

. . . and then the man pulled out his music box and handed it to the prostitute.

I stopped in my tracks not ten yards away and dropped flat to the cobbles.

"I won't need this any more," he said. "I want you to have it. I wish to have done one good deed before I leave this foul earth." Then he tipped his hat. "A very good evening to you, madame," he said and continued on his way.

That was it? No thwack? No murder? No intestinal art? (Why was I just a little bit disappointed? That's sick!)

"Hey, look what that kind gent gives me, and it works, too! I could get fifty quid for it," cackled the lucky whore as I passed her by. "Hey, you's looks just like 'im! You's his brother, then?"

I didn't answer her. My thoughts were with Old Toothless Sally Jenkins and the other victims as I followed in the murderous footsteps of the Thwacker, who for some unknown reason—perhaps some pang of true guilt, or perhaps simply out of boredom—had spared his final prey.

"Fine, don'ts answers me!" yelled the whore. Then she started to sing along with her music box. "Sweets, Rosies O's-Gradies . . . she's my's little . . . girls."

The sound of her harsh voice was eventually folded inside the thankfully obstreperous envelope of clomping horse carriages, slap-fighting sanitation workers, steam-powered gas lamps, and rustling mango-tree leaves. It began to feel less like I was following the man, and more like he was leading me. I trailed behind at a dangerously close distance now, and I didn't care. I was determined that this whole nasty business would end here, tonight.

We turned a corner on Nineteenth Street, and, halfway down the block, the man skipped up the steps of the nondescript brownstone. He pulled out a set of keys and unlocked the door. I scurried across the street to get a straight-on view of the building. Its façade was like the face of a sleeping murderer—menacingly unremarkable. He turned the key and the front door unlatched and opened slightly. Then he paused. *What the hell is he doing now?* I thought.

Then he turned and looked directly at me.

This was the first time that I saw the monster face to face. I gasped. His face was mine! He was me. I was him. We were identical!

I stood frozen in my spot as the murderer raised his arm and beckoned me—as if he were Ahab, lashed to the great white whale, his arm lifelessly entreating his crew to follow him to his watery grave. But I didn't follow. At least not at first.

He went inside and closed the door behind him. A moment

Then he turned and looked directly at me.

later a dim light shone through the foggy window on the third floor and I could see the killer's black silhouette moving back and forth. I knew I had to confront him, but I also knew that another life was in danger tonight, namely Elisabeth's.

It was 11:15; I didn't have much time. I needed to deliver my message—midnight at Castle Belvedere—but first I had important business in the nondescript brownstone.

Chapter the Fifteenth.

In which the slippery pettifogger is revealed, and the unchaste Madame Smith and the corpulent Mayor Roosevelt find themselves in a direful predicament that you may interpret more precisely as "doomful."

THE ROPES WERE CUTTING OFF LIZ'S CIRCULATION. SHE KNOCKED ABOUT trying to wake up her sleeping appendages. Time was running out. Midnight was fast approaching.

"Mmmm mmm rrrrrrr vvvv mmmurrrr," she moaned forlornly through the gag in her mouth.

Suddenly Roosevelt came bounding into the conservatory, apparently surprised to find Liz in such a dire predicament.

"Why, my dear woman, what have they done to you?" he bellowed as he opened the cage and hurried to undo her gag and bindings. "For heaven's sake, this is no way to treat a lady. Why, if any member of my regiment acted so uncivilized, I would have him horsewhipped . . . with a horsewhip!"

The moment the gag was out of her mouth, Liz began spewing.

"Get the hell away from me, you bastard!"

"But Miss Smith, it's me—Teddy!"

"Don't try to pretend. I know you're in on it! You're in cahoots with Tweed! I know all about it. I heard you talking in the parlor."

"I assure you, madame, I am an American patriot and a

wholehearted individualist in cahoots with no one but myself—and sometimes not even with him!"

"Look, Mr. Whoever-you-are, I heard the whole conversation. All that stuff about coming here to spy on the investigation, to throw us a couple of 'red herrings,' about your 'take' . . . 'the *contraption*'? Any of this ring a bell, Bippy-boy?"

Roosevelt raised three fingers.

"I swear to you, on scout's double-dutch honor, that I have positively no idea what you're talking about, madame, but I will admit to enjoying a red herring from time to time, as I find its sapidity far less salty than the more common finnan haddie."

"Nice try. Now get back! And get your hands up!"

She retrieved her pearl-handled whistle and held it like a derringer, pointing it at Roosevelt. He backed away with his hands in the air.

"But Lizzy-wizzy, I thought we were friends! To be honest, I thought maybe we were a little more than that. I've just been playing hard to get." He winked and blew her a kiss.

"Yes, but friends don't kidnap friends—or have you forgotten that part too?"

"My dear Miss Smith, I went to Delmonico's because I received an urgent message from Chief Spencer to bring you here. And the last thing I remember is helping you step up into a carriage, and then . . ."

"And then?"

Roosevelt rubbed the back of his head.

". . . and then, I must have been hit from behind and knocked out, because when I regained consciousness, I was lying on the cobblestones. Of course, the first thing I did was to immediately rush home."

"Oh, put a lid on it. Here, hogtie yourself!" She threw him the ropes. "And then get in the cage."

"As you wish, but may I be so bold as to ask you a question?"

"Yes, and when you're done, I have a few for you, too. Like where's the death ritual taking place?"

Roosevelt fumbled with the ropes.

"Well, first of all, how does one hogtie oneself?"

"Hands behind the back. Ankles to wrists, you'll figure it out."

"Yes, quite so." The big man plopped down on the floor, rolled over onto his side, and began to awkwardly experiment with the most efficient way to rope himself up. He flip-flopped back and forth like a beached whale, getting red in the face and percolating the famous Roosevelt sweat.

". . . and secondly, Miss Smith, did you actually *see* me abduct you?"

"What are you talking about? You kidnapped me! Now just shut up."

"Yes, but how do you know? I mean, did you actually see me?"

"How could I see you? You threw a hood over my head!"

"Me? No, not I. I was already unconscious. But perhaps one of those . . . mischievious monks did? Yes?"

Liz stared at the man writhing on the floor. Was she mistaken? She was positive that one of the voices she heard coming from the parlor belonged to Tweed—his lisp was unmistakable—but what about the other voice? Could she be certain it was Roosevelt's? Then she replayed the kidnapping in her mind.

When we walked out of Delmonico's, I was in front of Teddy. That means someone other than he could have thrown the hood over my head and pushed me into the carriage. I suppose it is possible.

Liz was inexorably cocksure of herself unless it involved people she cared deeply about.

"I can't take any chances," she said. "You've been acting awfully strange, Teddy. Now make those knots nice and tight."

"I've been acting strange because of the rap I took on the old

bean when I fell through the trapdoor. But I believe that last bastinado at Delmonico's has brought me back to my senses. Why, I can even quote myself again. Listen to this one: 'It is always better to be an original than an imitation!'" He burst out in a bountiful guffaw. "Rather apropos, I'd say, wouldn't you? It's bully! Isn't it? Weehoo!"

A slight smile crossed Liz's lips. Was this her real Teddy?

"I knew when you returned from Cairo that we were all in for an adventure, but I had no idea it would turn out to be this thrilling. Why, I do believe peril and confounding intrigue follow you where e'er you go, Miss Smith, correspondent par excellence for the *Evening Post*!"

That was exactly the same way he had introduced her to Caleb the night she showed up at Delmonico's. *It had to be him!*

"Teddy?" she said with tears welling up in her tired eyes.

"Why, of course it's me, my dear. It's been me all along." He dropped the ropes, stood up, and held out his arms.

"Oh Teddy." She allowed herself to be swallowed up in his big greasy bear hug.

"There, there now, sweet Lizzy-wizzy, everything is all right. Uncle Teddy will take care of you now."

"I'm so sorry I ever doubted you."

"That's all right, my dear. I'm sure you were more than a little bit influenced by that young Chief Spencer fella. He's a fine chief of police, but he's still a bit green behind the ears. He tends to fly off the handle, he's a little too quick on the draw, can't seem to focus on . . ."

Liz pulled away from Roosevelt.

"Caleb! I almost forgot about Caleb. He's gone to the Lyceum Theater to arrest Houdini. He believes Houdini and Archibald Campion are acting together as the Thwacker. I always suspected

Campion . . . but Houdini? . . . well, that might just be one of Caleb's little . . . you know . . . tangents."

"Yes, but that still doesn't tell us where the death ritual will occur. We need that Book of Names. I'm quite sure it's written down in there somewhere."

"Don't worry about the book."

"Yes, but we haven't much time. The death ritual is set for midnight." He took out his pocket watch. "That's less than an hour from now."

Suddenly they heard the mechanical ape's gregarious greeting.

"Howdy folks! Teddy will be right with you. In the meantime, why not take a load off in the parlor?"

They both froze. Then Liz whispered, "Someone's here."

"Be calm," said Roosevelt. "I can handle this." He pulled down a mounted Savage .22 hunting rifle from the wall and checked to make certain it was loaded.

"You sure you know how to use that?" whispered Liz.

"My dear young lady, I was splattering the brains of helpless wild animals all over the endangered species list back when you were still playing tiddlywinks, pinochle, and 'I'll show you my pangywangy if you show me yours'!"

He knelt and aimed the rifle at the entrance. He pulled back the hammer. Liz crouched behind him.

"Don't shoot until you see who it is," she cautioned.

They heard footsteps approaching.

"Steady," she whispered.

Suddenly the double doors burst open.

Bang!

Teddy fired and the rebound of the Savage sent him barreling backwards into Liz. They both splashed down into the koi pond behind them.

When the smoke had settled, an alien figure stood in the center of the conservatory.

Was it Caleb? Was it Professor Archibald Campion? Was it me? NO, *IDIOT!* It wasn't any of those guys!

It was the muddy, tattooed hobo in the loincloth, and he was still holding his spear, his burlap bag, and the wax figure that he had stolen from the Eden Musée—only the wax figure was missing its head, the blast from the rifle having blown it clean off. Its collar was now on fire.

"What in the name of the blessed virgin reading the latest *Harper's Weekly* is going on here?" bellowed the hobo. "Why, I seem to have lost my head!" He laughed and threw the mannequin to the floor. He stamped out the flames with his foot.

"Ow! Ow! Ow! Ow! Hot! Hot! Hot! This reminds me of the time my old chum Mahatma Gandhi and I took in a little too much black gungl and decided it would be jolly fun sport to dance barefoot in our campfire!"

Liz jumped back, grabbed the Savage .22, and stood between the two men, pointing the rifle at both of them.

"Okay, who wants to tell me what's going on?"

The two men faced off. They were positively identical—same build, same mustache, same squinty eyes—two absolutely indistinguishable Roosevelts, except that one of them was in a loincloth and had a lot of mud on his face.

"Good heavens! Mittie never told me I had an identical twin!" declared the hobo, then he reached out his burly arms. "Brother, give us a hug!"

"Stay the hell away from me," said the other man. "Liz, this guy's an impostor. *I'm* Teddy Roosevelt! Come on, we have to get that Book of Names!"

"An impostor? My dear sir, I am anything but," blustered the half-naked wanderer, his little round eyes going wild. He fanned

out his legs and replanted his feet solidly on the ground and placed his hands on his hips. "I'll have you know, sir, that I am the fourth child of the pulchritudinous Miss Martha 'Mittie' Bulloch of Roswell, Georgia, and my dear father, the great New York City philanthropist and ardent loyalist, Theodore Roosevelt, Senior. I was born upstairs in this very house not forty years ago, and I am the proud brother to Elliott, Bamie, and Corinne. I served this country honorably with my fellow Rough Riders during the Spanish-American War . . ."

"But that hasn't even . . ."

"Don't say it!" The tramp held up his index finger. "I have held public office as secretary of the Navy, police commissioner, and I am at present the mayor of this fine city, working hand in hand with the lovely Miss Smith and the brave Chief Spencer to solve the horrendous Thwacker murders. Now, I have been called many things in my day, sir, but never an impostor. I am the real article, I can assure you. 'For it's far better to be an original than an imitation!' Everyone knows that!"

There was a long, palpable pause before Liz finally cleared her throat.

"What, did he use that one already?"

"Yes I did," said the odd-acting Roosevelt, "becuause it is *my* quote. I am the one who said it. Because *I am* Teddy Roosevelt."

"Well, we seem to have ourselves quite a little bugaboo here, don't we?" Liz said. "I suppose there's really only one true way to be sure . . ."

"Now listen here," bellowed the hobo. "I did not get whacked on the head, swim five miles through the collective excrement of the entire population of the Mulberry Bend, endure the infamous and dreaded initiation rights of the Mud Tot tribe, and get tossed out alone on the streets without even a single memory of a fine leisurely summer afternoon shooting cans off the heads of

the natives of Zanzibar to call my own, only to have to play who's-your-Teddy with some half-wit dimestore knockoff who couldn't tell an endangered Armenian razorbacked pigowl from a quilled Argentinian owlypig if his life depended on it. I've spent too long without so much as knowing my name to lose it now, and I perhaps never would have recovered it, had it not been for the rather flattering wax likeness I happened upon at the Eden Museé. I carried it through the city's gloomy streets, holding the statue before me like the dowsing rods of the pygmy Nigerian waterseekers, now sadly eradicated due to the unfortunately high quality of their fur—"

"Your point, *impostor?*" said the other Roosevelt.

"All the while a voice whispered in my ear, 'Delmo, Delmo, Delmo . . .' And then I came upon it, that Avalon of eateries, that culinary Camelot, that which I remembered when I had forgotten even my own dear Mittie's name: Delmonico's. And, even better, it was the night they have their all-you-can-eat oyster bar. My senses were overpowered. Wielding that statue now as a shield, and my spear as—well, a spear, I mounted the steps. Yes, it is a black-tie-only establishment, but no force on earth could have kept me from those shellfish. They defended it with overturned chairs, fending off my spear blows with the lids of tureens, but I prevailed. And as I mounted the bar, victorious, kicking aside the scattered corpses of the vanquished, my treasured wax-work in one hand, in the other an entire upturned bowl of steamed mussels now racing down my gullet, shell and all, my memories returning one by one with each savory bite—then I knew, truly knew, who I was. And you sir, you miserable excuse for a Teddy Roosevelt, I shall tell you what I said then, and what I tell all my conquered enemies . . ."

With that he lifted his loincloth, revealing the piercing that

King Bowser Koopaloopa had given him so many years before in Fiji.

"Blackguards, knaves, and fools alike, *cower before my pearl!*"

Liz covered her eyes and giggled. Then Teddy (formerly the 'hobo', 'tramp', 'bum' etc.—boy am I glad that's over, I was running out of adjectives) turned to the impostor (formerly the 'odd-acting Teddy') and asked, "Have you one of these? My amigo?"

"You guys are all nuts!" cried the impostor, and he ran for the door.

"Quick Liz, the Savage!" Liz tossed the rifle to Roosevelt, and he took aim and fired. But the bullet missed, smashing his prized collection of porcelain sumo wrestlers instead.

"Dang it all!"

"Let him go, Teddy." said Liz. "He's just one of Tweed's henchmen. We have more important things to attend to."

"Tweed? What does he have to do with all of this?"

"You and I have a lot of catching up to do, Mr. Mayor."

"My dear lady, how could you have possibly believed that four-flushed pettifogger to be your true cuddly Teddy-weddy?"

"I knew he was an impostor all along," she said coyly, cocking her head to the side, "I just wanted to see your famous pearl."

Teddy blushed and looked down. He drew his big toe back and forth on the floor.

"All you ever had to do was ask," he said shyly.

Liz planted a sweet kiss on his cheek.

"Your gorilla out there didn't say 'howdy' before he came into the conservatory. That told me that he was already in the house and was undoubtedly the other voice I heard talking in the parlor. And, more importantly, he didn't know how to hogtie himself."

"Who doesn't know how to hogtie himself?"

"Exactly. But Teddy, where have you been?" she asked and

examined the cryptic tattoos on his back and brushed away the mud on his face.

"My dear, there isn't enough time to relay every detail. Suffice it to say that from now on I'm never sitting where any plug-ugly who has been trying his best to kill me all night asks me to."

"Yeah, we figured something like that had happened."

"So did Phossy Phil tell us anything useful?"

"Phossy Phil!" said Liz incredulously. "That name seems like a distant memory to me now."

"Hey, where has my little Ishi gone to?"

Liz rolled her eyes, "Ah, Teddy," she began with a patronizing tone in her voice. "Why don't you sit down and let me fill you in on what's been happening."

"Miss Smith, you *are* aware that there's been another murder, aren't you?" asked Teddy as he looked high and low for any sign of his missing pet Yahi.

"What?"

"Yes, a prostitute by the name of Blue Whale. And what's worse, Chief Spencer is accused of the crime."

"Good Lord! Why doesn't anyone ever tell me about these things?"

"He's being held at the Tombs as we speak." Teddy picked up his graffitied portrait and his face swelled with rage. "Now who would do such a dastardly deed? I want these teenagers found and hung up by their Buster Browns!"

"Teddy, come on. We have to rescue Caleb."

At that moment something rolled through the conservatory and came to a stop at their feet. Teddy picked it up. It was the animatronic gorilla's head.

"What the?"

Standing in the entrance to the conservatory were five hooded monks.

"Cower before my pearl!"

"I'm afraid that won't be pothible, Mith Thmith," said Boss Tweed, stepping from behind the evil bogeys.

"You thee, you two are coming with me. It'th almotht midnight and that meanth it'th time for the death ritual!"

Teddy asked meekly, "Could we at least stop at Delmonico's on the way? All those oysters have left me rather parched."

Chapter the Sixteenth.

In which concordant brothers-in-arms do the baneful Thwacker and the idle-headed author quite rapidly become (and woe is us at such an ungodly confluence!).

LOOKING BACK ON IT NOW, I DON'T KNOW WHY I FELT COMPELLED TO answer Mrs. O'Leary's prying questions in the voice of my evil twin. Maybe I was more afraid of being burned as a time-traveling witch than being hanged as a homicidal maniac. I've always preferred hanging to burning—ever since I was a child. Because burning takes a long time and it would also hurt, but when you're hanged, you just fall asleep.

"I have been to the Mince-About Hall, Mrs. O'Leary, and then out for a rather curtailed constitutional," I explained, standing in the foyer of the nondescript brownstone. "I hope that answers your query."

"Coming and going quite a bit then tonight, you have been, Doctor, have you not?" she remarked, nervously scrunching her apron in her hands.

"And is there any law against that, madame?" I said, sounding as sinister as I could. "For I would not want to break the law! And if I ever did break the law, I would hope that no one would take notice of the fact—for their own well being, that is."

Mrs. O'Leary's eyes grew wide with fright, and she gulped. "No

Chris Elliott

law against it, Doctor. No law 'tall. So will you be wanting me to wash any bloody . . . I mean soiled clothing for you, then?"

"That won't be necessary, Mrs. O'Leary." Then I moved menacingly close to her. "Why don't you just go about your own business?"

She picked up her bucket and mop.

"Yes, about my *own* business, I am. Mopping up, I was. Now off to put the chickens to bed I am, slop the pigs, I might . . . milk the cows, I will. Certainly not going to notify the authorities, I won't. A good evening to you, Doctor, I say. . . . Don't mind me now . . . on my way, I am . . ."

The skittish woman stumbled over her own feet as she exited through the back door. I couldn't help but giggle. *I was a pretty convincing Jack the Thwacker,* I thought. *Maybe that's what I should be next Halloween. (That is, if the book is a success.)*

I climbed the steps to the third floor. His chamber door was ajar, and I pushed it open. The only light in the room was coming from two candlesticks that he held beneath his face, making him appear less like me and more like a photo negative of me.

"Won't you come in?" he said in a kindly voice not unlike my own. As I entered, he handed me my own candlestick.

"It's amazing."

"Yes, it is, isn't it?" he said.

"You've got my semi-symmetrical eyes, my pasty complexion, my consistently running nose, and you even have the same scar that I got when I stuck my head in the rock polisher."

"Make yourself at home."

I shined the light around the room and observed that the walls were wrapped in newspaper clippings. Articles about Jack the Thwacker and his murderous deeds were mixed in with other disturbing headlines like "Homeless Man Stabs Three on Broadway," "Fire Engine Explodes, Killing Twelve," "Husband Kills

Wife," "Baby Kills Nanny," "Dog Shoots Cat," "Cat Kills Mouse," "Mouse Kills Cheese," "Cheese Kills Self."

One wall was devoted to outlandish Lincoln assassination conspiracy theories, such as the notion that a second gunman was firing from the orchestra pit, camouflaged as the conductor. Then I gasped: a curious clipping at the bottom corner near the floorboards read, "John Wayne Gacy Charged with Multiple Murders."

"Just one of the many cases that fascinate me," the Thwacker said pleasantly. "There are so many others."

He brightened a wall with his candle and I was shocked to find articles on the Green River killer, the Zodiac killer, the Boston Strangler, Charles Manson, Son of Sam, and Ted Bundy.

"I don't understand . . . ?" I said.

"Don't you? It's my homework. Do you care for a cup of tea?"

"Do you have anything stronger?" I asked, feeling like I needed a little help to get through the conversation. (You might need a strong drink to get through this chapter, too.)

"They sent me a basket of Skyy Vodka and assorted cheese and crackers after the success of the first murder," he remarked. "I find that it's the only alcohol that doesn't give me a hangover in the morning—something these nineteenth-century blowhards haven't yet figured out how to produce."

"Me, too. I mean it's my favorite vodka too."

"Well now, isn't that a coincidence." He poured us each a shot and then sat down in his easy chair. "Please sit." I sat on his bed. "To the future!" he toasted, and we downed our spirits and refilled our glasses.

"*They* sent you a basket? Who's *they*?"

"The Mummers, of course. Charming group of men . . . don't know them very well, except for the grand poobah."

"Tweed?"

"The Boss . . . my boss."

"You know, this variety of vodka and those newspaper clippings . . . they're all from the future," I observed. "So . . . are you me from the future?" Somehow I knew that wasn't right, because I was pretty sure that *I* was me from from the future, but I think I was just trying to work out some parallel-universe, Star Trek-y type of theory in my head.

"No, *you're* you from the future. I'm me from this time. Refill?" And he poured us each another shot.

"Quick, where was I born?" I quizzed.

"New York City."

"Year?"

"1960."

"Schooling?"

"Adam's Academy for the Literally Small-Headed."

"Burst onto the scene portraying who?"

"The lovable but chatty Thoroughbred Number Six in *Equus.*"

"Married?"

"Divorced."

"Why?"

"Because of . . . intimate issues."

"More specific."

"Sex."

"You bastard! Why?"

"Your wife didn't appreciate having to tie you up and blindfold you whenever the two of you made love."

"Double bastard! Why?"

"Because she worked for Amnesty International and found the practice a conflict of interest."

"How the hell do you know all this?" I shouted.

We downed our vodka and he filled our glasses again.

"Because I'm a nineteenth-century . . . you! Don't ask me

how, I don't get it myself! But let's drink to it! It's crazy!" So we threw back our poison and filled up our glasses.

"You can sure put it away!" I said.

"Only as much as you can!" he replied.

"I hear that!" And we both laughed.

"But there's one big difference between us . . . 'doctor,'" I said, beginning to feel the effects of the booze. "I would never kill anybody. I mean, mug, sure, who wouldn't, but never kill!"

He got up and moved to his desk, where he watered a small plant as he spoke. "I don't remember much about my early childhood. But at some point in my life, Boss Tweed took over raising me . . . or . . . brainwashing me. I was programmed to do the horrible things that I did. They put me in a cage with a wire mother who would refuse to hug me until I killed someone—and it couldn't be just anyone, but they didn't tell me that at first. And after I figured out what they wanted, it just got worse. 'Kill mamma another prossie, would ya, Chrissie?' she'd say. 'Ya love yer mamma, don't ye?' she'd say. And if my crimes weren't brutal enough, the hugs would adminster horrifying electric shocks. It was an arduous process of trial and error, but in the end I had an uncontrollable urge to make elaborate tableaus out of whore entrails. What they didn't count on was the fact that I was born with a conscience—your conscience, I suppose. So no matter how hard they tried to turn me into a mindless killer, there would always be that part of me that knew I was doing wrong. That's why I tried to leave clues behind to help Spencer, Smith, and Roosevelt."

He suddenly grabbed his head as if he were in pain.

"No, no, no . . . Mother, make it stop! Make it stop!"

"Like the letters to Liz Smith? And the cryptic poem on the wall implicating the Mummers?" I asked.

"Yes, that's right. Thanks to my—our conscience, I managed

to point the finger at those evil Mummer clowns, and believe you me, they weren't happy about it either."

"And the messages in the crime scene?"

"The morbid tableaux were meant just for *you* to decipher and then to eventually lead you back in time. If you ask me, it would have been a lot simpler just to throw you in a sack and toss you in, but who am I to say? I'm just a homicidal maniac, right?"

He downed his shot glass and refilled it. "There's much more, no doubt, but that's my part of it, kiddo."

Then his feet did a quick shuffle-riffle, stamp, brush-scuff. Possibly also a pull.

"It all seems so simple," I said. "And yet somehow I'm not understanding any of it. I guess it's the vodka."

I stood up and instinctively did a stomp, dig, slap, and a brush-ball (which was difficult with one shoe).

"Do you mind if I ask you a question?" he said.

"Shoot, baby!"

He did a triplet-down, heel drop, chug, flap-step, and ball change. I answered with the same, but added a cramp roll, dig-paddle, and time-step riff-drop.

"What's the future like? I'll never get a chance to see it!"

"Oh, it's not so great." And I did a fast flap-slap-stamp.

"Oh, I don't believe that," he answered with a flap, slap-stamp-*flap-slap-stamp-stump*. "Tell me, have reason and justice finally united to perfect human society into a glorious and enduring utopia?"

Flap—slap—stamp—stump—dig—paddle—clap.

"Ah, more or less."

Flap-ball change—shuffle—riffle!

And before we knew it we were both tap-dancing our asses off all around his flat, like two Fred Astaires in heat. We changed up steps, rhythms, and patterns, each challenging the other with

more intricate combinations. We were shim-sham-shimmying from one piece of furniture to the next until we both collapsed—he in his chair and I on his bed.

"By the way," he said, catching his breath and pouring us some more Skyy. "What the hell do you do about these damned plantar warts?"

"Oh, that's easy!" I answered, *really* feeling the booze now. "Here, pop a couple of thesessssss." I threw him my vial of antibiotics. "They never totally go away. They grow under the skin like potatoes, you know."

"I didn't know that," he said.

"And now I have a question for you, sir."

"Please proceed."

"Is this place rent-controlled?" I asked, admiring the high ceilings and the beautiful prewar moldings. "Because if I could get my name on the lease now, this would be one hell of an investment for when I get back to 2005."

"You're not going back."

"Yeah, I am, I just have to save Liz Smith first."

"The time machine only works one way. You can travel to the past, or you can travel to the future, but once you've done one or the other you can't return. It wasn't designed to go back and forth."

"What? That sucks!" I stood up and the room swayed to and fro. "What the hell am I supposed to do now?"

"Have another drink!" he replied, and I plopped back down on his bed and drank.

"This is horrible."

"By the way, you're also being framed!" he said.

"But by who? And why? What have I done to anyone? I've just tried to live my life as a gentle jester!"

"I don't know who. But Tweed is obviously working with

somebody from the future, that's how he gets me the Skyy Vodka and the newspaper articles about future serial killers."

"The future? Who could it be?"

"That's the question. To the future!" And we raised our glasses and downed some more hard liquor. "And now my friend, we must say goodbye, for my involvement in these wretched events is finally over. You see, I was programmed to commit suicide once all the murders had been accomplished."

"No!"

"And to dispose of my body myself."

"Huh?"

"Yeah, that was a little mistake in the programming—I shan't even venture to explain how they did that—but I finally figured out how to do it. I'm going to blow my head off near the incinerator opening, and then my body will just tumble down the chute and burn up."

With that he retrieved a .44 magnum from underneath his chair and laid it on his lap.

"But then I won't be able to prove my innocence!"

"I believe that was the plan. 'Wanted' flyers with your face on them are being distributed throughout the city as we speak." He grabbed his head in pain again. "No, I didn't have a drink, Mother, I swear, I'm going to do it right now! Keep your pants on!"

"I hate it here!" I yowled and stamped my foot.

"As do I, my friend. As do I. But fortunately for me I'm not long for this world."

He stood and started for the hallway.

"No, please, you have to help me. Don't kill yourself. You're my only hope! Please!" I pleaded.

"I'm sorry, friend. I'd like to help, but even if I weren't programmed to commit suicide, I would have to do it anyway. I can't live with the horrible things I have done."

Flap—slap—stamp—stump—dig—paddle—clap.

I was blocking his way.

"Oh come on, sure you can. They're not that horrible. They were prostitutes! For crying out loud! They get paid to get murdered by serial killers. It's a tradition! And I got to tell you, some of your later work with intestines was really quite interesting."

"Out of my way!" he demanded. "I don't want to have to hit you, because it would be like hitting myself, and I'm not into self-mutilation. Plus it would just be confusing."

"I can't let you do it!"

I hugged him by the torso and pushed him furiously back into the room. We scudded over his desk, knocking his potted plant to the floor, where the pot shattered. We wrestled, bouncing from one side of the room to the other, and I had a feeling that the match could last forever because our respective durability was precisely equal. But the battle would end much sooner than I thought.

Outside, in the backyard, Mrs. O'Leary was unaware of the violent struggle taking place in the upstairs apartment, but at approximately 11:25, when she heard the deafening *bang* of the .44 magnum cannon, she nearly had a heart attack—as did her chickens. She ran inside to see what had happened.

In her haste she ignored the oil lamp, which her cow had just kicked over.

For the moment only small bits of straw were in flames, but within two hours the entire city would be engulfed.

And that's how I started the Great Chicago Fire.

Chapter the Seventeenth.

In which all is explained (I think).

CALEB HAD COMMANDEERED A TOMBS PRISON VAN, ALSO KNOWN AS A "Black Maria," to hasten his travel uptown to Roosevelt's. Now, the horse-drawn van bounced mercilessly up and down on the cobblestones and listed dramatically, almost to the point of toppling over, whenever he swerved to the right or to the left. Its cargo of street vagrants, hoodlums, plug-uglies, and prostitutes was thrown about and propelled violently into one another in the back of the buggy—essentially becoming the ingredients in a Cuisinart blender of rogues. (Today, a Black Maria is a popular blended frozen cocktail that derives its name from the felonious ruck's unfortunate trek uptown.)

Caleb pulled up in front of Roosevelt's house at approximately 11:30 PM. With his .32 in hand, he approached the front door cautiously. It was unlocked as usual. Inside, the house was dark and the first thing he noticed was the headless torso of the gorilla, its mechanical arm still waving as if it were greeting guests.

"Hello?" Caleb called out and waited for a response—there was none.

He stepped into the parlor and looked around. *Nothing out of*

place. From above, the mounted beasts eyed his every move like medieval gargoyles. He headed back towards the conservatory and tripped over a stuffed capybara.

"God damn it, Roosevelt," he muttered.

Blue moonlight streamed through the panes of the skylight, illuminating a tall object standing in the center of the conservatory. As Caleb neared it, the object revealed itself as a figure in a hooded robe, standing stone-still and looking down.

"Campion?"

There was no response.

"Campion?"

"You won't need your pistol, Chief Spencer. At least not *yet*," it said, in a weak and curiously dispirited voice.

"I'll be the judge of that."

He lifted his head, and his long, bony fingers pulled back his hood. He was gaunt man with deep-set eyes, high, sharp cheekbones, and thick, dirty gray hair. He seemed emaciated and there was very little life left behind his sad umber windows. The creases framing his mouth were likely caused by years of pain, both physical and emotional. Still, there was just a slight hint of kindness lingering in the corners of his lips, and perhaps around the eyes and maybe behind his big ears.

"What are your thoughts about time, Chief Spencer?" he asked.

"I think I don't have much. So you better talk fast."

"Time and faith are one and the same. Each powerful, yet elusive; intangible and yet . . . capable of greatly distorting reality."

"I'm not here for a sermon, Professor."

"I need you to have faith in what I am about to tell you, Caleb, because it will be very difficult to believe, but understanding it is vital to saving Elisabeth's life."

"I'm waiting."

As he spoke, Campion paced back and forth, avoiding the snakes and iguanas and other wildlife that slithered on the tile floor at his feet.

"Some years ago—or some years from now, depending on how you look at it—I traveled back through time from the twentieth century to the nineteenth century."

Caleb rolled his eyes.

"My purpose back then was—or will be—to develop a method of reproducing human cells in the hope of curing many of the diseases that still plague mankind in the future. In order to do this, I needed help—financial help, that is—and so I turned to the Secret Society of Mummers, of which I was a proud member. The Mathematical Brigade was my coterie. The organization had financed my projects in the past—that is, my twentieth-century projects—but they refused to provide me with what I required to re-create—or clone, as it is, as it *will be,* called—an actual human being—a duplicate, an exact double of the original."

Caleb sighed. *What did I expect from an escaped lunatic?* But then he thought of the odd-acting Roosevelt.

"You see, human cloning is prohibited in my time," Campion continued. "And the Mathematical Brigade were a very conservative bunch of Mummers, very hesitant to tread such ethically uncharted waters. I realized that the only way to get funding for the morally questionable practice would be to find some group that possessed great wealth, as well as a slightly less scrupulous attitude towards the unwashed masses. I thought if cloning could be sold as a new-fangled innovation at a time when the great industrialists and capitalists were investing their fortunes in whatever the world of tomorrow might offer—well, with that kind of backing, it had a chance to succeed."

"Go on."

"So I built myself a time machine at the planetarium where I

worked, which by the way is not that difficult to do, and traveled back to the nineteenth century, and had my cloning research underwritten by the powerful and rich patriarchs of New York City, aka the Fancy Brigade of the Secret Society of Mummers."

Caleb pulled out his Edison tape recorder and wound it a few times.

"No one is going to believe this! So you're a time-traveling Dr. Frankenstein? You're telling me that you've created a human being out of thin air? Exactly how does one go about doing that, Professor?

"Somatic nuclear cell transfer. It's quite simple really. The nucleus of the cells—see, bodies, it will be discovered, are made of millions of little simple animals, called cells, and each cell has a nucleus. You take a single donor hair, harvest the cells from it, and implant them in an egg—" Campion could tell from Caleb's perplexed look that he still was not following. "You see, human life is created when a sperm from a man joins an egg from a woman—er, inside the woman's body. Each has half the DNA— oh dear, you wouldn't know what that is, either. Basically I took a little smidgeon of the magic goody life stuff from a grown man and placed it inside a woman—but, er, not the way that it's normally done. I used a needle and a microscope."

"You are one sick turkey, Campion."

"Oh, never mind. What is important is that the resulting chemistry created an embryo . . ." He frowned and his voice grew darker. ". . . an embryo with *him* inside."

"Him?"

"The Thwacker."

"Professor . . ."

"I beg you, have faith!"

The professor's plea was firm and Caleb backed off.

"As the years wore on, I married and I had a little daughter.

Oh, those were happy days—good times. That is, until I discovered that the Mummers were using me, and that I had unintentionally cloned a living person from the twentieth century, a man upon whom they were going blame the dreadful Thwacker murders. Boss Tweed, you see, has entered into a pact with an evil woman from the future, and it is *she* who wants to frame this poor soul."

"She?"

"She is the curator of the Museum of Natural History . . . at least in the future she is. She was my superior in the twentieth century . . . Mrs. Flutter."

"Why?"

"I don't know."

"You know, all you're doing is convincing me that you should be back in your cell at Bellevue."

"Alas, my powers to convince have faded along with my desire to live. There is only one thing I care about in this wretched world, and that is my daughter."

There was something about his sincerity at that moment that touched Caleb, and he decided to try to keep an open mind.

"So if what you are telling me is true, then this Mrs. Flutter is setting up a man from the future to go down in the history books as Jack the Thwacker?"

The professor's eyes brightened. "Yes, that's correct," he said. "For some selfish reason, I suspect."

"And the real murders were committed by this time-traveler's double, or clone?"

"Precisely, Chief Spencer."

"And what do Boss Tweed and the Mummers get out of this?"

Campion held out his arm and a bird landed on it.

"*Bucorvus abyssinicus,* more commonly known as the ground hornbill. Not an attractive bird, but . . ."

"Please, Professor, help me help you here. What could the Mummers possibly gain from all this?"

Campion sat on the edge of the piranha fountain and threw the fish tiny bits of orange rind.

"You know, when I was a schoolboy studying this period of history, I was struck by how ordinary men, men with no great brilliance about them, could amass such staggering wealth merely through speculation. Why were some, who were born into the same wretched poverty as the cursed inhabitants of the Mulberry Bend, able to rise to the surface, while others were not? Were they so much smarter than the rest? But now I know that it wasn't just speculation, it was information—information sent to them from the future."

"Mrs. Flutter is telling Tweed what happens in the future?"

"Tweed is just a pawn. She supplies him with foreknowledge of politics, economics, natural catastrophes, wars, inventions . . . anything that will ensure that the affluent patriarchs of the city stay rich and get richer. There is nothing more powerful than the power to see the future."

"But how?"

"My time machine works two ways, forwards and backwards. But it is also a communicator."

"A telephone to the future?"

"I constructed it first, before the machine. I had to be sure that someone here would finance my plans . . . but apparently in my absence it has fallen into the wrong hands."

Caleb ran his fingers through his thinning hair.

"Professor, I want to believe you, but . . . I mean . . . so why the death ceremony?"

"I left the organization when Boss Tweed and the patriarchs reverted back to the old, dark practices of ancient Mummery . . . practices that include human sacrifices."

"Yes, I know this part. I heard it from Tom Thumb and the little people."

"Oh, don't get me started on the little people. Those guys really got a raw deal."

He stroked Roosevelt's pet anaconda and sighed, forcing himself to relive a ghastly incident in his life.

"When they found out I intended to go to the authorities, to tell the whole story . . . about the clone, the human sacrifices, the time machine, they . . . well, they . . . they threatened to take my daughter . . . so I sent her far away."

"Where did you send her, Professor?"

"They claimed that my daughter's birth coincided with the ancient Mummerick calendar's prophecy of the arrival of the true earth goddess, Erce. I didn't want her mixed up with that evil cult . . . it was for her own safety."

"*Where* did you send her, professor?"

"I sent her to live with relatives . . . in Maine."

"Maine? . . . then that means . . ."

"Yes, Chief Spencer, Elisabeth Smith is my daughter."

Caleb furrowed his brow.

"Who else would it have been, really?"

"And you tried to warn her, didn't you?" Caleb was starting to put the pieces together.

"When the 'Great'—that's a laugh—Houdini informed me that the Thwacker scheme was afoot, I wrote to Liz in Cairo and warned her to stay away, but that plan backfired. I should have anticipated that her ceaseless need to satisfy her own curiosity would override any safety precautions on my part.

"I could have told you that was a bonehead move."

"So later I attempted another warning—firing a blank at you from up there. Yes, that was me. I apologize for being so dramatic."

"Well Professor, maybe it would have been simpler just to come out and tell Liz in person what was going on."

"Impossible. She would never believe me. She hates me, and I don't blame her. After all, I sent her away. And, frankly, up until that point I wasn't that great of a father." Campion sighed. "We mad scientists so rarely are. Now she believes me to be . . . *non compos mentis*. You see, Tweed had me committed to Bellevue to ensure that any future accusations on my part would be deemed the nonsensical ravings of a lunatic. I could not tell her the truth because I feared getting her involved . . ."

"So, at this moment, two identical human beings are walking around New York City, one of them a poor, hapless victim, and the other . . . the Thwacker!"

"That is correct."

"No it's not. The Thwacker is dead!" I declared from the doorway.

Caleb whipped around and pointed his .32 at me.

"Hold it right there!" he demanded.

"I just left the nondescript brownstone! He committed suicide!" I said, and then I hiccuped. "But he didn't fall down the incineratour . . . ter . . . incineraterrrr."

"Okay, Professor, which one is this? The Thwacker or the hapless victim?" Caleb pulled out the "wanted" flyer and compared it to my face.

"Caleb! Caleb! I can't believe it's really you!" I moved quickly to him and squished his face with my fingers, poked him, checked his teeth, and sniffed him vigorously.

He backed away from me, quite puzzled. "Do I know you?" he asked.

"There's only one way to be certain," said Campion, and he retrieved a large object out of a duffle bag. "I invented this for just such an occasion."

The object looked like a big wooden vacuum cleaner, and he had to tug exhaustingly several times on its cord to get the motor started. Then he ran the nozzle up and down my body.

"Stop it. Stop! It tickles!"

After a moment, he turned the machine off.

"He's the original all right."

"He's also inebriated," said Caleb.

"Hey, I represent that remark!" I slurred. "I just had a couple of li'l drinky-poos with the murderer, that's all. Hey, he's a hell of a dancer . . . *was* . . . *was* a hell of a dancer." Suddenly I became mournful and I took off my top hat and my *Get a Life* baseball cap, held them over my heart, and bowed my head. "Let us observe ten minutes of silence in honor of the dearly deceased Thwacker man!" Then I broke out into uncontrollable laughter.

Caleb furrowed his brow and glared at me.

"Why the hell would you clone *that*?" he asked Campion incredulously.

"I didn't know *whom* I was cloning, that's the point. I thought Tweed got the donor hair from a cadaver at the morgue, not off the head of a real live moron from the future."

"Hey, that's not very nice, El Professoratory!" I chimed in as I plopped down hard on the floor and crossed my legs Indian-style. "Me wannem wigwam!" I cried. Then I toppled over.

"All right, Campion," said Caleb, now anxiously pacing again. "Say I believe you. What do we do now?"

"The Mummers have Liz and the mayor, and I believe—with a level of certainty—that they mean to sacrifice Roosevelt to her, thus paving the way for the Mummers to rise to even greater glory. Ah, supersititious hogwash."

"I suppose you've eliminated all that nonsense by the twenty-first century," said Caleb. "It must be terribly trying to

your patience to be surrounded by religious zealots and small-minded, power-hungry men."

"Ah, yes, well not exactly, but we've made leaps and bounds in the mass production of small plastic knicknacks."

"Hey, don't you want to hear what *I* know?" I asked from the floor.

"If only we knew where the death ritual was to take place," ruminated Campion.

"We've been trying to uncover that for three days now, with no luck!" said a defeated Caleb.

"Hey fellers!"

"Yes, I know, they are very good at keeping secrets, for obvious reasons."

"We haven't much time, either," warned Caleb, looking at his pocket watch.

"Yoo hoo, fellers, I know where it takes place!"

"I missed something along the way, some clue." Caleb was beating himself up now. "And my ineptitude has put both Elisabeth and the mayor in great danger." He buried his face in his palms.

"Don't blame yourself, Caleb, you've done everything you can." Campion put his hand on the chief's shoulder.

"Okay, forget it," I said. "I give up. I guess you two don't want to hear about Belvedere Castle?"

"What did you just say? Did you mention Castle Belvedere?" asked Campion.

"You bet your sweet bippy I did! I overheard Vanderbilt and Astor talking about it at Madame Belmont's . . . moont's . . . and I'll tell you something else, I think they're gonna try some coup d'état or some shit to take over the Mummers! Good night!" And I fell back over.

"This all makes sense," said Campion. "Castle Belvedere is a

"Lucy!" I yelled from my prone position on the floor,
and then I passed out in my own vomit.

mystical place, the perfect setting for the saturnalia, and it also makes sense that Vanderbilt and Astor would want to merge the National Coalition of Mummers under one single banner. Their power would reach from coast to coast."

Campion and Caleb both paced now. "But the Mummers are spiritual men," continued the professor. "They're devoted to their idols, so . . . of course the only way the Fancies could seize ultimate power would be to destroy the idol that they all commonly worship—their divine feminine figure."

"Erce?"

"The earth goddess."

"Elisabeth."

"We must hurry to the Central Park and stop them."

"How are we going to do that? There's just the two of us and this idiot drunk! We're outnumbered!"

"Outnumbered perhaps," said Campion with a twinkle in his eyes. "But not outfoxed—I have an idea!"

"Oh, I hate it when she says that! Lucy!" I yelled from my prone position on the floor, and then I passed out in my own vomit.

Chapter the Eighteenth.

A warning to the fainthearted: included in these pages is the description of a battle fraught with such an inordinate amount of blood as to turn the stomach of even the most seasoned of readers. I pray you read at your own peril.

THE FIRE THAT MRS. O'LEARY'S COW STARTED HAD NOW SPREAD BEYOND the nondescript brownstone to consume the entire block on Nineteenth Street.

Meanwhile, in Central Park, at approximately 12:05 AM, a bizarre apparition began to form out of the fog that floated gracefully through the rambles just north of Belvedere Castle. From betwixt the giant redwood pines, ancient copper beeches, and massive walnut trees, out tromped Archibald Campion's mechanical soldier, Boilerplate, stamping forward with an unstoppable determination. (The professor's brilliant idea.)

The robot held human cargo in each hand. Caleb sat in Boilerplate's right palm, and I sat in its left, while Campion straddled its shoulders steering the contraption with a heavy control box.

Belvedere Castle (Italian for "deadly view"), sat perched high atop Central Park's grandest elevation, a jagged rock formation known as Vista Crag (meaning "rock of the deadly view").

The castle, a prime example of imposing Gothic architecture, was replete with battered stone walls, numerous terraces, and ominous-looking towers. It was built by Frederic Law Olmstead

and Calvert Vaux on the ruins of an old Druid temple. Native Americans who inhabited Central Park long after the Druids had returned home to . . . um . . . Liverpool . . . believed the location to have been haunted by the ghosts of strange creatures who appeared to them as half man and half animal, as well as "the big-headed gray midgets who came down from the stars to stick magic arrowheads in the bottoms of the worthy."

Today, like Stonehenge, crop circles, and daylight savings, no one is certain what purpose it served. But the Castle Belvedere remains a Mecca for hosts of teen goths, Wiccans, and all manner of misguided youths hopped up on the dope and the crack and the Coolattas, looking for answers in this crazy, mixed-up place we call Earth.

In 1882 Belvedere Lake, a small armlet of the old Croton reservoir, sat at the base of Vista Crag. Today, the lake is called Turtle Pond, and its serene character belies its ugly past. Back then, more than just cute turtles inhabited the murky pool. A myriad of deadly reptiles, insects, and scaly amphibians abounded. Hungry alligators cruised its face or snoozed along its banks while huge boa constrictors hid amid the bulrushes in its shallows. Fierce-looking dragonflies skimmed the top, and hideous vultures kept a constant vigil, waiting for anything deceased to float to the surface.

Taken all together, the castle and its surrounding death pond offered the ideal location for the Mummers' midnight bacchanalia.

"Okay, close enough," Caleb whispered, and we stopped beneath a rustic bentwood pagoda just out of sight of the castle.

Boilerplate made a soft hydraulic sound as his right arm descended slowly, gently lowering Caleb. Then it made a rickety rattling noise and turned its left palm upside down, dropping me straight into the mud below.

"Sorry," tittered Campion. "I guess it's still got a couple of kinks to work out."

From our vantage point we could make out torches burning outside the castle. A banner welcoming "Brother Mummers of 1882" hung above the castle's giant Gothic doors.

At the other end of the lake, we noticed activity around the base of the statue of King Wladyslaw Jagiello, the fifteenth-century Lithuanian count who supposedly crucified thousands of Teutonic Knights of the Cross during the battle for Grunwald in 1410 and then claimed afterwards that he had been sleepwalking when he did it. I know this because I'm a big King Wladyslaw Jagiello buff—always have been, always will be.

"They're gathering," said Caleb. "I need to get a better look."

Campion picked up the control box and pushed a couple of buttons. Suddenly, Boilerplate grabbed Caleb by his underarms and hoisted him straight up in the air.

"How's that?" asked Campion.

"Perfect. If anyone sees me, they'll just think I'm monkeying around on the statue of Hans Christian Anderson."

I was still pretty looped and I was peering through Caleb's binoculars, looking directly at the back of Campion's head, which was only about six inches away, when Caleb called for his field glasses.

Campion pulled them away from me.

"Hey, I was looking at those, meanie!"

"Welcome to the world of conjunctivitis," the professor said to me, and then he chuckled and handed the binocs up to Caleb.

"What the hell is wrong with you nineteenth-century people? You just want to spread your filthy diseases . . . all around the . . . universe?" I babbled, not entirely sure what the hell I was saying.

Caleb focused on the other side of the lake. A slow procession began making its way towards the castle.

"It's beginning," he said. "They've got those mechanical monks posted on all levels of the crag."

"They're expecting something, then," said Campion. "We'll have to be careful."

The parade was led by a man holding a torch and dressed in brightly colored rags. Behind him was a figure covered from head to toe in straw. He held a banner emblazoned with the insignia of the Fancy Brigade (a crossed sword and banjo). One after another, hundreds of gaily attired Mummers, some carrying torches and some carrying banners delineating their specific brigade, marched contiguously towards the castle. We could hear their low murmuring as they approached.

"Erce, *Terra Mater*. Erce, *Terra Mater*."

Caleb shook his head.

"What a ridiculous batch of front-page clodpolls," he muttered.

"Can you see anything?" whispered the professor to Caleb.

"Nothing illegal. Unless they don't have a parade permit!"

I started laughing hysterically at his joke. It wasn't that funny, I just couldn't control myself, but then my laughter turned quickly to tears.

"I miss Wendell," I hiccuped. "He's my best friend . . . and . . ."

"Shhh! Shhh!" Both Caleb and the professor admonished me for being so loud.

"Ooh, me so sorry!" I said in an Asian accent for no apparent reason.

"Okay. Get me down," said Caleb.

Boilerplate again lowered Caleb gently to the ground. I can't be sure, but it seemed the robot turned to me and smirked.

"All right," said Caleb, "stay low and follow me."

We crouched down as we navigated the thorny hemlock bushes that encircled the lake, sneaking around to the far side of

the forbidding castle. Boilerplate moved quickly and quite adeptly for a robot of its girth and weight. *Campion really knows his robots,* I thought to myself, as we hunkered down behind a large boulder and scanned out our next move.

A hooded bogey stood watch on a stone outcropping just above our hiding spot.

"We have to get by him," whispered Caleb. "Then we'll have to climb."

"Look what I found," I said, picking something white out of the pond. It was a lady's bra and it had the initials *E.S.* embroidered on it. I winked at Boilerplate and he made a lascivious whirring sound. Caleb and Campion looked at the undergarment with trepidation, and then looked at each other. *Could it be the same bra from the evidence box?* I wondered. I took a magic marker out of my pocket and wrote, "Stop sniffing me, you pervert!" *Hah! That'll really mess with future me's head!*

"I'll take care of the Ghost of Christmas Future, first," said Caleb. He climbed up Boilerplate's rigid body and moved onto the rocks about ten feet below the guard. He inched his way up to within reach of the fiend's lower extremities. Then, in true Spencer fashion, he pulled out his nightstick and swung it hard at the phantom's ankles, sending him flying off the ledge. The sentinel plummeted down into the murky lake below.

The splash was small and surprisingly quiet, and immediately, a throng of ravenous, not to mention stupid, alligators converged on the spot and attempted to devour the metal wraith.

"All clear!" whispered Caleb. And we began to ascend Vista Crag.

The earlier rain had left the rocks damp and slippery, and it was difficult to get a grip.

"I remember doing this in high school," I whispered.

"Shh, quiet!"

"I was drunk back then, too."

Suddenly I lost my footing and fell backwards. I tumbled in midair a few thousand times before I felt a sharp, painful tug around my neck. I was strangling—I couldn't breathe. Boilerplate had caught me by the collar. He pulled me up and I clung to his back, holding on to his shoulders with my legs wrapped around his iron torso for the rest of the climb. He may have been made of metal, but he was my friend.

We scaled the southern wall of the castle, and then one by one we slipped over the parapet wall and secreted ourselves behind a large column on a balcony that overlooked the grand courtyard below, mindful not to be discovered by the shrouded monks who paced back and forth on the same overlook.

The procession of Mummers had now gathered and the yard was filled to the brim with every species of clown known to man: Auguste clowns, White Face clowns, Tramps, Merry-Andrews, Zanies, Buffoons, Lawyers. They were all there.

The Fancy Brigade, the most feared of the Mummers, consisted of men wearing colorful masks and huge feathered wings. They hoofed it up, flawlessly performing their famous Mummer's strut, or "fancy walk," while the String Brigade played "I'm Looking Over a Four-Leaf Clover." The Straw Man danced around a bonfire like a witch doctor, while the Comic Brigade, masquerading as women, aped an outlandish burlesque striptease. Large wooden kegs lined the outer walls, and the beer flowed freely.

The elaborate costumes, the dazzling colors, and the orgy of boisterous jocundity suggested a harmless party thrown by a bunch of happily inebriated conventioneers. But in truth, this was the beginning stages of an ancient pagan fertility rite that had been practiced throughout the ages by the Babylonians, Sumerians, Egyptians, and Celtics (that's right—the basketball team), and its inevitable, awful finale would not include bursting

open a piñata shaped like a donkey, but rather a human sacrifice—two to be exact.

"Full moon," said Campion softly. "The symbol of the power of the goddess."

Caleb looked up and smirked. "Orion—the symbol of the power of the hunter!" Then he hit his chest with his fist.

"Milky Way," I said. "The symbol of the way-too-fried-to-do-this-shit time-traveler," and then I giggled.

Boilerplate looked up too, but alas, the contraption was not capable of speaking, so we will never know what brilliant obiter dictum the gentle giant was thinking at that particular moment.

"There's Liz," Caleb said, relieved. "She's alive!"

Elisabeth was sitting cross-legged on a raised bamboo platform that appeared to be some sort of altar. She was half naked, wearing a sort of feathery tribal lingerie that will miraculously cover any parts you might have been interested in seeing for the remainder of this chapter. Her body was decorated with brightly colored hieroglyphics. Around her neck hung a myriad of tribal necklaces, and she wore copper wrist and ankle bands. Her giant headdress was made out of peacock feathers and it was obviously too heavy for her neck to support, as her head swayed back and forth. Her eyes were shut and she looked either drugged or under some sort of spell or both.

"But I don't see Roosevelt."

"If he's to be made a sacrifice, they're probably anointing his body with almond oil right now," said Campion.

"Why do I think he'd be enjoying that?"

The party reached an orgiastic pitch. The String Brigade was now playing "I'm a Yankee Doodle Dandy." The level of volume made by the noisemakers, the whoops, the howls, and the banjo music was positively deafening.

The Straw Man reached into a barrel and pulled out a handful

of black powder, which he threw into the bonfire. Immediately it exploded, sending burning cinders shooting into the universe.

Suddenly everything stopped.

Not a sound.

I tried to surpress a laugh. There wasn't anything funny going on, but you have to remember the condition I was in.

"I'm going around to the other side. Wait for my signal," whispered Caleb. Campion nodded, Boilerplate saluted, and I belched.

Campion removed his monk's robe, revealing his frayed Bellevue crazed-person's pajamas, and handed the robe to Caleb.

"You might need this. Now go save my daughter. And good luck."

The young police chief hunched down and dashed from one column to the next, making his way to the side of the yard where Liz sat below on the altar.

From high atop the castle towers came the exotic moans of the didgeridoo (or something like that), an ancient Aboriginal wind instrument. The horns were blown three times, signaling the mass of Mummers to supplicate and begin chanting:

"Erce, Erce. *Terra Mater, Terra Mater.*"

"Erce, Erce. *Terra Mater, Terra Mater.*"

Caleb slipped into the robe and pulled the hood over his head. He walked the parapet undetected by the other guards. He was in his true element now, in which he was always the most capable—cross-dressing.

While the Mummers were occupied by their chanting, he sidled down a stairwell that brought him to the courtyard level.

Moving quickly, he positioned himself near Elisabeth, sneaked up behind the monk guarding her, and opened his switchblade knife. Gently slicing the back of the monk's robe, he located a small door in the robot's lower back and pried it open with his knife. He stuck his hand in and yanked out a fistful of

wires. Sparks flew out, smoke emanated from the opening, and
the monk collapsed in a smoldering heap.

"*Terra Mater. Terra Mater. Terra Mater,*" chanted the crowd quietly and rhythmically as they swayed back and forth. Someone
struck a tambourine.

Caleb was just about to grab Liz when—

Boom!

A loud explosion rocked the yard, and out of the billowing
smoke appeared the Grand Poobah of the Mummers—William
"Boss" Tweed.

The big man's face was painted all white, and he was covered
in white feathers and frilly boas. His head was topped with an
all-white Indian chief's headdress, and to each arm were attached giant white feathered wings.

"Look at this muggins," I said to Boilerplate.

"Don't be fooled," warned Campion. "Tweed is the Plutocrat—very powerful. He orchestrates the entire ritual, and it is
said that he has the evil eye . . . the power to kill . . ." Campion
bulged out his eyes and pushed his face into mine, ". . . just by
looking at you!"

"Hey, back off, you nut. I still say he's a muggins." I offered
my hand to Boilerplate to slap me five, but he didn't.

Tweed addressed the assembly:

In comes I but wonth a year.
Pray give me room to rhyme.
For I will show you activities, my dears,
That shall make the theeing man blind!"

A stentorious cheer rose from the rabble, shaking the old
castle walls. Caleb pulled Liz off the platform, and she fell into
his arms.

"Liz, Liz? It's me, Caleb." He slapped her face several times. She woke with a start and slapped him back.

"Ow, jeez, Liz. I'm trying to save you, here."

"Caleb? Oh Caleb, I thought you were Tweed." She threw her arms around him and gave him a long and sensuous kiss.

"Okay, honey, keep it in your pants till we get out of here, will ya?" he quipped.

"Before we begin," announced Tweed,"I want to let you all know that thankth to our thuccthethfull parade and our convention at Madithon Thquare Garden, we have raised a record two hundred and twenty-thikth dollars and eighty-three thenth to be put towards our annual convention next year. Congratulations one and all!"

Another cheer rose from the kneeling Mummers. Caleb shrouded Liz in the defrocked monk's robe, and they hurried up the steps to the parapet.

"Oh, and on a personal note: a thpecial thankth to the Thnack Brigade—those brownies were thimply to die for!"

The Mummers all laughed, and the Snack Brigade patted each other on their backs.

Caleb and Liz were moving swiftly and unnoticed towards us. The Plutocrat pulled out the big book of names, opened it, and began a monotoned incantation:

By De Temporum Ratione we pray to
those who thelebrate with uth Imbolce, Beitane,
Lugnathda, and of course my favorite holidays,
Lammath and Thamhain.
We pray to Hezmonath and
all the Valkyries to bring forth
our true virgin goddeth, for she walkth
the earth even now . . .

Liz stopped short. She appeared to be enthralled by the ceremony.

"Liz, we have to hurry," Caleb whispered.

"Wait. The shape-shifters are coming."

As the big man with the lisp continued to babble, queer behavior possessed some of the costumed participants in the yard. One began to convulse and another seemed to levitate a few inches off the ground, although as Caleb looked closer, it was obvious that the guy was just standing on his toes. Another Mummer began to howl at the moon, and still another was on all fours hopping up and down and making frog sounds.

The String Brigade started up a snappy version of "Toyland," and a fast-moving procession of morbidly obese albinos wearing nothing but white dhotis entered the yard led by Rob Roy, the albino freak from Coney Island. Teddy was with them, tied by his wrists and ankles to a pole. He was also naked except for his loincloth.

Caleb whispered, "Liz, we need to move."

But Elisabeth didn't respond. Her eyes seemed glazed over. She barely blinked as she stared straight ahead. She was lost in a trance. Something unseen had control over her mind and body.

"It is I. It is I," she repeated softly.

"Something's wrong," Campion said, and I elbowed Boilerplate as if to say "Get a load of this guy."

In the yard, Tweed brandished a knife as the albino goons affixed Roosevelt to a makeshift wooden rotisserie suspended above the bonfire. The Straw Man danced around it, whooping it up, and shaking a rattle in Teddy's face.

"Good Lord. D'you mean to roast me alive? Weehoo!" And with that the flames grew momentarily higher, singeing the bottom of his loincloth. Tweed moved menacingly close to Roosevelt and began his final incantation:

Hail to thee, *Terra Mater*
Mother of men.
Be fruitful in our embrathe.
Filled with food for the uthe of men.

"Tweed, now I know we've had our differences in the past, but why not be a dove and cut my bindings, and let's be done with this half-assed pagan goosery!"

"Teddy, my old friend, I've been wanting to cut your throat ever thinth the day I met you!" And he put the knife under the mayor's jaw.

"It is I!"

Silence fell over the yard—and all heads turned upwards.

Elisabeth was standing on the parapet in plain view, having discarded the monk's robe. At that moment a brisk wind blew over the crag, so that her feathers ruffled dramatically. (But you still couldn't see anything good.)

"Liz, what the hell are you doing?" Caleb hissed.

Cornelius Vanderbilt and John J. Astor were standing amidst their fellow Fancy Brigadiers, and they pulled off their masks and began to retrieve their daggers from beneath their feathers.

"It is I you seek! I am she—virgin mother of Mummers! . . . Well the virgin part . . . not so much. Anyway, it is I! Let the true festival of Saturnalia begin!"

With that, she spread her arms open wide like wings, bent her knees, tightened her buttcheeks, and hurled herself off the parapet.

"Liz, no!" cried Caleb.

She landed below in the arms of the Fancy Brigade and was passed forward to the Plutocrat mosh-pit style. Vanderbilt and Astor were on either side of Tweed with their daggers drawn.

"Hold it right there! You are all under arrest!" yelled Caleb, but no one could hear him over the boisterous yelps from the mob.

"Quiet! It is she, Erthe!" declared Tweed. "But look upon her, my brother Mummers. She is no goddeth . . . she is merely mortal. Let uth dithpatch her now, and thend her back to the netherworld, and worship no falthe idols ever again. Let uth unite as one. One nation of Mummers. Under *one* banner. The banner of the Fanthy Brigade!"

The only brigade to cheer was of course the Fancies. The other Mummers began to murmur amongst themselves in dissatisfaction.

"It must be done quickly, before they revolt," said Vanderbilt to Tweed, and as Astor held Liz, Vanderbilt raised his dagger.

Caleb fired his pistol, but the bullet didn't even come close to Vanderbilt. He looked at his pathetic little gun. "One of these days they have to come up with a weapon that has a little more oomph to it."

Sensing his moment (as much as any robot can), Boilerplate pushed Campion and me aside and stepped from behind the column. He made a hydraulic noise and his arms cocked at the elbows. His wrists clanked open and two Gatling-gun nozzles extended out. He began to blast away.

Bang bang bang bang bang bang bang bang bang bang . . .

Pandemonium broke out as the Mummers sprinted for cover. Vanderbilt and Astor dropped Elisabeth, and she snapped back to reality.

"What in the name of Charles Dickens in heat is going on?" she cried.

"Boilerplate!" exclaimed Roosevelt. "You're finally out of the closet!"

The beer barrels were blasted apart, sending tidal waves of

frothy brew into the panicking harlequins. Bullets were landing dangerously close to the barrel of black powder as the iron machine kept firing. A rain of spent shells fell smoking at its feet.

"Attack!" shouted Vanderbilt, and the Fancy Brigade pulled out spike-covered tambourines and banjos with affixed bayonets. They began to do battle with the other Mummer brigades.

"Good gracious! The scarecrow has Liz!" Roosevelt observed while his fat roasted over the bonfire. Young Police Chief Caleb R. Spencer dashed toward her, and with a swift kick he sent the Straw Man sailing backwards, into the bonfire. His costume in flames, the scarecrow rolled around trying to extinguish himself.

Liz grabbed Caleb's knife and cut Teddy's ropes.

Before he fled the castle, Tweed shot Caleb, Roosevelt, and Smith the evil eye, but it didn't kill them, so he gave them the evil middle finger instead and quickly escaped under cover of the smoke from the Gatling guns.

"Hurry to the parapet. We must flee!" commanded Spencer.

"Yes, of course," said Roosevelt. "'As dry leaves before the wild hurricane fly' and so on and so on. But wait!" He stopped. "Do my eyes deceive me or is that little Ishi?"

The strawman's straw, having burned away, now revealed the smoldering Indian standing before them.

"Ishi, bad! Bad boy!" scolded Roosevelt.

"I'm terribly sorry, old chap. No hard feelings. It's just that you're such a bloody bore. That's all." And then the wild Indian let out a frightening war-cry and threw his tomahawk at Teddy. The projectile bounced off T. R.'s head with a loud *clank* and Ishi bolted away.

"I never trusted the Yahi. Dreadful race of savages," said Roosevelt.

They were hemmed in by an overwhelming number of Fancy

Brigadiers. Caleb did his best to bash heads with his nightstick, and Liz turned into a red-faced madwoman, kicking feathered groins right and left, while Roosevelt held his own, ramming his hard head into his attackers' bellies—but it was still a losing battle.

"There's too many of them!" Liz shouted.

"We have to get to the parapet!" said Caleb.

"You two go, this is grand sport!" declared Teddy as he knocked the wind out of another mountebank with his cannon-ball cranium.

"You're coming with us, Teddy," demanded Elisabeth.

"My dear Chief Spencer, please be so kind as to escort Miss Smith to the parapet. Don't worry about me. If I have to, I am more than willing to sacrifice my life. For it is what evil men count upon the good men doing!"

Spencer had already retrieved the bottle of chloroform that he had pocketed at Bellevue, and now he held its lip under the mayor's nose. Teddy immediately fell into his arms and, with Liz's assistance, Spencer dragged him up to the parapet.

In Washington Heights, the carriage doors to the old medieval Cloisters creaked open and out marched row after row of mechanical hooded monks—hundreds and hundreds of them in ranks of ten across. They marched down Fort Tryon Park, across Broadway over to Fifth Avenue, and then into Central Park, headed for Belvedere Castle to abet the Fancy Brigade's attempt to seize power.

Bang bang bang bang bang bang bang bang bang bang!

"What? Who said that? Where am I?" blustered Teddy. "Why Boilerplate, it's good to see you back in action, my old mechanical mule!" He smacked the tin man on its back and the robot shot out another blast of bullets.

Chris Elliott

Caleb glanced at the label on the bottle of chloroform. "I thought it was supposed to put a person out for two hours," he said to himself. "I guess it must go by weight."

Archibald Campion stepped from behind the column and faced his daughter.

"Hello, Elisabeth."

Liz froze.

"Daddy?"

At that moment—even in the midst of the violent chaos—the world stopped turning for her. Campion's melancholic orbs conveyed a sincere mea culpa for the sad chronicle of events that had ordered their lives thus far, as well as a heartfelt plea for forgiveness and a prayer for reconciliation hereafter. Elisabeth needed no particulars at that moment, for she felt, as he did, the undeniable pain and loss that the years of estrangement had caused them both, and she understood intrinsically the heavy burden that he had carried so selflessly for all this time—out of love for her . . . and at that moment, as the world stood still, all she needed was a hug from Daddy.

The two embraced.

I was bawling uncontrollably. Boilerplate opened a compartment in its arm and handed me a tissue before returning to firing its missiles.

"There is so much I need to say," Campion told Liz.

"Not now, Daddy. Just tell me: you're not the Thwacker, right?"

I answered for him: "No, *I* am," I said, wiping the sniffles away from my red nose. "Well not really me, but my double, but he's dead. So don't worry."

Liz looked confused by me, and perhaps a little grossed out as well.

"I'm sorry, allow me to introduce myself, I am your humble servant, ma'am. Chris Elliott's the name—actor, writer, bon vi-

vant from the twenty-first century." I clicked my heels and took her hand and French-kissed it.

"Eew," she said, quickly pulling it away.

"I'm sorry, I'm also a little pickled."

"Don't worry, he's harmless," said Caleb. "I'll explain later. Right now we have to get out of here."

"Easier said than done, my good chief!" roared Roosevelt, for the army of monks was crossing the Great Lawn and advancing rapidly on the castle.

"Good heavens, there must be thousands of them," said Caleb.

"Then all is lost," moaned Liz.

"Not necessarily. You underestimate the power of . . . the . . . *Mud Tots!*" declared Roosevelt. He opened a compartment in Boilerplate's back and pulled out his old battered bugle. He blew the instrument and shouted, "Charge!"

From out of the thick hemlock bushes surrounding the castle, the entire Mud Tot tribe emerged, armed and ready for battle. Chickabiddy glanced up at the mayor. They smiled at each other. Then Teddy pointed towards the Great Lawn and the young chief responded by giving him the "okay" sign.

"But they're just children . . . and . . . babies," said an astonished Liz.

"Yes, children and babies that are quite a adept at the art of war, my dear," said Roosevelt, pushing a monk off the parapet into the yard.

"Umm, that's kind of a sad commentary on your society, don't you think?" I said, but no one was even listening. "Hello? Hey everyone, I'm still here!" I shouted—nothing. So I managed a sad, surly "twenty-first century rules!" under my breath.

The mammoth army of monks and the ragtag tribe of Mud Tots charged toward each other at breakneck speed, the Tots screaming at the top of their lungs.

"This is a bad idea," yelled Molly Coddle, raising her club 'n' spikes.

"Oh come on," shouted Bambino. "We haven't maimed and mutilated in a long time. We need the practice!"

"Runabout! Get your butt back here!" bellowed Chickabiddy. The little infant was in her diaper and smoking a cigar, crawling ahead of the pack, but she fell back at his command. "You stay close to us."

The two armies collided in the middle of the Great Lawn and a wall of dust rose up, concealing the action, but we could hear horrible, unearthly sounds emanating from the haze covering the melee.

The battle was short and sweet, and when the dust settled, the Mud Tots were standing on top of a giant scrap-metal heap of ass-whipped monks. They let out their triumphant war cry, and Chickabiddy waved to Roosevelt. Teddy saluted in return and gave him the thumbs up.

"That was unexpected," said Vanderbilt to Astor. "Without the monks, we are completely outnumbered. Oh well, I suppose we always have next year's convention to seize ultimate Mummer power."

"Yes, I suppose we do," replied Astor.

"Call for the retreat. I'm returning to my Fifth Avenue mansion, for I'm quite fagged out. What say you we take over the Mummers *next year,* and spend the rest of this waste of a year in beautiful Barbados."

Astor called for retreat, and the Fancy Brigadiers laid down their weapons. The fighting ceased. The rest of the Mummers cheered.

"Hurray!" "Yay!" "Yippee!" We were all jumping for joy. Roosevelt hugged Campion, Liz made out with Caleb, I smacked Boilerplate on his back, and . . .

A huge explosion ripped through Castle Belvedere.

Bang bang bang!

One final volley blasted out of the automaton's guns and, unfortunately, straight into the barrel of black powder. A huge explosion ripped through Castle Belvedere, and a box in the corner of the yard marked FIREWORKS FOR AFTER THE SACRIFICE erupted as well.

"Jump!" yelled Caleb, and all five of us leaped off the parapet into the black lake below, just as Olmstead and Vaux's Gothic folly blew up in an awesome display of fireballs, glittering crossettes, blue pearl comets, and sparkling roman candles.

Chapter the Nineteenth.

In which occurs a denouement so controversial that it will rock the very foundations of religion, politics, and New York City real estate.

As all this was happening in Central Park, most of lower Manhattan was now ablaze thanks to Mrs. O'Leary's clumsy cow.

In 1882, the municipal fire department had not yet been established, so the city relied heavily on volunteer organizations to fight its infernos. Unfortunately these organizations were made up of goons and cutthroats with strong ties to various rival political factions. They basically amounted to nothing more than street gangs with hoses. The fire companies went by colorful names like the Charter Oaks, the Shad Bellies, the Old Junk, and the Lady Washingtons, and their members were all loyal to their own constituencies and political leaders.

Consequently, the members of the Big Lisp (which was Boss Tweed's company) spent more time spraying water at the members of the Fatheads with Small Glasses and Big Mustaches (which was Roosevelt's company) than at the inferno.

And so, since there was no adequate means of extinguishing it, the Great Fire of 1882 began to move steadily north.

A MYRIAD OF BROKEN ROCKS, CRAZY HEADDRESSES, BENT INSTRUMENTS, smoldering costumes, shrouded monks, Mummers, and albinos splashed down into Belvedere Lake.

On the far shore, we dragged ourselves out of the lagoon and collapsed at the feet of King Jagiello. We were lucky to have escaped the alligator and boa constrictor attacks, the hungry animals preferring the blubbery albinos to our lean, muscular bodies. Now, as we watched the castle disintegrate into a pile of rubble, white feathers floated down all around us and the park became awash with sad clowns.

"Such a shame," said Teddy.

"I'm sure they'll rebuild it," said Liz.

"No, not that. I mean I would've liked to wrassle some of them gators."

Spencer sighed.

"You're welcome, you know," he groused.

"Young man, I'd like to congratulate you," Roosevelt roared, and Spencer puffed out his chest, this time ready and willing to receive some well-deserved accolades.

"You've finally come around about our little lady here, haven't you?" the mayor said, putting his big arm around Elisabeth and squeezing her. "She's quite the little lifesaver, isn't she?"

Liz smiled sheepishly at Caleb.

"I wouldn't be surprised if we don't make her a deputy in your little police department."

Caleb rolled his eyes.

"Look over there! I believe that's Boss Tweed fleeing!" observed Campion, peering through the binoculars.

The fat Mummer was bolting in the direction of the famous Central Park landmark Cleopatra's Needle.

"Hurry, we must apprehend him," shouted Caleb, and we all took off in pursuit.

The 70-foot-tall obelisk still stands on Greywacke Knoll today. It dates back to 461 BC and was given as a gift to New York City in 1869 from the khedive of Egypt. Although it's called Cleopatra's Needle, it was actually a tribute to Thutmose III and has absolutely nothing to do with Cleopatra whatsoever. Some people believe that it's not even Egyptian, but rather a leftover set piece from the popular musical *Joseph and the Amazing Technicolor Dreamcoat,* which first wowed audiences on Broadway back in 1866.

We trotted through the dense Japanese yews, magnolias, and crab apple trees up the steep embankment to Greywacke Knoll, and then looked around for Tweed. But he had vanished.

"Where is he?" I asked.

"I think I have a pretty good idea," said Liz.

She felt around the base of the obelisk, her hands gliding over its raised hieroglyphics. When she found the two symbols she was looking for, she grasped them and turned each one counterclockwise until something clicked.

With one hand Boilerplate heaved open the two-foot-thick stone door, and before us was a steep staircase heading downward.

"How did you know about this?" Caleb asked Liz.

"One of the benefits of working with archaeologists. Howard Carter and I were having afternoon crumpets and figs in my suite when he told me that they didn't just bring the obelisk over from Alexandria, they brought its entire underground catacomb system as well. It was part of some drunken fraternity prank at his archaeology school. The tunnels down there lead to an exit somewhere on the west side. Let's find out where."

"Sounds like you and Howard Carter were pretty chummy," Caleb said jealously.

"What if we were?"

"Oh please. Let's not start *this* hooey again," complained Roosevelt. "Miss Smith, since you seem to know so much about this old thing, why don't you lead the way?"

"Gladly." She lit a torch and started down the stairs.

Where and if we would ever come out was anyone's guess. (What do you think?)

AT THE MUSEUM OF NATURAL HISTORY, THE LITTLE FELLOW IN THE BUR-gundy bellhop's uniform paced nervously back and forth in front of the double doors to the planetarium. They were locked from the inside, and he could hear peculiar noises emanating from within. A flickering blue light shot out from underneath the doors and spilled across the floor in front of him.

"No no no, it's past closing time. No one should be in the celestial dome. I'm quite vexed. Yes, I'm quite vexed, indeed."

Then he heard what sounded like rapping coming from the coat-check room, and he went to investigate. He stood in the empty room, spooked by the persistent sound, then, glancing at the floor, he noticed a trapdoor. He unlatched it and opened it up.

Immediately Liz climbed out, in midsentence.

". . . so what you're telling me is that my father invented a time machine—*and* created a living human being?" The usher was shocked to see such a scantily dressed lady climbing out of the floor—in fact, he would have been shocked to see *any* lady climbing out of the floor, even a fully attired one.

"Oh, my apologies, good evening to you, sir," Liz said, and she curtsied.

"Yes. A very good evening to you too, madam," said the confounded usher.

"That's exactly what I'm telling you," stated Caleb, as he, too,

climbed out from beneath the floor. He was followed by Roosevelt and Campion. "Good evening," Campion said to the usher.

"I say, that's a spiffy uniform!" bellowed Roosevelt, tugging the epaulettes on the usher's jacket. "What regiment are you with?"

"Regiment, sir?" said the overwhelmed usher. "I'm with no regiment, sir." He was so confounded that the trapdoor slipped out of his fingers and came down hard on my head.

"Ow!"

"Oh, I didn't see you there," he said, pulling it open again.

"And out of all the people in the world . . . you duplicated *that*?" Liz pointed at me as I stepped out from beneath the floor, rubbing my head.

"I was tricked," explained Campion, not for the first time.

Next Boilerplate climbed out of the hole and towered over the little usher, who took one look at the giant iron man, said "G-g-g-good evening," and promptly fainted straight away.

"So the question remains—why would this Mrs. Flutter want to frame this poor simpleton?" concluded Liz.

"That's right," said Caleb.

"Hey guys, I'm not that simple. In fact, some people find me rather complex." I was feeling sober now after the cold dunk in Belvedere Lake. "You people aren't as nice as I describe you in the book."

"Son," bellowed Teddy, gripping my shoulders with his small but powerful round hands. "Remember, envy is as evil a thing as is arrogance!" Then he smacked my face with his open palm.

"Ow."

Boilerplate chuckled and let out a blast of steam.

"Perhaps we shall find the answers we seek right here," said wise old Professor Campion. "Look where we are."

"The museum!" observed Elisabeth.

Caleb moved to the locked double doors. "And behind these doors lies the planetarium."

"Yes! And my ticket home!" I yelped.

Campion raised his index finger. "I must remind you that the time machine . . ."

"Yeah, yeah, I know" I said. "It only works one way. You know, for being such a brilliant guy, you would think you could have figured out a way to get it to go back and forth."

"I'm working on it," he groused. "You try warping the space-time continuum on a professor's salary some time . . ."

Boilerplate yanked hard on the handles, and the heavy doors tore away from their hinges. A blast of hot air burst out of the planetarium, and from somewhere shone a blinding blue light.

The round room was glowing and alive with static electricity. Boss Tweed stood in the middle under the dome, next to the mechanism that projects the stars on the ceiling (I've tried to find out what it's called, but I don't think it has a name; anyway, at this point I'm sick of doing research). He was holding the Book of Names, as well as a gun.

"Please come in. You're jutht in time."

We walked halfway down the aisle.

"That'th clothe enough. Take a theat."

"Just in time for what, Tweed?" asked Caleb.

"To witneth my grand departure from thith backwards period in time. Do you know that in the future they have thomething called television, where one can enjoy a minthtrel show in the comfort of one's own parlor? They also have 'expeditiouth edibles' . . ."

Everyone looked puzzled.

"Fast food," I explained under my breath.

". . . therved quickly and in mammoth proportions. New

York Thity is no longer divided between the haves and the have-noth—it belongs entirely to the haves! And I plan to be a part of it!"

He was about to pull a lever on the celestial projector (hey, that's the name of that thing . . . here comes another smooch for the old forearm) when suddenly the dome came alive with bright lights and shooting stars. Harrison Ford's voice began to narrate.

"A long, long time ago . . ."

"Bunk in," I whispered to Roosevelt. "I've seen this before. It's really dull." I slumped down in my seat and rested my head on his shoulder. He moved to another seat.

Suddenly there was a loud *boom* like something had broken the sound barrier, and a giant portal, rimmed by electromagnetic charges, materialized in the middle of the room.

In the center of the portal, an image began to take shape. We watched as the picture became clearer and clearer, until the un-mistakable wrinkly visage of Mrs. Flutter, the museum curator, appeared. It was like we were watching a giant TV screen broad-casting from the future (like maybe some shitty PBS show).

"What the hell is taking so long?" asked Mrs. Flutter in an ir-ritated voice.

"That's her! That's Mrs. Flitter!" I shouted, as I stood and pointed.

"Flutter," she corrected, rolling her eyes.

"She's the witch that sent me back in time!" Teddy moved yet another seat away.

"Yes, that's her," said Campion.

"Oh, hello there, Professor," she said. "I thought you were in the nut house? Have you figured out how to make the contrap-tion go back and forth yet?"

"I'm working on it," he muttered. "It's actually more com-plicated than you might think."

"Stay here," Caleb whispered to Liz. He moved through the row of seats, making his way around to flank Tweed.

"Caleb! Where are you going?" she whispered, but he didn't answer. Her curiosity got the better of her, as usual, and she sneaked down the aisle after him.

"So, do you have an answer for me, Tweed?" asked Mrs. Flutter. "Or are you just going to stand there like a big tub of lisping lard?"

"I'm thorry, Madame Flutter. But the plan has failed. The clone had a conscienthe! He implicated not only the thimpleton, but the Mummers as well!"

"I could give a shit about the Mummers! Why is the kid not in jail?"

"Because everyone believes me! Ha ha!" I said triumphantly, "And now I'd like an answer from you, Madame Fluffer-nutter . . ."

"Oh shut up, jerk, and just sit down," she commanded, but I ignored her.

"Why me?" I asked. "Why did you want to frame *me*?"

"Yes, why him?" asked Liz, popping up in the front row.

"Liz, stay back!" demanded Caleb, revealing himself positioned only a few feet from Tweed. Tweed spun around and pointed his gun at Caleb.

"Thtay back Thpenther, or I'll shoot!"

"What did I ever do to you?" I asked the giant lady in the swirling portal.

"Yes, do tell him why! In fact, tell us all why!" said a new voice from somewhere in the darkened auditorium. And then out of the shadows stepped the fake Roosevelt. "Tell them everything!"

"Why, look who's here! It's the bogus me!" exclaimed Teddy. "Young man, I oughta take you out to the woodshed and give you a good thrashing!"

"You cloned him, too?" I asked Campion.

"All right, who cloned Roosevelt?" said a confused Professor Campion. "I know I didn't do it."

"But I'm *not* a clone." The fake Roosevelt put his fingers behind his ears and began to pick away the mask that he was wearing.

It only took a moment before I knew who it was.

"Wendell!"

"Who's Wendell?" asked Liz.

"He's only my bestest friend in the whole wide world. But what are you doing here? I thought you were shacked up with your new girlfriend!"

"Chris, allow me to introduce you to my new girlfriend . . . Ms. Flutter."

There was an awkward pause, and it was obvious that Mrs. Flutter was flustered.

"Oh, what the hell . . . everything's gone to shit anyway."

And then she pulled away her own mask revealing an even more disarming countenance hiding underneath.

"Yoko!"

"Who's Yoko?" asked Liz.

"My neighbor. She lives next door to me in the Dakota."

"Tell him why, Yoko!" said Wendell.

Yoko seemed bothered, like she didn't have the time for this kind of crap.

"Tell him!"

"Because I needed a bigger recording studio, all right?" she said.

I paused, trying to absorb this new data. "Wait a second. Are you saying that all of this . . . *everything* . . . was just about you wanting my *apartment*?"

An annoying twitch that Caleb had abandoned many years before returned to the crow's-feet around his eyes.

"Yeah, well . . . you never leave!" said Yoko. "You don't die . . . you don't move . . . you don't do nothing! I had to think of something else . . . I want your *place!*"

"You see, Chris," said Wendell, "a few select New Yorkers know about Campion's time machine."

"But Wendell, why are you involved in this?"

"She came on to me, man. It was that day, that day in the elevator. The day that I suggested you try to solve the old Jack the Thwacker case. It was all a plan to get you back in time and arrested for the murders so that she could get your digs . . . and then I was supposed to live happily ever after with her."

Yoko snickered.

"But you were my best friend!" I said, my voice beginning to crack.

"Yeah, but you never listened to me! It was always about you! Plus you were constantly putting that stupid image of the

 Cavalier King Charles spaniel drinking the bottle of root beer in my head . . . it got to the point where that was all I could think about, even when I was . . . having my Wendell time."

"But—"

"You have to understand, Chris . . . I *loved* her."

Yoko laughed. "What a sap!"

"It wasn't until Tweed informed me that you can only go one way in the time machine that I realized she was trying to get rid of me—just like she was trying to get rid of you."

Caleb sighed and pinched his eyes shut, struggling to control the twitching.

Yoko began to converse with someone 'off-camera' (as it were).

"No! You don't put that there! Idiot! That's shampoo, not salad dressing. Out! You're fired! Get out! Out!"

There was a long pause, and the first person to finally speak was Professor Campion. He seemed to be working his thoughts out aloud.

"But . . . since my machine only works one way . . ."

"Yes . . . ?" said Yoko impatiently.

". . . then why would you have to go to such extremes to frame the innocent Elliott boy? He would have been stuck back in 1882 anyway."

Yoko pondered this.

"That's true, I didn't think of that," she said. "Maybe it's because I don't like him. Oh well, I got his place anyway, so screw all of you, and see you in the funny papers." With that her face vanished, replaced by a pulsating pattern of colors in the middle of the portal.

"What a mean lady," I said.

"I'm so sorry, Chris. I was just pissed at you, that's all," sniffled a contrite Wendell. "Can we still be friends?"

"Sure we can, Wen. Hey, I'm gonna need some company back here in the nineteenth century, right?" And we gave each other a hug.

"Well I'm glad everyone's happy. Bon voyage one and all. I'm off to the future!" And Tweed began to step into the vortex of the portal.

"Hey, fat man, you ain't going anywhere, 'cept straight to hell!"

We all turned around to see little Mammy standing in the aisle pointing Tom Thumb's hornlike gun at Tweed.

"This is for Charley," she said, "and for the glory of the Organization of Hateful Midgets!"

"Watch it!" shouted Caleb.

Blam!!!!

Mammy's gun fired.

Caleb's instinct to "serve and protect"—even if he was protecting a less than outstanding citizen—clicked in, and he jumped for Tweed.

"Caleb, no!" shouted Liz.

The bullet missed the two men, but Caleb and Tweed tumbled backward together into the pulsating vortex and disappeared.

Liz screamed and buried her face in her palms.

"Christ," cursed Mammy. "Us little people can't get a friggin' break, this way or that." She waddled back up the aisle muttering to herself about big white people always screwing things up.

"He's gone! He's gone!" Liz cried, and she pounded her father's chest with her fists. "Bring him back! Bring him back!"

Campion tried to comfort her.

"I can't, my dear, I'm sorry." Clearly his comforting skills were poor.

"Then I'm going too!" she announced.

"Do you know what that means, my child?"

"Yes, I know what it means. It means I can't come back—that is, until you figure out how to do it. But Daddy, I lost him once. I can't lose him again. I love him! And . . . he loves me!"

Wendell and I started to tear up.

"I don't suppose that after being an absent father for twenty years I can expect you to obey my paternal wishes. Plus it wasn't like I was a very good father when I was around . . . and I was an even worse husband. I mean, no wonder your mother killed herself . . . have I mentioned that yet? A lot happened while you were in Maine—but we don't have time for that! You must follow your own heart, my dear! My love goes with you, always."

"So do I!" bellowed Roosevelt. "I go with you always, too!" And he came bounding down the aisle.

"Teddy, no! You can't come. You have a political career ahead of you. You have to stay. The country needs you!"

"But my dear Miss Smith, it is *adventure* that I crave! Not politics! Besides, you and that young chief of police need someone to look after you! From what I've seen thus far, the future looks like a mighty dangerous jungle." He cupped his mouth and leaned in to Liz. "By the way, have you noticed that Caleb is slightly incontinent?"

"Oh Teddy," she said and hugged her big bear.

"I'm going too!" shouted a man in a black top hat, carrying a cane and carpetbag. "Wheeeee!!!!!!!" he cried as he ran down the aisle and jumped straight into the twirling vortex.

"Who the hell was that?" asked Wendell.

"It was his clone!" said Campion, pointing his finger at yours truly.

Everyone glared at me.

"I guess . . . it was just a flesh wound. Hard to imagine with a .44 magnum, but he was pretty sauced."

"Bully!" blustered Roosevelt. "All the more reason for me to accompany Miss Smith to the future. After all, we're a *team,* and we have a new charge; we must now apprehend the Thwacker in the twenty-first century! I just pray they have an adequate equivalent to Delmonico's!"

"They do." I said. "It's called Applebee's!"

"*Adieu,* all!" T. R. vociferated "And remember, we are now face to face with our destiny and must meet it with a high and resolute courage!" With that he let out one final weehoo, stepped into the vortex, and vanished.

"Wow, that quote actually made sense," said Liz, holding her nose.

Then she saluted goodbye to Boilerplate, whose round metal eyes, I don't mind saying, were shedding little drops of oil. It dabbed them with a tissue.

She nodded and smiled to Wendell, who waved good-bye.

Then she wrapped her arms around Professor Campion, stood on her toes, and hugged her daddy—possibly for the last time.

She started down the aisle towards the vortex—but then stopped and turned around and approached me.

"Good-bye, humble servant Elliott. I'm not sure I will ever truly understand you, but I'm a fine judge of character, and you obviously have a . . . good heart."

"Yeah. I haven't had it checked recently, but I think it's all right; it's my prostate I'm more worried about . . . and liver spots." I extended my hand for her to shake, but she ignored it and leaned in and gave me a soft kiss on my cheek.

We smiled at each other, and my front cap fell out.

Then she stepped into the vortex and disappeared into the future.

"Because I needed a bigger recording studio!"

In the new country a city will rise,
and from the dark the Twayker will surprise.
An idiot will his first novel compose,
and the popular opinion will concur that it blows.

—Nostradamus, Quatrain Number Six. Some
people believe that the city he refers to is New York
and that "Twayker" is really the Thwacker. No one
knows who the idiot author is that he refers to.

Chapter the Twentieth.

In which, alas, a great fire consumes the grand city and begins its long journey west to . . . Chicago.

"FIRE! FIRE!" CRIED THE USHER. "THE ENTIRE CITY IS ABLAZE!"

As if on cue, the planetarium filled with billowing smoke.

"Hurry, we must flee!" commanded Campion.

"Wendell, what are you doing? We have to get out of here!" I shouted.

Wendell was busy reapplying his Teddy Roosevelt makeup.

"If I have to live back in this shitty time period, I'm gonna live here as a white man. I'm getting into the *good* restaurants!"

I couldn't blame him. All four of us rushed out of the museum.

The air outside was dim and oily. We stood aghast with slack jaws as we looked south down Central Park West. Most of New York City, including the Museum of Natural History, was indeed in flames.

"Wow, it's all going up in smoke," I said. "All that beautiful architecture—lost."

"And my time machine."

We watched the horrific spectacle for a moment.

"What will you do now, Professor?" I asked.

"I suppose, if it's still standing, I'll return to Bellevue Madhouse and continue my work."

"Bellevue? Why would you go back to that hole?"

"It's not so bad, really. I have my own private room, the porridge is hot, and I only pay tuppence for rent—which is unheard of in this city."

"You pay rent to be locked up like that?"

"Of course. Everything costs money in this town. You know that. I'm just hoping my cell goes co-op, so I can buy."

"Yeah, I suppose it would be a good future investment."

"Good luck to you, young man. This period in time takes a little getting used to, but you'll get the hang of it. As did I. Just stay away from the cold hindquarters buffet at Delmonico's and you'll be fine."

Campion climbed up on Boilerplate's shoulders.

"Farewell Wendell, or should I say, Mr. Roosevelt!"

Wendell obviously liked the sound of that. He puffed out his chest and bellowed,"Bully! Bull-eeee! Bully, bully, bully, bull*eee*!"

"Let's go through the park, Boilerplate," said Campion. "I believe it's the quickest route."

Boilerplate nodded to me and let out a loud steam whistle, as if to say good-bye. Call me a sentimentalist, but I think the big lug had grown quite fond of me in our time together. Campion pushed a button on the control box, and the robot and his passenger began to clomp across the street to Central Park.

At the curb they turned around and Campion called out,

"And a very fine good evening to you both!"

THE GREAT FIRE OF 1882 BURNED FOR THREE DAYS AND THREE NIGHTS before finally surrendering to a late-summer rain.

Afterward much of the city lay in smoldering ashes, but thankfully the Dakota was spared, as well as the Flatiron Building, the Nabisco Pork Fat and Hardtack company, and Conrad Röntgen's Race Transformation Salon.

The massive calamity overshadowed the perplexity of the Thwacker murders, and any investigation into the strange events at Castle Belvedere was shelved. With the right pockets lined with sufficient amounts of payola, Vanderbilt and Astor escaped arrest and circumvented any possible Mummer-related prosecutions. In fact, the Mummers were welcomed year after year, as their conventions and parades brought desperately needed revenue into the striving city.

In time, New York would rebuild itself and life would return to normal, or as normal as it gets for me.

Wendell went on flawlessly impersonating Roosevelt and was considered a well-respected and beloved mayor. He was awarded the medal of honor after fighting side by side with Boilerplate and his fellow Rough Riders in the Spanish-American war, which finally happened in 1898. Eventually he would go on to become the first African-American president of the United States—although luckily for him, the country didn't know it.

As for me, my destiny was spelled out the night I stood on Central Park West and watched the city burn—spelled out in big red letters on wanted posters plastered all over the grand metropolis. (Somehow they were fireproof.)

I have since worked odd jobs for meager pay. I was last seen portraying Judy in a hastily slapped-together streetcorner production of *Punch Comes Home Drunk and Mad,* and for my efforts spent a month at Bellevue recovering.

The truth is, most of my days and nights are spent on the lam as a fugitive stuck in another era—constantly changing locations, forever on the lookout for that single-minded juggernaut who

refuses to give up the pursuit: the officious detective Thomas A. Byrnes, who, after becoming chief of police, vowed to track me down no matter what it took.

Which explains the despicable habitat in which I now reside—and in which I now write these final words.

You see, in 1882 there were over ten thousand opium dens, Chinese hop houses, and yummy-brain-food joints in New York City, located mostly downtown. Chief among these was Lee Kay's on Pearl Street.

The dingy basement establishment offered customers a hard shelf to lie on with a wooden wedge for a pillow and a variety of mind-altering substances ordered from a large menu decorated with red tassels.

For all his cursing in Chinese and spitting loogies at the back of my head, Lee Kay is actually an all-right boss. He recently promoted me to maitre d'.

"Welcome to Lee Kay's, where there's always something unique to satisfy your yen. Allow me to tell you our specials. Tonight we have fresh Li Yuen served in a tall Yen Tsing bong, which is rather expensive and reserved for you high-hatters, but I recommend it highly. Highly . . . get it? We're also offering Yen Pock, Yen Hop, and Yen Dung—all moderately priced and presented with a set of yen shee gows, which you may take with you for use on another visit. Of course, if you're low on finances you're welcome to just inhale whatever might be floating around the room."

At night I lie awake on my bottom shelf and wonder about my friends in the twenty-first century. I'm not particularly worried about Caleb and Liz. I'm sure Caleb is head of Homeland Security by now, and Liz is probably writing a gossip column for some New York newspaper. Hopefully they're living happily ever after. Teddy? I'm not sure what Teddy's doing—probably holding court

at Applebee's and posing naked for the students at the Art League. But I know if he ever decided to try show business, there's a great part for him in *Arsenic and Old Lace.*

It's more the 'doctor' whom I'm curious about. I wonder if he's living in my apartment at the Dakota, and I wonder if he's pretending to be me and reaping all the copious benefits and rewards that go along with being me. I also sometimes wonder if he walks the dark streets of New York City, indulging once again in his grisly business.

And so, dear reader, at the beginning of this story I promised you a shocking denouement, and I believe that I have delivered on that promise. But now you must promise me something. Promise me that if this manuscript ever makes it back to the twenty-first century, and you read it, that you will please alert the authorities. Tell them that Chris Elliott—the rich and famous actor whom everybody loves—is a fraud! Tell them that the real Chris Elliott is stuck in the past and is doomed to remain there unless you send help. It is up to you, dear reader, if you ever want to see the original again. You are my only hope!

And now I must put down my quill and don my overcoat and top hat, for the evening is cold, and the wind rustles relentlessly through the narrow cobblestone streets, beckoning to me like the ghosts of an old History Channel documentary on Jack the Jolly Thwacker, and I must hurry to my first midnight confluence.

You see, not long ago I applied and was happily accepted into the Pinhead Brigade of the Secret Society of Mummers. It's a fairly new and quickly growing brigade—right now it's just the two of us, me and the enigmatic Zip, Barnum's favorite freak. Our first get-together is tonight at the bandshell in Central Park, and I don't want to be late. I'm quite sure it will prove most enlightening.

And so, my benevolent readers, it is therefore incumbent

upon me to thank you most fervently for indulging my pathetic efforts to burden you with this humble scroll, and I therefore wish, with the utmost heartfelt sincerity, that all who can will hesitate not to enjoy with my blessings . . . a very fine good evening.

Praise be to Erce.

Epilogue.

HELLO, MY NAME IS MYRON STOLPER. I REPRESENT CHRIS ELLIOTT AS well as a slew of other fabulously talented celebrities-slash-entertainers.

One day, I was napping in my tanning bed when I received a surprise collect call from an individual who, while preferring to remain anonymous, wanted to wish me a happy birthday. Considering that my birthday had already passed, and since I was born into a leap year and my next birthday was not for another four years, it was difficult for me not to be a little suspicious. However, I enjoy surprises and I felt sure this was a practical joke being perpetrated on me by my fellow agents at United Superboy Talent, Inc. (222 Beverly Drive, between La Boboleeto and Yor Binaca), so I decided to accept the charges.

The connection was staticky and it was difficult to understand what the voice was saying.

"Go to the Rose Center, Myron. Go to the Rose Center, Myron," was all I could make out.

The only Rose Center I was familiar with was the Rose Marie Center for Aged Actresses Who Resemble Aged Actors, and there

was no way in hell I was going back there. The last time I went I accidentally called Kaye Ballard "Mr. Borgnine."

So I forgot about the collect call until the end of the month when the phone bill came—*"Impossible! The conversation only lasted thirty seconds!"* But AT&T assured me that there was no mistake—that interstellar time-differential rates had gone up (I've never understood the plan I signed up for). Fortunately, Superboy Talent allowed me to dip into my income savings, so I was able to cover the phone bill as well as my alimony nut and the liposuction for my St. Bernard.

Fast-forward two weeks and I'm in New York City to celebrate my numero uno main man Chris Elliott's triumphant return to Broadway as the Blue Spruce in Eugene O'Neill's *Ah, Wilderness!* The opening-night party was an extravagant affair held at Club Freckles (formerly Charcoal, which used to be Gold Toe, but was originally Resnick's Happy Jangle-Bangle and Mince-About Hall back in the 1800s).

As soon as I arrived I realized that the show was throwing a nineteenth-century-themed opening-night party. *Oh come on, this is so gay!* I thought, but, theme party or not, it was time to do some schmoozin'.

It was so crowded, I couldn't even get close to Elliott. He was surrounded by a bevy of creamy babes, and I decided that it was not the most opportune moment to congratulate him on his stellar performance. (I have never seen anybody stand that still for that long in all my life. It was breathtaking.)

The place was decorated to approximate the club's look back when it was the Mince-About Hall (the legendary hot spot that used to take ordinary people off the streets and make them into the likes of stars). Paper lanterns swayed this way and that, gas-powered rotating mirror balls hung from the ceiling, and, behind a long bar, the bartenders—or as they were called back in

the old days, 'mixologists'—tried unsuccessfully to juggle giant wooden barrels of booze. The place was filled with a more youthful faction of costumed celebrities who were swamping the dancefloor and grooving to the hot turn-of-the-century piano tunes. Some were doing the funky Viennese Waltz, some the frenetic Quick Step, some the sexy Virginia Reel, and still others were attempting to recreate the steamy and often forbidden El Taco De Belle.

The contagious vibration of the ragtime beat infiltrated my body right down to the very marrow inside my pelvic bones, and I couldn't stop my head from bebopping back and forth as I checked out the evening's merchandise. There were some mighty fine foxes (wearing sepia makeup) getting funky out there—straight up.

I glided across the dancefloor, snapping my fingers and strutting my stuff—scanning out any potential fourth Mrs. Myron Stolpers—and headed over to the music master.

He wasn't just playing Scott Joplin's rags, he was impersonating Joplin as well, and doing a pretty convincing job of it. Not that I know exactly what Scott Joplin was like, but the guy was dressed in a high-collared shirt and bowler, and he had that old-school African-American thing down pat.

I watched his swift hands as they raked fluently up and down the keyboard, creating the unhinged "Elite Syncopations." When he was done I just had to give him my card.

"Hey man, you are great! If you ever need representation, please give us a call. We handle Chris Elliott as well as a slew of other fabulously talented celebrities-slash-entertainers."

"That's not Chris Elliott," the guy said.

"No?" I replied, chuckling at his sense of humor. "Okay, I'll play along. Who is it?"

"He's impersonating him."

"Uh-huh, I see. Like you're impersonating Scott Joplin?"

"I *am* Scott Joplin. We have to talk, Stolper."

"Hey, how did you know my name?" A sudden chill ran down my spine. *Was this guy really the famous piano player reincarnated?*

"You just gave me your card," he said.

"Oh yeah, I forgot."

He led me over to a corner and we talked.

"Chris wanted me to give you this," he said and handed me a heavy legal-sized leather envelope.

"What's this?"

"A book. The book he was working on. It's finished. Also there's some nickelodeon receipts that he wants you to send to his accountant."

"You know, that's funny. I was just thinking about that the other day. A while back he told me that he was researching something for a book, but then he never mentioned it again. I figured that he just gave up on it, because you really have to know what you're doing when you write a book—I mean you really have to be *very* talented and *extremely* intelligent to write a book—as well as being intoxicatingly, boyishly charming . . . and did I mention talented?"

"Just read it, crackerhead. You'll understand everything." He started back towards his piano.

"Wait a second. How is it that you have the book?" I asked.

"I'm a friend of his."

"Yeah, but I'm Chris Elliott's agent."

"Not the real Chris Elliott."

"Look, buddy, I know you musicians are a little fluffy in the old brainworks department, but . . ."

"You should have gone to the Rose Center, Myron," he interrupted.

"Hey, was that *you*? Listen, you owe me some bling for that call."

"Why didn't you go?" he asked.

"Because that place smells like baby wipes."

The Joplin look-alike retrieved a pouch of tobacco and proceeded to roll his own cigarette.

"Wow. That's really a lost art," I observed.

He ignored me, lit his smoke, and took a long drag off it. I realized it wasn't tobacco.

"Professor Campion invented a way to call the future—collect. So Chris called and told you to go to the Rose Center at the Museum of Natural History. He was planning on sending you the manuscript through the vortex in the planetarium."

"Uh-huh."

"He can't return until Campion figures out how to make the time machine go back and forth. But when you didn't show up, he was devastated. So I told him I'd deliver the book for him. I figured I owed him one, since he wrote the opening riff to 'The Entertainer' for me."

I began to laugh.

"This is good. This is really good," I said. "So Elliott put you up to this, huh? How much is he paying you? It's great. It's like some old-time, Andy Kaufman, antiperformance, 'is it real or is it Memorex?' shit. I love it!"

The piano man took a puff off his joint and continued.

"Unfortunately, now I'm stuck here, and let me tell you something, your future ain't all it's cracked up to be. I'd rather be back in the old Jim Crow world that I came from. At least there people appreciated my music. Here it's relegated to silly theme parties like this and the occasional closing credit sequence in a Woody Allen movie."

"Look, guy. Thank you for delivering the book. I'll tell Chris that you did a superb job and recommend you for . . ."

"You don't have to recommend me for anything. Just read the goddamn book. Your client's life depends on it."

And with that he scuttled off, threw on his overcoat, and left the party.

I never did get a chance to speak with Chris that night, but when I returned to L.A., I took advantage of every two-hour Botox session to read at least a few lines out of each chapter. A year or so later, I was finished with the book, and I have to say that my life was changed. I was blown away.

Yes, it's inconceivable, probably impossible, and quite possibly just the ramblings of a mentally disturbed person—but hell's bells, I do believe it all.

I rushed the book over to Miramax for publishing, but along the way I came face to face with a dilemma. A rather large dilemma, at least a six-footer weighing close to three hundred pounds, but instead of walking around it, I decided to address it straight on.

"What do you want from me?" I asked.

"You know," said the dilemma. "You have to make a choice."

"I've made my choice."

"Have you?"

"Yes. I must save my real client and inform the authorities of the Thwacker's whereabouts. Right now he's in Canada shooting an episode of *CSI Miami*."

"Are you positive about that choice?"

"Yes, of course I am. Absolutely. It's the right thing to do. It's the only thing to do."

"I don't remember the real Chris Elliott ever being booked on an episode of *CSI*. Was he?"

"No. He auditioned once, but Daniel Stern beat him out for the role."

"And you've just made a three-picture deal with the Thwacker, haven't you?"

"Yeah, so, what are you saying?"

"It just seems to me that you're doing a little better with your new client than with the old one. Dare I say that Jack the Jolly Thwacker is more talented than his previous incarnation?"

"Well, I mean . . ."

"You have a hefty alimony payment every month, don't you, Myron?"

"Yes, but I can usually make it . . . just about."

"I'd think about this, if I were you. You and the Thwacker could do great things together!"

I thought about it for . . . thirty seconds. He was right. What's the point of bringing Chris Elliott back from the past? The statute of limitations has run out and the Thwacker would never be charged with any crime at this point, so we would just be stuck with another (less talented) Chris Elliott running around, and I ask you, does the world need another, *less talented*, Chris Elliott? I don't think so. I thanked my dilemma and told him we should get together for a beer some time.

A few months later, Miramax published *The Shroud of the Thwacker*, and I am happy to report that Jolly Jack (and I) are making a bundle off it. I'm not sure that was Chris's intention, but it's just the way things worked out, right?

The Thwacker lives in the Dakota with his new squeeze, Yoko Ono. They broke down the walls between their apartments and built a brand-new recording studio.

As for me, I'm a survivor and always will be. You would think I'd be wracked with guilt, having left Chris to rot in his own

filth . . . you would think that, but I'm not. Remember, I'm an agent. I've never looked back. It was the right thing to do. The only thing I feel bad about is that once I made up my mind, my dilemma, whom I had grown quite fond of, suffered a massive coronary and expired (he sure loved his greasy foods). His funeral was attended by only a handful of family members and, of course, yours truly. He was buried at Forest Lawn under a simple headstone, which reads: "Herein lies my dilemma."

(Oh wait, my dilemma seems to be sending me a psychic transmission, post-mortem. He says maybe if I wanted to keep all this a secret I shouldn't have written all that down. How do you delete on this thing? . . . Er, I mean, it was all a joke. There is no fake Chris Elliott. But if there *were,* I certainly wouldn't go trying to rescue him, if I were you. I've got this one's name trademarked, his work copyrighted, and his DNA patented. Hypothetically speaking, it would be just awful to be stuck in a protracted infringement suit with Superboy Talent, Ltd., wink-wink. Get my drift?[5])

My life goes on, I've married my fourth wife, Zee, and I've since signed a whole new slew of celebrity-slash-entertainers. At the top of the list is Scott Joplin himself, and I know he wouldn't mind me telling you, because he's too shy to boast himself, that if you listen very closely, you can currently hear "The Entertainer" playing in the background of a really cute—and, I think, quite tasteful—national spot for Stainmaster carpeting.

And believe you me, my main man Scott Joplin could not be prouder.

---

5. I'll sue your pants off!

Acknowledgments

As much as I'd like to take full credit for this flawless manuscript, I feel compelled to acknowledge the vital contributions made by others who stand equally complicit and deserve to be hanged as much as I do.

True accountability lies with my editors, the imperious Jonathan Burnham and the unimpeachable Rob Weisbach as well as my publisher, the sensational Kathy Schneider—their unwavering support and gentle guidance throughout this surprisingly pleasurable process has been deeply appreciated and their notes were refreshingly intelligent and remarkably concise. Although, at first, I had no idea what they meant by *"ad nauseam."*

While guilty and just as exposed as the rest of us to the inevitable onslaught of petty lawsuits, my deepest gratitude goes out to Kristin Powers, JillEllyn Riley, Claire McKinney, Andrew Bevan, Carrie O'Maley, Noah Levy, and Richard Florest, all of whom along with a host of others at Miramax—whose names I haven't bothered to memorize—worked so tirelessly to transform this book into the highly polished hunk of steaming . . . um, *perfection* that it is today.

My friend Johnny Schmidt bears a large degree of culpability as well. On board from the begining, not only did he assist me in navigating through the befuddling twists and turns of my intricate story, but he also glued together and re-sanded any rough dialogue, polished any lackluster prose, and made sure I kept the ending where it belonged—at the end. (How positively brilliant!)

I'm certain that this book would not be as exhilarating a read were it not for my sister Amy Elliott Andersen's amazing illustrations (that took a lot longer than she thought they would—at least that's what she keeps telling me in her nonstop e-mails—I think she'angling for more cash).

My wife, Paula Niedert Elliott, deserves a special thanks for proofreading all my rough drafts and recognizing words that even spell-check had given up on and my daughters Abby and Bridey get a big thank-you for being my true inspiration—college tuition can be a great motivator.

Thanks to my friends Adam Resnick, John Altshuler, Dave Krinski, and John Collier for their punch-up efforts (*efforts,* that's a laugh) and also to my brother Bob Elliott Jr. for his in-depth research. (Yes, believe it or not, there was actual research done—you can't make up something like *Boilerplate*—well you can, but it's a lot easier when your brother just shows you a picture of it). And thanks go to my brother-in-law, Steve Higgins—whose positive reaction to the first half of the book prompted me to finish the second half.

Of course thanks go to my manager Tom Demko, who gave me the idea to write a book in the first place (basically because the rest of my career was in the shitter).

And a special heartfelt thank-you goes out to a guy who barely glanced at his Blackberry during all those nerve-racking pitch sessions— my literary agent, the lovely and effervescent David Vigliano, who makes every day of my life worth living—mainly because they're so much better than any day of his.

Finally this book is dedicated to my Mom and Dad (the popular comedy team of Bob and Lee). Thanks for raising me in New York City, folks—I so wish I could afford to move back!

Daffy-down-dilly

Daffy-down-dilly has come up to town
In a yellow petticoat and a green gown.

I Sing, I Sing

I sing, I sing,
From morn till night,
From cares I'm free,
And my heart is light.

Three Little Kittens

Three little kittens, they lost their mittens,
And they began to cry,
"Oh, Mother dear, we sadly fear
    Our mittens we have lost!"

"What! Lost your mittens, you naughty kittens!
Then you shall have no pie."
"Meow, meow, meow!"

The three little kittens found their mittens,
And they began to cry,
"Oh, Mother dear, see here, see here,
    Our mittens we have found."

"What! Found your mittens, you good little kittens!
Then you shall have some pie."
"Purr, purr, purr."

I Saw a Ship A-Sailing

I saw a ship a-sailing,
A-sailing on the sea;
And, oh! It was all laden
With pretty things for thee!

There were comfits in the cabin,
And apples in the hold;
The sails were made of silk,
And the masts were made of gold.

The four-and-twenty sailors
That stood between the deck
Were four-and-twenty white mice
With chains about their necks.

The captain was a duck,
With a packet on his back;
And when the ship began to move,
The captain said, "Quack! Quack!"

Hark! Hark!

Hark! Hark! The dogs do bark,
Beggars are coming to town;
Some in rags and some in tags,
And some in velvet gowns.

Humpty Dumpty

Humpty Dumpty sat on a wall,
Humpty Dumpty had a great fall;
All the king's horses and all the king's men
Couldn't put Humpty Dumpty together again.

Dance, Thumbkin, Dance

Dance, Thumbkin, dance;
Dance, ye merrymen, everyone.
For Thumbkin, he can dance alone,
Thumbkin, he can dance alone.

Dance, Foreman, dance;
Dance, ye merrymen, everyone.
For Foreman, he can dance alone,
Foreman, he can dance alone.

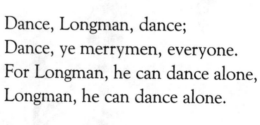

Dance, Longman, dance;
Dance, ye merrymen, everyone.
For Longman, he can dance alone,
Longman, he can dance alone.

Dance, Ringman, dance;
Dance, ye merrymen, everyone.
But Ringman cannot dance alone,
Ringman cannot dance alone.

Dance, Littleman, dance;
Dance, ye merrymen, everyone.
For Littleman, he can dance alone,
Littleman, he can dance alone.

Tommy Tonsey

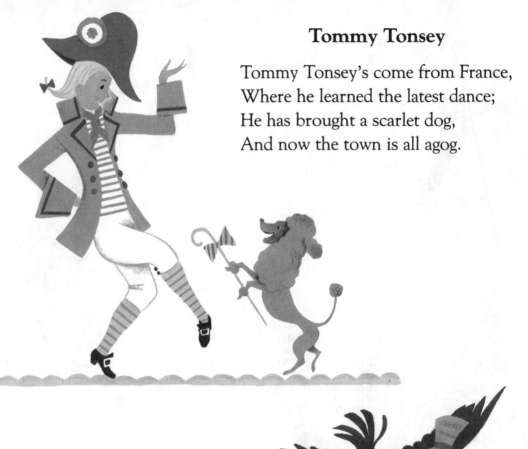

Tommy Tonsey's come from France,
Where he learned the latest dance;
He has brought a scarlet dog,
And now the town is all agog.

Tweedle-dum and Tweedle-dee

Tweedle-dum and Tweedle-dee
Resolved to have a battle,
For Tweedle-dum said Tweedle-dee
Had spoiled his nice new rattle.

Just then flew by a monstrous crow
As big as a tar-barrel,
Which frightened both the heroes so,
They quite forgot their quarrel.

Where Are You Going, My Pretty Maid?

"Where are you going, my pretty maid?"
"I'm going a-milking, sir," she said.
"May I go with you, my pretty maid?"
"You're kindly welcome, sir," she said.

Ifs and Ands

If "ifs" and "ands"
Were pots and pans,
There'd be no need for tinkers' hands.

London Bridge

London Bridge is falling down,
Falling down, falling down,
London Bridge is falling down,
My fair lady.

Build it up with iron bars,
Iron bars, iron bars,
Build it up with iron bars,
My fair lady.

Iron bars will bend and break,
Bend and break, bend and break,
Iron bars will bend and break,
My fair lady.

I Had a Little Nut Tree

I had a little nut tree; nothing would it bear
But a silver nutmeg and a golden pear.
The king of Spain's daughter came to visit me,
And all was because of my little nut tree.
I skipped over water, I danced over sea,
And all the birds in the air couldn't catch me.

Margaret Wrote
a Letter

Margaret wrote a letter,
Sealed it with her finger,
Threw it in the dam
For the dusty miller.

Dusty was his coat,
Dusty was the siller,
Dusty was the kiss
I'd from the dusty miller.

A Family Drive

Old Bob, young Bob,
Little Bob and big,
Molly Bob and Polly Bob,
And Polly Bobby's pig,
All went for a drive one day
And, strange as it may seem,
They drove six miles and back again
And never hurt the team.

Dance to Your Daddie

Dance to your daddie,
My bonnie laddie;
Dance to your daddie,
My bonnie lamb;
You shall have a fishy,
On a little dishy;
You shall have a fishy,
When the boat comes home.

The North Wind

The north wind doth blow,
And we shall have snow,
And what will the robin do then,
  Poor thing?

He'll sit in the barn
And keep himself warm,
And hide his head under his wing,
  Poor thing!

The Schoolroom Clock

There's a neat little clock—
In the schoolroom it stands—
And it points to the time
With its two little hands.
And may we, like the clock,
Keep a face clean and bright,
With hands ever ready
To do what is right.

Ride Away, Ride

Ride away, ride away,
Johnny shall ride,
And he shall have pussycat
Tied to one side;
And he shall have little dog
Tied to the other,
And Johnny shall ride
To see his grandmother.

Twinkle, Twinkle,
Little Star

Twinkle, twinkle, little star,
How I wonder what you are!
Up above the world so high,
Like a diamond in the sky.

When the blazing sun is gone,
When he nothing shines upon,
Then you show your little light,
Twinkle, twinkle, all the night.

Three Young Rats

Three young rats with black felt hats,
Three young ducks with new straw flats,
Three young dogs with curling tails,
Three young cats with demi-veils,
Went out to walk with two young pigs,
In satin vests and sorrel wigs;
But suddenly it chanced to rain,
And so they all went home again.

A Farmer Went Trotting

A farmer went trotting upon his gray mare,
Bumpety, bumpety, bump!
With his daughter behind him, so rosy and fair,
Lumpety, lumpety, lump!

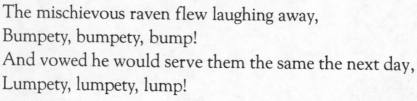

A raven cried croak! And they all tumbled down,
Bumpety, bumpety, bump!
The mare broke her knees and the farmer his crown,
Lumpety, lumpety, lump!

The mischievous raven flew laughing away,
Bumpety, bumpety, bump!
And vowed he would serve them the same the next day,
Lumpety, lumpety, lump!

Three Blind Mice

Three blind mice! Three blind mice!
See how they run! See how they run!
They all ran after the farmer's wife;
She cut off their tails with a carving knife.
Did you ever see such a sight in your life
As three blind mice?

The News of the Day

"What is the news of the day,
Good neighbor, I pray?"
"They say a balloon
Is gone up to the moon!"

The Cats of Kilkenny

There were once two cats of Kilkenny,
Each thought there was one cat too many;
So they fought and they fit,
And they scratched and they bit,
Till, excepting their nails
And the tips of their tails,
Instead of two cats, there weren't any.

The Cats' Serenade

The cats went out to serenade
And on a banjo sweetly played;
And summer nights they climbed a tree
And sang, "My love, oh, come to me!"

Two Gray Kits

Two gray kits and the gray kits' mother
All went over the bridge together.
The bridge broke down, they all fell in;
"May the rats go with you," says Tom Bolin.

Ding, Dong, Bell!

Ding, dong, bell!
Pussy's in the well!
Who put her in?
Little Johnny Green.
Who pulled her out?
Little Johnny Stout.

What a naughty boy was that
To try to drown poor pussycat,
Which never did him any harm,
But killed the mice in his father's barn!

The Muffin Man

O do you know the muffin man,
The muffin man, the muffin man,
O do you know the muffin man
That lives in Drury Lane?

To Market, To Market

To market, to market, to buy a fat pig,
Home again, home again, jiggety-jig.

To market, to market, to buy a fat hog,
Home again, home again, jiggety-jog.

To market, to market, to buy a plum bun,
Home again, home again, market is done.

Yet Didn't You See

Yet didn't you see, yet didn't you see,
What naughty tricks they put upon me?
They broke my pitcher
And spilt my water
And buffed my mother
And chid my daughter
And kissed my sister instead of me.

The Little Mice

This little mousie peeped within;
This little mousie walked right in!
This little mousie came to play;
This little mousie ran away!
This little mousie cried, "Dear me!
Dinner is done and it's time for tea!"

Hickory, Dickory

Hickory, dickory, dock!
The mouse ran up the clock;
The clock struck one,
And down he run,
Hickory, dickory, dock.

One, Two, Buckle My Shoe

One, two, buckle my shoe;
Three, four, shut the door;
Five, six, pick up sticks;
Seven, eight, lay them straight;
Nine, ten, a good fat hen;
Eleven, twelve, dig and delve;
Thirteen, fourteen, maids are courting;
Fifteen, sixteen, maids in the kitchen;
Seventeen, eighteen, maids are waiting;
Nineteen, twenty, my platter's empty.

Sing Song!
Merry Go Round

Sing song! Merry go round,
Here we go up to the moon, O!
Little Johnny a penny has found,
And so we'll sing a tune, O!

On Christmas Eve

On Christmas Eve I turned the spit;
I burnt my fingers, I feel it yet;
The cock sparrow flew over the table,
The pot began to play with the ladle;
The ladle stood up like an angry man
And vowed he'd fight the frying pan;
The frying pan behind the door
Said he never saw the like before;
And the kitchen clock I was going to wind
Said he never saw the like behind.

Old Mother Goose

Old Mother Goose,
When she wanted to wander,
Would ride through the air
On a very fine gander.

Old Mother Goose
and Other Nursery Rhymes

Illustrated by
Alice and Martin Provensen

A Golden Book • New York
Western Publishing Company, Inc., Racine, Wisconsin 53404